CONTENTS

DISCRIMINATION

A GUIDE TO THE RELEVANT CASE LAW

TWENTY-SIXTH EDITION

Michael Rubenstein

Michael
Rubenstein
Publishing

Published by Michael Rubenstein Publishing Ltd

PO Box 61064
Southwark
London
SE1P 5BQ

www.rubensteinpublishing.com
www.eordirect.co.uk
www.eqlr.co.uk

© Michael Rubenstein Publishing Ltd 2013

ISBN: 978-0-9558224-5-2

Printed by Hobbs the Printers Ltd, Totton, Hampshire

CASE INDEX

INTRODUCTION

The 26th edition of the *Discrimination Guide* takes into account the effect on the case law of 65 employment discrimination cases reported during 2012.

Discrimination has assumed ever-increasing prominence in the world of employment law. This was one of the main reasons why we launched *Equality Law Reports* (EqLR) in October 2010. This edition of the Guide covers both cases reported in *Industrial Relations Law Reports* (IRLR) during 2012 and also employment discrimination cases included in EqLR.

A major purpose of this Guide is to extract from the thousands of discrimination cases decided over the years the main principles concerning employment discrimination that still can be regarded as binding authority. My hope is that this will assist those advising, acting or adjudicating in this jurisdiction on the current approach of the courts to the range of problems of interpretation posed by the statutes.

The Guide is organised according to cross-strand issues, with separate sections on particular protected characteristics focusing on principles specific to that characteristic. In 2012 the appellate courts dealt with an increasing number of cases brought under the Equality Act 2010 rather than under the former discrimination legislation.

During 2012, EqLR and/or IRLR reported three judgments of the Court of Justice of the European Union on discrimination law, one judgment of the European Court of Human Rights, four from the Supreme Court, nine from the Court of Appeal, two each from the Inner House of the Court of Session and the Court of Appeal in Northern Ireland, and 44 judgments from the Employment Appeal tribunal on aspects of discrimination law.

The reported EAT judgments came from courts presided over by 11 different judges: nine judgments from the new President, Mr Justice Langstaff; seven judgments from HH Judge Richardson, six from HH Judge McMullen QC, five from Mr Justice Underhill and from HH Judge Clark, three from HH Judge Birtles, two from Mrs Justice Slade, Lady Smith, Mr Justice Wilkie and HH Judge Serota QC, and one from Mr Recorder Luba QC.

So far as causes of action are concerned, in 2012, we reported 19 cases involving race discrimination issues, 17 sex discrimination cases, 14 cases on disability discrimination, 12 on equal pay, 10 on age discrimination, three on pregnancy discrimination, two on marriage discrimination and religion or belief discrimination, and one on sexual orientation discrimination.

To take the judgments reported in 2012 into account has meant deleting 34 entries which appeared in the 25th edition of the Guide, but which are no longer considered relevant, while adding 71 new principles in light of the new case law.

Where essentially the same point has been enunciated in more than one reported case, the highest authority has been cited or, where that is not possible, the most recent or the most frequently quoted decision. For this and other purposes, therefore, the Guide distinguishes between the principle and the case. The principle, if still relevant, should be found in the Guide. A particular case may not be referred to either because it is no longer relevant or because the principle enunciated is better captured by another reference.

Finally, since there has to be a cut-off point in preparing a publication such as this, I have only included cases reported in IRLR or EqLR up to the end of 2012. Inevitably, however, because this area of the law is developing so rapidly, the Guide may include some principles which been have overruled by the courts by the time this edition reaches your hands. For those who wish to keep up-to-date, the Guide thus should be seen as an adjunct to *Industrial Relations Law Reports* and *Equality Law Reports*, rather than a replacement for regular perusal of these journals. *Equal Opportunities Review* will continue to provide expert analysis of many of these key decisions.

Michael Rubenstein
January 2013
Michael@rubensteinpublishing.com
Twitter: @mhrubenstein

1. EXCLUSIONS, EXCEPTIONS AND PRELIMINARY ISSUES

MEANING OF "EMPLOYMENT"

Employment" means –
(a) employment under a contract of employment, a contract of apprenticeship or a contract personally to do work;

EQUALITY ACT 2010 – s.83

Jivraj v   **[2011] IRLR 827 UKSC**
Hashwani   **[2011] EqLR 1088 UKSC**
In order to come within the scope of the definition of "employment", the relevant employment relationship must be "employment under" a contract personally to do work. It is not sufficient to ask simply whether the contract was a contract personally to do work, nor is it sufficient to ask what the dominant purpose of the contract was, although the dominant purpose may well be relevant in arriving at the correct conclusion on the facts of a particular case.

Mingeley v   **[2004] IRLR 373 CA**
Pennock and Ivory
On the plain words of the statute and the authorities, a claimant has to establish that his contract placed him under an obligation "personally to execute any work or labour".

Jivraj v   **[2011] IRLR 827 UKSC**
Hashwani   **[2011] EqLR 1088 UKSC**
In *Allonby v Accrington and Rossendale College*, the Court of Justice drew a clear distinction between those who are in substance employed and those who are "independent providers of services who are not in a relationship of subordination with the person who receives the services". There is no reason why the same distinction should not be drawn for the purposes of domestic law between those who are employed and those who are genuinely self-employed. In determining which of these two categories an individual falls into, the essential question to ask is whether, on the one hand, the person concerned performs services for and under the direction of another person in return for which he or she receives remuneration, or whether, on the other hand, he or she is an independent provider of services who is not in a relationship of subordination with the person who receives the services.

Quinnen v   **[1984] IRLR 227 EAT**
Hovells
The inclusion in the definition of "employment" of a third limb covering employment under "a contract personally to execute any work or labour" is a wide and flexible concept and was intended to enlarge upon the ordinary connotation of "employment" so as to include persons outside the master-servant relationship.

Muschett v   **[2010] IRLR 451 CA**
HM Prison Service
Mutuality of obligation is not a condition of a contract for services.

BP Chemicals Ltd v   **[1995] IRLR 128 EAT**
Gillick
The extended definition of "employment", referring to employment under a contract personally to execute work,

must be taken to refer to a contract between the party doing the work and the party for whom the work is done. A contract worker does not enter into an "employment" relationship with the principal.

Burton v   **[2003] IRLR 257 EAT**
Higham t/a Ace Appointments
All that the statutory definition of employment requires is for there to be an obligation to do work. In this case, those engaged by an employment agency under a temporary worker's contract fell within the wider definition of "employment", notwithstanding that they provided their services to the client. The obligations set out in their contract corresponded to those envisaged in the statutory definition. The temporary worker's contract required them, when accepting an assignment, to do work. They could not substitute another person to take their place. That the work was performed for the client did not take it outside the scope of the statutory definition.

X v   **[2011] IRLR 335 CA**
Mid Sussex Citizens Advice Bureau   **[2011] EqLR 309 CA**
Volunteers at the Citizens Advice Bureau who are unpaid and have no binding contract fall outside the scope of the Disability Discrimination Act and the Framework Employment Equality Directive 2000/78. Volunteers do not fall within the meaning "occupation" in Article 2 of the Directive. The concept of "worker" has been restricted to persons who are remunerated for what they do. The concept of "occupation" is essentially an overlapping one, and there is no reason to suppose that it was intended to cover non-remunerated work. Nor could it be held that obtaining a voluntary post was a stepping stone to access to employment and therefore was an "arrangement" made for the purpose of determining who should be offered employment. An arrangement is not for the purpose of determining who should be offered employment if that is not what it is designed to achieve. The purpose of the arrangement in the present case was to secure advisers to provide advice to clients of the CAB; the purpose was not to create a potential pool from which full-time staff could be drawn.

Percy v   **[2006] IRLR 195 HL**
Church of Scotland Board of National Mission
An associate minister's relationship with the Church of Scotland constituted "employment" within the meaning of the statutory definition in that she was employed under a contract "personally to execute" work. Accordingly, she was entitled to bring her claim of sex discrimination against the church in an employment tribunal.

Percy v   **[2006] IRLR 195 HL**
Church of Scotland Board of National Mission
Holding an office and being an employee are not inconsistent. A person may hold an "office" on the terms of, and pursuant to, a contract of employment.

Hall v   **[2000] IRLR 578 CA**
Woolston Hall Leisure Ltd
Where the performance by the employer of a contract of employment involves illegality of which the employee is aware, public policy does not bar the employee, when discrim-

inated against on grounds of sex by dismissal, from recovering compensation. A complaint of sex discrimination by dismissal is not based on the contract of employment. Although the employee must establish that she was employed and was dismissed from that employment, it is the sex discrimination which is the core of the complaint. The correct approach is for the tribunal to consider whether the claimant's claim arises out of or is so inextricably bound up with her illegal conduct that the court could not permit the claimant to recover compensation without appearing to condone that conduct.

Hounga v   **[2012] IRLR 685 CA**
Allen   **[2012] EqLR 679 CA**
The fact that a claimant may be barred by illegality from enforcing her contract of employment will not automatically lead also to the conclusion that she will be barred from claiming compensation for a discriminatory dismissal from her employment. The correct test for dealing with illegality in discrimination cases is the tortious approach set out by the Court of Appeal in *Hall v Woolston Hall Leisure* and applied in *Vakante v Governing Body of Addey and Stanhope School (No.2)*.

Hounga v   **[2012] IRLR 685 CA**
Allen   **[2012] EqLR 679 CA**
An illegal immigrant, who had no right to be employed in the UK, could not claim that she had been unlawfully discriminated against when she was dismissed because there was a direct link between the discriminatory treatment of which she complained and the vulnerability to which she was subject by reason of her illegal employment contract. Her claim was clearly connected with her own illegal conduct and was barred on public policy grounds.

CLAIM IN TIME

(1) Proceedings on a complaint within section 120 may not be brought after the end of –
> *(a) the period of 3 months starting with the date of the act to which the complaint relates, or*
> *(b) such other period as the employment tribunal thinks just and equitable.*

(2) Proceedings may not be brought in reliance on section 121(1) after the end of –
> *(a) the period of 6 months starting with the date of the act to which the proceedings relate, or*
> *(b) such other period as the employment tribunal thinks just and equitable.*

(3) For the purposes of this section –
> *(a) conduct extending over a period is to be treated as done at the end of the period;*
> *(b) failure to do something is to be treated as occurring when the person in question decided on it.*

(4) In the absence of evidence to the contrary, a person (P) is to be taken to decide on failure to do something –
> *(a) when P does an act inconsistent with doing it, or*
> *(b) if P does no inconsistent act, on the expiry of the period in which P might reasonably have been expected to do it.*

EQUALITY ACT 2010 – s.123

Dodd v   **[1988] IRLR 16 EAT**
British Telecom plc
In order to be a valid complaint sufficient to stop time running, the written application must contain sufficient to identify who is making it and against whom it is made, and must contain sufficient to show what sort of complaint it is. An application whose contents did not comply with those broad minimum requirements would not be capable of being described as an originating application at all. However, the requirements of rule 1(a), (b) and (c) of the Employment Tribunals Rules of Procedure, which specify that an originating application shall set out the name and address of the claimant and of the person against whom relief is sought and the grounds, with particulars thereof, on which relief is sought, are not mandatory but are directory only. Therefore, where an application indicates that the claimant is making a complaint of discrimination in relation to her rejection for a particular post, a failure to specify whether the complaint is of sex discrimination or race discrimination or both is not fatal to the efficacy of the originating application.

Ali v   **[2005] IRLR 201 CA**
Office of National Statistics
Direct discrimination is one type of unlawful act and indirect discrimination is a different type of unlawful act. Accordingly, a claimant who alleged on his originating application that he had been less favourably treated on racial grounds needed permission to amend his claim of race discrimination to add a claim of indirect discrimination since this was a new claim, which was brought out of time.

Redhead v   **[2012] EqLR 628 EAT**
London Borough of Hounslow
Whether or not an ET1 contained claims of direct or indirect race discrimination is a pure question of fact. When pleading a claim of race discrimination, it may be unnecessary to refer to a specific section or subsection of the legislation, provided that the claim form asserts in plain language an act of race discrimination or gives sufficient particulars from which one can spell out such a claim. The ticking of a box is but one feature of construing whether, as a whole, an ET1 form does or does not contain a complaint of a particular type.

Cast v   **[1998] IRLR 318 CA**
Croydon College
A decision by an employer may be a separate act of discrimination for time limit purposes, whether or not it is made on the same facts as before, providing it results from a further consideration of the matter and is not merely a reference back to an earlier decision. If the matter is reconsidered in response to a further request, time begins to run again. Therefore, the appellant's complaint that the respondents had discriminated against her on grounds of sex by refusing to permit her to work part-time after she returned from maternity leave was not out of time, even though her request to work part-time was first refused prior to her maternity leave, and her originating application was not submitted until after she returned from maternity leave when her further requests to work part-time were again refused. Each decision amounted to a fresh refusal of a fresh request to work part time.

Swithland Motors plc v   [1994] IRLR 276 EAT
Clarke
An unlawful act of discrimination by omitting to offer employment cannot be committed until the alleged discriminator is in a position to offer such employment.

Aniagwu v   [1999] IRLR 303 EAT
London Borough of Hackney
A claimant must be able to identify the detriment to which he has been subjected before he can present a complaint. Therefore, the time limit for bringing a complaint of discrimination in respect of an employer's refusal to accept a grievance began to run from the date the decision of a grievance panel was communicated to the employee rather than the date on which that decision was taken.

British Gas Services Ltd v   [2001] IRLR 60 EAT
McCaull
Time does not run in respect of a discriminatory dismissal until the notice of dismissal expires and the employment ceases. In dismissal cases, it is when the individual finds himself out of a job that he suffers detriment as a result of the discrimination.

Matuszowicz v   [2009] IRLR 288 CA
Kingston upon Hull City Council
A failure to make reasonable adjustments is an omission, not an act. The time-limit provisions relating to "deliberate omissions" apply even where the failure to make a reasonable adjustment is inadvertent. In such a case, where a person has not done an act inconsistent with making a reasonable adjustment, the tribunal must determine when, if the employer had been acting reasonably, it would have made the reasonable adjustment.

Extension

Robertson v   [2003] IRLR 434 CA
Bexley Community Centre
An employment tribunal has a very wide discretion in determining whether or not it is just and equitable to extend time. It is entitled to consider anything that it considers relevant. However, time limits are exercised strictly in employment cases. When tribunals consider their discretion to consider a claim out of time on just and equitable grounds, there is no presumption that they should do so unless they can justify failure to exercise the discretion. On the contrary, a tribunal cannot hear a complaint unless the claimant convinces it that it is just and equitable to extend time. The exercise of discretion is thus the exception rather than the rule.

Chief Constable of Lincolnshire Police v   [2010] IRLR 327 CA
Caston
The statement in *Robertson v Bexley Community Centre* has been latched on to by commentators as offering "guidance", but in essence is an elegant repetition of well-established principles relating to the exercise of a judicial discretion. What the case does is to emphasise the employment tribunal's wide discretion.

Mills v   [1998] IRLR 494 EAT
Marshall
The words "just and equitable" in the discrimination legislation giving power to extend time could not be wider or more general. The discretion to extend time is unfettered and may include a consideration of the date from which the complainant could reasonably have become aware of her right to present a worthwhile complaint.

Malcolm v   [2012] EqLR 363 CS
Dundee City Council
Employment tribunals are not required to use the discretionary power to extend time sparingly. In exercising the discretion, employment tribunals must consider whether it is "just and equitable" to exercise it in the claimant's favour. The discretion afforded to an employment tribunal is a wide and unfettered one. A tribunal will err if it proceeds on the basis that an extension will be refused in all but exceptional circumstances.

London Borough of Southwark v   [2003] IRLR 220 CA
Afolabi
In considering whether it is just and equitable to extend time, a tribunal is not required to go through the matters listed in s.33(3) of the Limitation Act 1980, provided that no significant factor has been left out of account by the tribunal in exercising its discretion.

Bahous v   [2012] EqLR 4 EAT
Pizza Express Restaurants
When deciding whether or not it is just and equitable to extend time for presentation of a discrimination complaint, the merits of the complaint do not require separate consideration but are part of the exercise of balancing the prejudice likely to be suffered by the respective parties should time not be extended.

Mills v   [1998] IRLR 494 EAT
Marshall
Where a person was reasonably unaware of the fact that they had the right to being proceedings until shortly before the complaint was filed, whether it is just and equitable to extend time is for the employment tribunal to determine, balancing all the relevant factors, including whether it is possible to have a fair trial of the issues raised by the complaint. Unawareness of the right to sue might stem from a failure by the lawyers to appreciate that a claim lay, or because the law "changed" or was differently perceived after a decision of another court.

Chohan v   [2004] IRLR 685 EAT
Derby Law Centre
Delay in bringing a claim in time due to incorrect legal advice ought not defeat a claimant's contention that the claim ought to be heard. The failure by a legal adviser to enter proceedings in time should not be visited upon the claimant for otherwise the defendant would be in receipt of a windfall.

Robinson v   [2000] IRLR 904 EAT
Post Office
An employment tribunal was entitled to find that it was not just and equitable to extend the time limit for presenting the claimant's disability discrimination complaint in respect of

his dismissal, notwithstanding that his complaint was out of time because he was pursuing an internal appeal against dismissal. Parliament deliberately has not provided that the running of time should be delayed until the end of the domestic processes. When delay on account of an incomplete internal appeal is relied upon as a reason for failing to lodge a tribunal application in time, it will ordinarily suffice for the employment tribunal to put this into the balance when the justice and equity of the matter is being considered.

Apelogun-Gabriels v **[2002] IRLR 116 CA**
London Borough of Lambeth
The correct law for whether it is just and equitable to extend the time limit for presenting a discrimination complaint which is out of time because the claimant was pursuing internal proceedings was laid down by *Robinson v Post Office* rather than by *Aniagwu v London Borough of Hackney*. The fact, if it be so, that the employee had deferred proceedings in the tribunal while awaiting the outcome of domestic proceedings is only one factor to be taken into account. To the extent that *Aniagwu* lays down some general principle that one should always await the outcome of internal grievance procedures before embarking on litigation, it was plainly wrong.

Department for Constitutional **[2008] IRLR 128 CA**
Affairs v
Jones
Although there is no general principle that a person with mental health problems is entitled to delay as a matter of course in bringing a claim, there is an additional factor in disability discrimination not present when some of the other discretions come to be exercised, which is that the disability must be a 12-month disability as defined in the Act. Any person with a mental condition has therefore to predict whether he is likely to come within the definition. In this case, an employment judge was entitled to exercise his discretion to extend time where the true reason for the delay which occurred in presenting the claim was that the claimant did not want to admit to himself or to others that he was disabled within the meaning of the Act.

Continuing discrimination

Barclays Bank plc v **[1991] IRLR 136 HL**
Kapur
To maintain a continuing regime which adversely affects an employee is an act which continues so long as it is maintained.

Hendricks v **[2003] IRLR 96 CA**
Commissioner of Police for the Metropolis
In determining whether there was "an act extending over a period", as distinct from a succession of unconnected or isolated specific acts, for which time would begin to run from the date when each specific act was committed, the focus should be on the substance of the complaints that the employer was responsible for an ongoing situation or a continuing state of affairs. The concepts of policy, rule, practice, scheme or regime in the authorities were given as examples of when an act extends over a period. They

should not be treated as a complete and constricting statement of the indicia of "an act extending over a period".

Robertson v **[2003] IRLR 434 CA**
Bexley Community Centre
To establish a continuing act it must be shown that the employer had a practice, policy, rule or regime governing the act said to constitute it.

Cast v **[1998] IRLR 318 CA**
Croydon College
Application of a discriminatory policy or regime pursuant to which decisions may be taken from time to time is an act extending over a period. There can be a policy even though it is not of a formal nature or expressed in writing, and even though it is confined to a particular post or role.

Cast v **[1997] IRLR 14 EAT**
Croydon College
The mere repetition of a request cannot convert a single managerial decision into a policy, practice or rule.

Hendricks v **[2003] IRLR 96 CA**
Commissioner of Police for the Metropolis
The burden is on the claimant to prove, either by direct evidence or by inference from primary facts, that alleged incidents of discrimination were linked to one another and were evidence of a continuing discriminatory state of affairs covered by the concept of "an act extending over a period."

Tyagi v **[2001] IRLR 465 CA**
BBC World Service
A job claimant cannot complain of a policy of "continuing discrimination" extending over a period. The statutory language relating to selection arrangements, which refers to discrimination in the arrangements which the employer makes "for the purpose of determining who should be offered that employment", makes it clear that what is being complained about is not employment generally but the particular employment that is being offered.

Examples

Sougrin v **[1992] IRLR 416 CA**
Haringey Health Authority
A grading decision is a one-off act with continuing consequences rather than a continuing act of discrimination.

Rovenska v **[1997] IRLR 367 CA**
General Medical Council
If the General Medical Council's regime for exemption from a test set for registration as a medical practitioner was indirectly discriminatory, then it would be committing an act of unlawful discrimination on every occasion that it refused to allow the claimant limited registration without first taking the test.

Owusu v **[1995] IRLR 574 EAT**
London Fire & Civil Defence Authority
In alleging a failure by the employers over a number of years to re-grade him and a failure to give him an opportunity to

act-up when such opportunities arose, the complainant was alleging a continuing act in the form of maintaining a practice which resulted in consistent discriminatory decisions.

Calder v   [1989] IRLR 55 EAT
James Finlay Corporation Ltd

By constituting a mortgage subsidy scheme under the rules of which a woman could not obtain benefit, the employers were discriminating against the appellant woman in the way they afforded her "access" to the benefit. It followed that so long as she remained in the employers' employ, there was a continuing discrimination against her. Alternatively, it could be said that so long as her employment continued, the employers were subjecting her to "any other detriment". As the rule of the scheme constituted a discriminatory act extending over the period of the appellant's employment, it was therefore to be treated as having been done at the end of her employment rather than on the last occasion on which she was deliberately refused access to the scheme. Consequently, as her complaint had been presented within three months of leaving her employment, the employment tribunal had jurisdiction to entertain it.

Littlewoods Organisation plc v   [1993] IRLR 154 EAT
Traynor

A complaint of racial discrimination in respect of alleged racial abuse was not out of time, notwithstanding that the last incident took place more than three months before the complaint was filed, in circumstances in which remedial measures promised by the employers had not been fully implemented when the respondent resigned and made his complaint to the tribunal. So long as the remedial measures which had been agreed on were not actually taken, a situation capable of involving racial discrimination continued and allowing that situation to continue amounted to a continuing act.

CONTRACTING OUT

(1) A term of a contract is unenforceable by a person in whose favour it would operate in so far as it purports to exclude or limit a provision of or made under this Act.

(2) A relevant non-contractual term (as defined by section 142) is unenforceable by a person in whose favour it would operate in so far as it purports to exclude or limit a provision of or made under this Act, in so far as the provision relates to disability.

(3) This section does not apply to a contract which settles a claim within section 114.

(4) This section does not apply to a contract which settles a complaint within section 120 if the contract –
(a) is made with the assistance of a conciliation officer, or
(b) is a qualifying compromise contract.

(5) A contract within subsection (4) includes a contract which settles a complaint relating to a breach of an equality clause or rule or of a non-discrimination rule.

(6) A contract within subsection (4) includes an agreement by the parties to a dispute to submit the dispute to arbitration if –

(a) the dispute is covered by a scheme having effect by virtue of an order under section 212A of the Trade Union and Labour Relations (Consolidation) Act 1992, and
(b) the agreement is to submit the dispute to arbitration in accordance with the scheme.

EQUALITY ACT – s.144

(1) This section applies for the purposes of this Part.

(2) A qualifying compromise contract is a contract in relation to which each of the conditions in subsection (3) is met.

(3) Those conditions are that –
(a) the contract is in writing,
(b) the contract relates to the particular complaint,
(c) the complainant has, before entering into the contract, received advice from an independent adviser about its terms and effect (including, in particular, its effect on the complainant's ability to pursue the complaint before an employment tribunal),
(d) on the date of the giving of the advice, there is in force a contract of insurance, or an indemnity provided for members of a profession or professional body, covering the risk of a claim by the complainant in respect of loss arising from the advice,
(e) the contract identifies the adviser, and
(f) the contract states that the conditions in paragraphs (c) and (d) are met.

EQUALITY ACT – s.147

Clarke v   [2006] IRLR 324 EAT
Redcar & Cleveland Borough Council

Where the parties make a contract that follows any attempt by an ACAS conciliation officer to promote a settlement, the contract is made with the assistance of that ACAS officer. Whether a settlement is effective to preclude a claim being brought before a tribunal depends on whether what the ACAS officer has done corresponds to the functions which a conciliation officer has a duty, or power, to discharge. In determining whether the conciliation officer exercised her functions in order to effect a valid conciliation contract, the following principles apply:

a. The ACAS officer has no responsibility to see that the terms of the settlement are fair on the employee.

b. The expression "promote a settlement" must be given a liberal construction capable of covering whatever action by way of such promotion as is applicable in the circumstances of the particular case.

c. The ACAS officer must never advise as to the merits of the case.

d. It is not for the tribunal to consider whether the officer correctly interpreted her duties; it is sufficient that the officer intended and purported to act under the section.

e. If the ACAS officer were to act in bad faith or adopt unfair methods when promoting a settlement, the agreement might be set aside and might not operate as a bar to proceedings.

Clarke v   [2006] IRLR 324 EAT
Redcar & Cleveland Borough Council

An ACAS conciliation officer is not under a duty to give advice, to evaluate the claims or to ensure that the claimants understand the nature and extent of all their potential claims.

McWilliam v   **[2011] IRLR 568 EAT**
Glasgow City Council   **[2011] EqLR 554 EAT**
The requirement that a compromise contract must relate to a "particular complaint" does not mean that a complaint could only be validly compromised if either it was set out in a pre-existing Tribunal claim or if it had been articulated orally or in writing or in a prior grievance. Giving the words of the statute their ordinary meaning, the term "a complaint" is wide enough to include circumstances where there was nothing more than an expression of dissatisfaction about something. The purpose of the words "particular complaint" are to ensure that there was adequate specification in the compromise agreement itself of the complaint to which it related to so that both parties knew which particular complaint could not be litigated in the future. The employment judge in the present case had correctly concluded that what was required was that the complaint to be compromised should be sufficiently identified either by statutory provision or generically so that the employee was not asked to sign a blanket waiver of all possible claims he or she may have.

Lunt v   **[1999] IRLR 458 EAT**
Merseyside TEC Ltd
The requirement that a compromise agreement "must relate to the particular complaint" is not limited to complaints that have been presented to an employment tribunal. However, a "blanket" agreement compromising claims which had never been indicated in the past is not permitted.

Lunt v   **[1999] IRLR 458 EAT**
Merseyside TEC Ltd
A single compromise agreement can cover claims under more than one statute.

McWilliam v   **[2011] IRLR 568 EAT**
Glasgow City Council   **[2011] EqLR 554 EAT**
The requirement that the employee must have received advice from a relevant independent adviser as to the "terms and effect of the proposed agreement" did not require the relevant independent adviser to offer a view on whether or not the deal on offer was a good one or whether or not the adviser thought that the employee should accept it.

IMMUNITY

Heath v   **[2005] IRLR 270 CA**
Commissioner of Police for the
  Metropolis
Proceedings before a police disciplinary board constituted under the Police (Discipline) Regulations are sufficiently "judicial" to fall within the rule of absolute immunity from suit that attaches to judicial or quasi-judicial proceedings and excludes complaints about unlawful discriminatory conduct in the course of such proceedings to other judicial bodies, including employment tribunals.

DEATH OF CLAIMANT

Harris v   **[2000] IRLR 320 CA**
Lewisham & Guys Mental Health
  NHS Trust
A complaint brought under the discrimination statutes survives the death of the complainant.

BANKRUPTCY OF CLAIMANT

Khan v   **[2004] IRLR 961 CA**
Trident Safeguards Ltd
A claim for race discrimination is a "hybrid" claim, since it includes both a claim for pecuniary loss, which is property that is part of the bankrupt's estate, and a claim for injury to feelings, which is "personal" and does not form part of the bankrupt's estate, and therefore the whole of the hybrid claim vests in the trustee in bankruptcy in accordance with the decision in *Ord v Upton*. However, there is a public interest in claims of race discrimination being fully examined. Therefore, a bankrupt should be permitted to limit their claim for relief to a declaration and compensation for injury to feelings only. If that is done, the claim ceases to be a hybrid one.

ACTS AUTHORISED BY STATUTE OR THE EXECUTIVE

1(1) This paragraph applies to anything done –
  (a) in pursuance of an enactment;
  (b) in pursuance of an instrument made by a member of the executive under an enactment;
  (c) to comply with a requirement imposed (whether before or after the passing of this Act) by a member of the executive by virtue of an enactment;
  (d) in pursuance of arrangements made (whether before or after the passing of this Act) by or with the approval of, or for the time being approved by, a Minister of the Crown;
  (e) to comply with a condition imposed (whether before or after the passing of this Act) by a Minister of the Crown.

(2) A person does not contravene Part 3, 4, 5 or 6 by doing anything to which this paragraph applies which discriminates against another because of the other's nationality.

(3) A person (A) does not contravene Part 3, 4, 5 or 6 if, by doing anything to which this paragraph applies, A discriminates against another (B) by applying to B a provision, criterion or practice which relates to –
  (a) B's place of ordinary residence;
  (b) the length of time B has been present or resident in or outside the United Kingdom or an area within it.

EQUALITY ACT 2010 – Sch. 23, para. 1

Hampson v   **[1990] IRLR 302 HL**
Department of Education and Science
An act is done "in pursuance of" an enactment, order or instrument only if it is specified in the enactment, order or instrument.

Page v [1981] IRLR 13 EAT
Freighthire (Tank Haulage) Ltd
The interests of safety are not a justification for discrimination on grounds of sex unless the act was done to comply with a pre-existing statutory requirement.

Page v [1981] IRLR 13 EAT
Freighthire (Tank Haulage) Ltd
In order to satisfy the statutory test, an employer does not have to show that debarring a woman from taking up a job was inexorably the only method available to him of satisfying the requirements of the Health and Safety at Work Act to ensure, so far as is reasonably practicable, the health, safety and welfare at work of his employees. It is important to consider all the circumstances of the case, the risk involved and the measures which it can be said are reasonably necessary to eliminate the risk. There may be cases where one course which is suggested as being sufficient may leave open some doubt as to whether it is going to achieve the desired level of protection. In such a case, it may be that an employer is complying with the requirements of the legislation if, in all the circumstances, he thinks it right not to allow an employee, for his (or her) own protection or safety, to do the particular job.

DISCOVERY AND PARTICULARS

General principles

Nasse v [1979] IRLR 465 HL
Science Research Council
Vyas v
Leyland Cars
In discrimination cases, the necessary information and material to support or refute a claim will rarely be in the possession of the employee, but, on the contrary, is likely to be in the possession of the employer. Discrimination often involves an allegation that, although the unselected complainant is as well qualified as the person selected, or indeed better qualified, he was not chosen, an allegation which almost necessarily involves a careful comparison of qualifications and an inquiry into the selection process. The employer is likely to have information on these matters. There is a clear public interest, accepted and emphasised by Parliament in the Sex Discrimination and Race Relations Acts, that the fullest information should be before the tribunals.

Canadian Imperial Bank of [2009] IRLR 740 CA
Commerce v
Beck
The law on disclosure of documents is very clear, and of universal application. The test is whether or not an order for discovery is necessary for fairly disposing of the proceedings. Relevance is a factor, but is not, of itself, sufficient to warrant making an order. Confidentiality is not, of itself, sufficient to warrant the refusal of an order and does not render documents immune from disclosure.

West Midlands Passenger Transport [1988] IRLR 186 CA
Executive v
Singh
Statistics of the number of white and non-white persons who applied for similar posts with the employers over a period, categorised as to whether or not they had been appointed, are discoverable by an unsuccessful claimant for promotion since they are logically probative of whether the employers discriminated against him on racial grounds when they denied him promotion. The statistical material was relevant in that it might assist the complainant in establishing a positive case that the treatment of non-white employees was on racial grounds, which was an effective cause for their, and his, failure to obtain promotion and it might assist the complainant to rebut the employers' contention that they operated an equal opportunities policy and applied it in his case.

Perera v [1980] IRLR 233 EAT
Civil Service Commission
Since it is rare for there to be direct evidence or a direct admission of racial discrimination, tribunals will have to probe the facts which are put forward initially by the person against whom the proceedings are brought to consider whether there has been discrimination. Therefore, a claimant is entitled to have the opportunity of looking, in such form as is convenient and fair, at such material which is in the possession of the employer and which is necessary for the tribunal to consider the matter.

Rasul v [1978] IRLR 203 EAT
Commission for Racial Equality
A complainant is entitled to discovery of documents from the respondents, which will enable him to make a comparative analysis between his own qualifications and history and that of his competitors for a job for which he applied unsuccessfully, in order that an employment tribunal can legitimately draw the inference that the reason for his non-success was that the respondents had discriminated against him on grounds of his race. It is not easy for a complainant in a discrimination case to give direct evidence to establish whether somebody has practised discrimination, since it is what happens in the decision-making process of the prospective employer that is, or is not, discrimination.

Commissioner of Police of [1993] IRLR 319 EAT
the Metropolis v
Locker
Discovery of statements made in the course of the grievance procedure dealing with the employee's allegations of discrimination in respect of her non-selection for a post was necessary for fairly disposing of her employment tribunal complaints, notwithstanding that the statements sought to be inspected were about events which may have preceded the discriminatory conduct complained of, since the allegations went significantly wider than the conduct of the interview when she was not selected. She relied upon a background of discriminatory treatment which would, if proved, clearly be admissible material from which inferences could be drawn of discrimination on racial grounds, and the grievance procedure may well have produced statements that would tend to prove such background facts.

West Midlands Passenger Transport   **[1988] IRLR 186 CA**
    Executive v
Singh
A tribunal may decide that a request for discovery is oppressive and not order discovery even where it is relevant if it is of the opinion that it is not necessary for disposing fairly of the proceedings or for saving costs. Discovery may be oppressive if it requires the provision of material not readily to hand, which can only be made available with difficulty and at great expense, or if it requires the party ordered to make discovery to embark on a course which will add unreasonably to the length and cost of the hearing.

Carrington v   **[1990] IRLR 6 EAT**
Helix Lighting Ltd
There are no powers under the Employment Tribunals Rules of Procedure to require an employer to prepare a schedule of evidence disclosing details of the ethnic composition of its workforce where this information is not available and can only be produced by carrying out a survey of the workforce. "Discovery" is limited to the production of documents in being.

Confidential documents

Nasse v   **[1979] IRLR 465 HL**
Science Research Council
Vyas v
Leyland Cars
There is no principle of law by which documents are protected from discovery by confidentiality in and of itself. If an employment tribunal is satisfied that discovery of a document is necessary in order to dispose fairly of proceedings or for saving costs, it must order the document to be disclosed, notwithstanding that the document is confidential.

Nasse v   **[1979] IRLR 465 HL**
Science Research Council
Vyas v
Leyland Cars
Where there is an objection by an employer to the disclosure of documents on the grounds of confidentiality, the employment tribunal should inspect the documents to decide whether disclosure is necessary for the fair disposal of the case or for saving costs. An employment tribunal should not order discovery without first inspecting the documents concerned. In exercising its discretion as to whether to order disclosure, the tribunal should have regard to the fact that documents are confidential and should consider whether the necessary information can be obtained by other means, not involving a breach of confidence. It should consider whether justice can be done by special measures such as "covering up" or substituting anonymous references for specific names.

British Railways Board v   **[1979] IRLR 45 EAT**
Natarajan
Before deciding whether an examination of confidential documents is necessary, an employment tribunal chairman should decide whether there is any prima facie prospect of the confidential material being relevant to an issue which

arises in the litigation. If there is not, the examination of the documents should not take place. If it is reasonable to expect that there is a real likelihood of relevance emerging from the examination, it is a matter of convenience in each case as to whether the examination should take place at the interlocutory stage of discovery or immediately the matter arises at the trial.

The British Library v   **[1984] IRLR 306 EAT**
Palyza
In considering whether discovery sought is necessary for disposing fairly of the proceedings, a tribunal should confine its attention to matters which are, or might be, of assistance to the claimant. The tribunal is not required to order the disclosure against the employer's wishes of material which would or could help the employer's case. The "fair disposal of the proceedings" means a disposal which is fair to the claimant. The justification for ordering the disclosure of information which would otherwise remain confidential is that Parliament has seen fit to place upon the complainant of racial or sexual discrimination the burden of proving his or her case, notwithstanding that the bulk of the relevant evidence is likely to be in the possession of the respondent to the complaint. The procedure of discovery is designed to offset the probative disadvantages which the complainant would otherwise suffer. It is designed to do justice to the complainant, and there is no reason why it should seek to go further than that. The governing concept is fairness, not absolute justice, and it would be strange if one of the adversaries was compelled to adduce favourable evidence which he would rather withhold.

The British Library v   **[1984] IRLR 306 EAT**
Palyza
The decision of an employment tribunal as to whether or not it is necessary for fairly disposing of the proceedings that confidential reports should be disclosed in cases of alleged discrimination is one which the EAT is free to review and to substitute its own view. The decision whether discovery should be ordered is of such importance as to make it highly desirable that its review by the appellate court should be unfettered.

Commissioner of Police of   **[1993] IRLR 319 EAT**
    the Metropolis v
Locker
Whether public interest immunity exists depends upon whether the court is satisfied that the nature and status of the procedure in which the class of documents was generated is of a type to which public interest immunity should apply. On that basis, public interest immunity does not attach to statements made during the course of a police grievance procedure.

Particulars

McKinson v   **[2011] EqLR 1114 EAT**
Hackney Community College
An Employment Judge is entitled to ask the claimant to identify in schedule form precisely what his complaints of discrimination and victimisation were.

McKinson v   **[2011] EqLR 1114 EAT**
Hackney Community College

An Employment Judge does not have the power to require a claimant to select which few of a large number of complaints he would pursue at a final hearing.

Carrington v   **[1990] IRLR 6 EAT**
Helix Lighting Ltd

An employment tribunal does not have power in a case of alleged discrimination to require a schedule of evidence to be produced by an employer where there is no documentation upon which the schedule is to be based and where the production of the schedule is in the nature of creating evidence. Such information cannot be regarded as "particulars" as particulars are the basis whereby a party may ascertain the way the other side is putting their case so that they can prepare accordingly. Particulars are not evidence.

Obtaining information

(1) In this section –
    (a) P is a person who thinks that a contravention of this Act has occurred in relation to P;
    (b) R is a person who P thinks has contravened this Act.

(2) A Minister of the Crown must by order prescribe –
    (a) forms by which P may question R on any matter which is or may be relevant;
    (b) forms by which R may answer questions by P.

(3) A question by P or an answer by R is admissible as evidence in proceedings under this Act (whether or not the question or answer is contained in a prescribed form).

(4) A court or tribunal may draw an inference from –
    (a) a failure by R to answer a question by P before the end of the period of 8 weeks beginning with the day on which the question is served;
    (b) an evasive or equivocal answer.

EQUALITY ACT 2010 – s.138

Carrington v   **[1990] IRLR 6 EAT**
Helix Lighting Ltd

The statutory procedure by way of questionnaire is the way in which the legislature has made provision for a claimant to advance his or her case of discrimination. Tribunals are encouraged by the statutes to take a serious view of any unsatisfactory answering of questionnaires and have ample power to draw adverse inferences.

D'Silva v   **[2008] IRLR 412 EAT**
NATFHE

There is a tendency for respondents' failures in answering a questionnaire, or otherwise in providing information or documents, to be relied on by claimants, and even sometimes by tribunals, as automatically raising a presumption of discrimination. An inference can be drawn from failures of this kind only in appropriate cases, and the drawing of inferences from such failures is not a tick-box exercise. It is necessary in each case to consider whether the failure in question is capable of constituting evidence supporting the inference that the respondent acted discriminatorily in the manner alleged; and if so whether in the light of any explanation supplied it does in fact justify that inference. Such failures are only relevant to the extent that they potentially shed light on the actual discrimination complained of and thus, necessarily, on the mental processes of the decision-taker. There will be many cases where it should be clear from the start, or soon becomes evident, that any alleged failure of this kind, however reprehensible, can have no bearing on the reason why the respondents did the act complained of.

Carrington v   **[1990] IRLR 6 EAT**
Helix Lighting Ltd

It is a sensible and necessary part of the procedure that after any initial questionnaire, a claimant should be able to seek leave, on notice, to administer a further questionnaire.

Oxford v   **[1977] IRLR 225 EAT**
Department of Health and
   Social Security

There is no obligation on an employer, in answer to a form for questioning, to provide a complainant with the names and addresses of successful claimants for the position for which the complainant applied. Information as to the qualifications of successful claimants and other relevant information should generally be disclosed, with the identity of the individuals being concealed and their address withheld

Meister v   **[2012] EqLR 602 CJEU**
Speech Design Carrier Systems GmbH

A Russian national who believed that she had been discriminated against on grounds of age, sex and ethnic origin when she applied unsuccessfully for a position with a German company, for which she claimed, plausibly, to be qualified, could not rely upon EU discrimination legislation as entitling her to have access to information indicating whether the company engaged another applicant at the end of the recruitment process.

2. DEFINITIONS OF DISCRIMINATION

DIRECT DISCRIMINATION

(1) A person (A) discriminates against another (B) if, because of a protected characteristic, A treats B less favourably than A treats or would treat others.

EQUALITY ACT 2010 – s.13

(1) This section applies to any proceedings relating to a contravention of this Act.

(2) If there are facts from which the court could decide, in the absence of any other explanation, that a person (A) contravened the provision concerned, the court must hold that the contravention occurred.

(3) But subsection (2) does not apply if A shows that A did not contravene the provision.

EQUALITY ACT 2010 – s.136

BURDEN OF PROOF

Igen Ltd v   **[2005] IRLR 258 CA**
Wong
The burden of proof requires the employment tribunal to go through a two-stage process. The first stage requires the claimant to prove facts from which the tribunal could, apart from the section, conclude in the absence of an adequate explanation that the respondent has committed, or is to be treated as having committed, the unlawful act of discrimination against the complainant. The tribunal is required to make an assumption at the first stage which may be contrary to reality, the plain purpose being to shift the burden of proof at the second stage so that unless the respondent provides an adequate explanation, the complainant will succeed. It would be inconsistent with that assumption to take account of an adequate explanation by the respondent at the first stage. The second stage, which only comes into effect if the complainant has proved those facts, requires the respondent to prove that he did not commit or is not to be treated as having committed the unlawful act, if the complaint is not to be upheld. If the second stage is reached, and the respondent's explanation is inadequate, it will be not merely legitimate but also necessary for the tribunal to conclude that the complaint should be upheld.

Igen Ltd v   **[2005] IRLR 258 CA**
Wong
Although there are two stages in the tribunal's decision-making process, tribunals should not divide hearings into two parts to correspond to those stages. Tribunals will generally wish to hear all the evidence, including the respondent's explanation, before deciding whether the requirements at the first stage are satisfied and, if so, whether the respondent has discharged the onus which has shifted.

Hewage v   **[2012] IRLR 870 UKSC**
Grampian Health Board   **[2012] EqLR 884 UKSC**
It is important not to make too much of the role of the bur-den of proof provisions. They will require careful attention where there is room for doubt as to the facts necessary to establish discrimination. But they have nothing to offer where the tribunal is in a position to make positive findings on the evidence one way or the other.

MEANING OF "LESS FAVOURABLE"

R v   **[1989] IRLR 173 HL**
Birmingham City Council ex parte
  Equal Opportunities Commission
In order to establish that there was less favourable treatment of members of one sex by reason of their having been denied the same opportunities as the other sex, it is enough that they are deprived of a choice which was valued by them and which (even though others may take a different view) is a choice obviously valued, on reasonable grounds, by many others. It is not necessary to prove that that which was lost was "better".

London Borough of Islington v   **[2009] IRLR 154 EAT**
Ladele
It cannot constitute direct discrimination to treat all employees in precisely the same way.

Simon v   **[1987] IRLR 307 CA**
Brimham Associates
Words or acts of discouragement can amount to treatment of the person discouraged which is less favourable than that given to other persons.

Burrett v   **[1994] IRLR 7 EAT**
West Birmingham Health Authority
The fact that a complainant honestly considers that she is being less favourably treated does not of itself establish that there is "less favourable treatment". Whether there is less favourable treatment is for the employment tribunal to decide.

Stewart v   **[1994] IRLR 440 EAT**
Cleveland Guest (Engineering) Ltd
There is room for disagreement as to what is or is not less favourable treatment and the employment tribunal, as industrial jury, is best placed to make a decision on the facts of a particular case. If the error of law relied upon is the argument that the employment tribunal reached a decision which no reasonable tribunal, on a proper appreciation of the facts and law, would have reached, an overwhelming case to that effect must be made out.

DISCRIMINATORY TREATMENT

Nagarajan v   **[1999] IRLR 572 HL**
London Regional Transport
The crucial question in a case of direct discrimination is why the complainant received less favourable treatment. Was it on grounds of race? Or was it for some other rea-

son? If racial grounds were the reason for the less favourable treatment, direct discrimination is established. The reason why the discriminator acted on racial grounds is irrelevant when deciding whether an act of racial discrimination occurred.

Shamoon v   [2003] IRLR 285 HL
Chief Constable of the Royal
  Ulster Constabulary
Per Lord Nicholls: Employment tribunals may sometimes be able to avoid arid and confusing disputes about the identification of the appropriate comparator by concentrating primarily on why the claimant was treated as she was, and postponing the less favourable treatment issue until after they have decided why the treatment was afforded. Was it on the proscribed ground or was it for some other reason? If the former, there will usually be no difficulty in deciding whether the treatment afforded to the claimant on the proscribed ground was less favourable than was or would have been afforded to others.

James v   [1990] IRLR 288 HL
Eastleigh Borough Council
The question to be considered is: "would the complainant have received the same treatment from the defendant but for his or her sex?" This test embraces both the case where the treatment derives from the application of a gender-based criterion and the case where it derives from the selection of the complainant because of his or her sex.

Amnesty International v   [2009] IRLR 884 EAT
Ahmed
There is no real difficulty in reconciling *James v Eastleigh* and *Nagarajan*. In some cases, such as *James*, the ground for the treatment complained of is inherent in the act itself. In cases of this kind, what was going on inside the head of the putative discriminator will be irrelevant. In other cases, of which *Nagarajan* is an example, the act complained of is not in itself discriminatory but is rendered so by a discriminatory motivation – ie by the mental processes (whether conscious or unconscious) that led the putative discriminator to do the act. In both cases, the ultimate question is what was the ground of the treatment complained of, or the reason why it occurred. The difference between them simply reflects the different ways in which conduct may be discriminatory.

Cooperative Centrale Raiffeisen   [2011] EqLR 580 EAT
  Boerenleenbank BA v
Docker
There is a danger in elevating the "reason why" question as first formulated by Lord Nicholls in *Nagarajan v London Regional Transport* to a level at which the statutory provisions become immaterial.

R (on the application of Elias) v   [2006] IRLR 934 CA
Secretary of State for Defence
Direct and indirect discrimination are two different statutory torts. Although, in a general sense, discrimination with a discriminatory purpose, regardless of the particular form it takes, can be perceived as treating a person less favourably

"on racial grounds", in the present state of the law, the particular *form* of discrimination matters, even if there are present in the circumstances of the case a discriminatory purpose and discriminatory effects.

Jaffrey v   [2002] IRLR 688 EAT
Department of Environment, Transport
  and Regions
The facts of a case might give rise to claims both in respect of direct and indirect discrimination if different facts demonstrate the different types of discrimination, and the factual circumstances overlap but not precisely coincide.

Motive

R (on the application of European   [2005] IRLR 115 HL
  Roma Rights Centre) v
Immigration Officer at Prague Airport
If a person acts on racial grounds, the reason why he does so is irrelevant.

R (on the application of E) v   [2010] IRLR 136 SC
Governing Body of JFS
The grounds for discrimination are the factual criteria applied by the discriminator in reaching his decision rather than the motive for taking the decision. The motive for discriminating is not relevant.

James v   [1990] IRLR 288 HL
Eastleigh Borough Council
The correct test for direct discrimination is objective, not subjective. Whether or not the treatment is less favourable on the ground of sex is not saved from constituting unlawful discrimination by the fact that the defendant acted from a benign motive.

Moyhing v   [2006] IRLR 860 EAT
Barts and London NHS Trust
Direct discrimination cannot be justified. The fact that there may be good and sound reasons for distinguishing between men and women is no defence.

Singh v   [2011] EqLR 1248 CS
Biotechnology and Biological
  Sciences Research
There was no direct race discrimination where the employment tribunal concluded that the undoubtedly unreasonable behaviour on the part of the employers was wholly motivated by a desire to be rid of the Claimant as a "wholly unsatisfactory employee".

Stereotypical assumptions

R (on the application of European   [2005] IRLR 115 HL
  Roma Rights Centre) v
Immigration Officer at Prague Airport
The object of the legislation is to ensure that each person is treated as an individual and not assumed to be like other

members of the group, whether or not most members of the group do have such characteristics. A person may be acting on beliefs or assumptions about members of the sex or racial group involved which are often true and which if true would provide a good reason for the less favourable treatment in question, but what may be true of a group may not be true of a significant number of individuals within that group.

Aylott v [2010] IRLR 994 CA
Stockton on Tees Borough Council [2010] EqLR 69 CA
Direct discrimination can occur when assumptions are made that a claimant, as an individual, has characteristics associated with a group to which the claimant belongs, irrespective of whether the claimant or most members of the group have those characteristics.

Horsey v [1982] IRLR 395 EAT
Dyfed County Council
The statutory definitions of discrimination cover cases where the reason for the discrimination was a generalised assumption that people of a particular sex, marital status or race possess or lack certain characteristics. They do not only cover cases where the sole factor influencing the decision of the alleged discriminator is the sex, marital status or race of the complainant. Most discrimination flows from generalised assumptions and not from a single prejudice dependent solely upon the sex or colour of the complainant. Therefore, a decision to treat a complainant in a particular way for reasons which, as an essential ingredient, contain a generalised assumption about a woman's behaviour is a decision made "on the ground of" her sex.

Causation

Owen & Briggs v [1982] IRLR 502 CA
James
That a racial consideration was an important factor in an employer's decision is sufficient to found a case of discrimination. It is not necessary that the racial factor be the sole reason for the employer's decision.

Nagarajan v [1994] IRLR 61 EAT
Agnew
Where there are mixed motives for the doing of an act, not all of which constitute unlawful discrimination, there will be unlawful discrimination if the unlawful motive was of sufficient weight in the decision-making process to be treated as a cause of the act thus motivated. An important factor in the decision is well within that principle.

London Borough of Islington v [2009] IRLR 154 EAT
Ladele
There will be unlawful discrimination where the prohibited ground contributes to an act or decision even though it is not the sole or principal reason for the act or decision. It follows that there will inevitably be circumstances where an employee has a claim for unlawful discrimination even though he would have been subject to precisely the same

treatment even if there had been no discrimination, because the prohibited ground merely reinforces a decision that would have been taken for lawful reasons.

Lewis Woolf Griptight Ltd v [1997] IRLR 432 EAT
Corfield
There is sex discrimination where the principal reason for dismissal is gender-neutral, but the means by which the employer sought to effect the termination of employment are gender-specific, such as reliance upon the statutory maternity leave provisions, and could not be relied upon in the case of a man. Therefore, the claimant was discriminated against when the employers used the expiry of the four-week period after maternity leave as an excuse for terminating the employment.

Seide v [1980] IRLR 427 EAT
Gillette Industries Ltd
In determining whether there has been unlawful discrimination, the question is whether the activating cause of what happened is that the employer has treated a person less favourably than others on racial grounds. Where there is more than one ground for an employer's action, it might be enough if a substantial and effective cause for the action is a breach of the statute. However, it is not sufficient merely to consider whether the fact that the person is of a particular racial group is any part of the background or is a *causa sine qua non* of what happened. Therefore, an employee who was transferred in order to preserve good working relationships had not been discriminated against on racial grounds, notwithstanding that he might not have been transferred had he not been Jewish, since his being Jewish was not the activating cause of his transfer.

Statutory comparison

(1) On a comparison of cases for the purposes of section 13, 14, or 19 there must be no material difference between the circumstances relating to each case.

EQUALITY ACT 2010 – s.23

Hewage v [2012] IRLR 870 UKSC
Grampian Health Board [2012] EqLR 884 UKSC
Whether situations are comparable is a question of fact and degree.

Macdonald v [2003] IRLR 512 HL
Advocate General for Scotland
Pearce v
Governing Body of Mayfield Secondary School
All the characteristics of the complainant which are relevant to the way his case was dealt with must be found also in the comparator. They do not have to be precisely the same, but they must not be materially different. That is the basic rule, if one is to compare like with like. Characteristics that have no bearing on the way the woman was treated can be ignored, but those that do have a bearing on the way she was treated must be the same if one is to deter-

mine whether, but for her sex, she would have been treated differently.

Birmingham City Council v   [2012] EqLR 910 EAT
Millwood
A tribunal is entitled to come to a conclusion as to comparability and express broadly why it regards two people as being in materially similar circumstances. It does not have to dot every "i" and cross every "t" when dealing with the evidence.

Ahsan v   [2008] IRLR 243 HL
Watt
The treatment of a person who does not qualify as a statutory comparator (because the circumstances are in some material respect different) may nevertheless be evidence from which a tribunal may infer how a hypothetical statutory comparator would have been treated. This is an ordinary question of relevance, which depends upon the degree of the similarity of the circumstances of the person in question (the "evidential comparator") to those of the complainant and all the other evidence in the case.

Ahsan v   [2008] IRLR 243 HL
Watt
It is probably uncommon to find a real person who qualifies as a statutory comparator. In most cases, however, a tribunal should be able, by treating the putative comparator as an evidential comparator, and having due regard to the alleged differences in circumstances and other evidence, to form a view on how the employer would have treated a hypothetical person who was a true statutory comparator.

Madden v   [2005] IRLR 46 CA
Preferred Technical Group Cha Ltd
The hypothetical comparator does not have to be a clone of the claimant in every respect (including personality and personal characteristics) except of a different race. If that were right, every case of alleged race discrimination in which there was a hypothetical comparator and less favourable treatment would result in a finding in the claimant's favour.

Central Manchester University   [2012] EqLR 318 EAT
  Hospitals NHS Foundation Trust v
Browne
The use of a hypothetical comparator raises three questions: what are the attributes of the comparator, would such a comparator have been treated differently, and was that difference in treatment on a prohibited ground? Comparing the treatment of those in non-identical but not wholly dissimilar cases is a permissible means of judging how a hypothetical comparator would have been treated.

Central Manchester University   [2012] EqLR 318 EAT
  Hospitals NHS Foundation Trust v
Browne
It is not always necessary to deal with arid questions as to the characteristics or treatment of hypothetical comparators when those questions are sufficiently answered by identifying the reason for the treatment.

Showboat Entertainment   [1984] IRLR 7 EAT
  Centre Ltd v
Owens
In judging whether there has been discrimination, although like has to be compared with like, the comparison is between the treatment actually meted out and the treatment which would have been afforded to a man having all the same characteristics as the complainant except his race or his attitude to race. Only by excluding matters of race can it be discovered whether the differential treatment was on racial grounds. Therefore, in a case where an employee was dismissed for refusing to carry out an unlawful discriminatory instruction, the correct comparison was between the employee dismissed and another employee who did not refuse to obey the unlawful discriminatory instruction rather than between the employee and how the employers would have treated another employee who refused to obey the instruction.

B v   [2007] IRLR 576 EAT
A
The appropriate comparators in respect of a female personal assistant who had a consensual sexual relationship with her male employer and was dismissed when he became jealous of her relationship with another man was a homosexual male employer and a homosexual male employee. Since such an employee would have received exactly the same treatment – ie he would have been dismissed when his apparent infidelity was discovered, driven by feelings of jealousy – there was no discrimination on grounds of sex.

Evidence

Standard of proof

Igen Ltd v   [2005] IRLR 258 CA
Wong
The guidance issued by the EAT in *Barton v Investec Henderson Crosthwaite Securities Ltd* in respect of Sex Discrimination Act cases, which has been applied in relation to race and disability discrimination, would be approved in amended form, as set out below:

(1) ... it is for the claimant who complains of sex discrimination to prove on the balance of probabilities facts from which the tribunal could conclude, in the absence of an adequate explanation, that the respondent has committed an act of discrimination against the claimant which is unlawful ... These are referred to below as "such facts".

(2) If the claimant does not prove such facts he or she will fail.

(3) It is important to bear in mind in deciding whether the claimant has proved such facts that it is unusual to find direct evidence of sex discrimination. Few employers would be prepared to admit such discrimination, even to themselves. In some cases the discrimination will not be an intention but merely based on the assumption that "he or she would not have fitted in".

(4) In deciding whether the claimant has proved such facts, it is important to remember that the outcome at this

stage of the analysis by the tribunal will therefore usually depend on what inferences it is proper to draw from the primary facts found by the tribunal.

(5) It is important to note the word "could" in [s.136(2)]. At this stage the tribunal does not have to reach a definitive determination that such facts would lead it to the conclusion that there was an act of unlawful discrimination. At this stage a tribunal is looking at the primary facts before it to see what inferences of secondary fact could be drawn from them.

(6) In considering what inferences or conclusions can be drawn from the primary facts, the tribunal must assume that there is no adequate explanation for those facts.

(7) These inferences can include, in appropriate cases, any inferences that it is just and equitable to draw from an evasive or equivocal reply to a questionnaire or any other statutory question.

(8) Likewise, the tribunal must decide whether any provision of any relevant code of practice is relevant and if so, take it into account. This means that inferences may also be drawn from any failure to comply with any relevant code of practice.

(9) Where the claimant has proved facts from which conclusions could be drawn that the respondent has treated the claimant less favourably on the ground of sex, then the burden of proof moves to the respondent.

(10) It is then for the respondent to prove that he did not commit, or as the case may be, is not to be treated as having committed, that act.

(11) To discharge that burden it is necessary for the respondent to prove, on the balance of probabilities, that the treatment was in no sense whatsoever on the grounds of sex, since "no discrimination whatsoever" is compatible with the Burden of Proof Directive.

(12) That requires a tribunal to assess not merely whether the respondent has proved an explanation for the facts from which such inferences can be drawn, but further that it is adequate to discharge the burden of proof on the balance of probabilities that sex was not a ground for the treatment in question.

(13) Since the facts necessary to prove an explanation would normally be in the possession of the respondent, a tribunal would normally expect cogent evidence to discharge that burden of proof. In particular, the tribunal will need to examine carefully explanations for failure to deal with the questionnaire procedure and/or code of practice.

Hewage v   **[2012] IRLR 870 UKSC**
Grampian Health Board   **[2012] EqLR 884 UKSC**
The guidance given by the Court of Appeal in *Igen Ltd v Wong* requires the employment tribunal to assume that there is no adequate explanation for the primary facts when deciding what inferences or conclusions can be drawn from them. The assumption at that stage is simply that there is no adequate explanation and does not in any way diminish the burden on a claimant of proving facts from which the tribunal could conclude in the absence of an adequate explanation that the respondent has committed an act of discrimination against the claimant which is unlawful. There is no assumption as to whether or not a prima facie case has been established. The purpose of the assumption

is to shift the burden of proof at the second stage of the test, but the prima facie case must be proved, and it is for the claimant to discharge that burden.

Madarassy v   **[2007] IRLR 246 CA**
Nomura International plc
The burden of proof does not shift to the employer simply on the claimant establishing a difference in status (eg sex) and a difference in treatment. Those bare facts only indicate a possibility of discrimination. They are not, without more, sufficient material from which a tribunal "could conclude" that, on the balance of probabilities, the respondent had committed an unlawful act of discrimination.

Hussain v   **[2011] EqLR 699 EAT**
Vision Security Ltd
The statement by the Court of Appeal in *Madarassy v Nomura* that a prima facie case of discrimination is not established merely by showing a difference of status and a difference of treatment was rejecting a submission that this was sufficient to reverse the burden of proof automatically in all cases, and was not intended to be a rule of law. Drawing an inference of discrimination is a matter for factual assessment and is situation-specific.

Madarassy v   **[2007] IRLR 246 CA**
Nomura International plc
Although the burden of proof provisions involve a two-stage analysis of the evidence, it does not expressly or impliedly prevent the tribunal at the first stage from hearing, accepting or drawing inferences from evidence adduced by the respondent disputing and rebutting the claimant's evidence of discrimination. The respondent may adduce evidence at the first stage to show that the acts which are alleged to be discriminatory never happened; or that, if they did, they were not less favourable treatment of the claimant; or that the comparators chosen by the claimant or the situations with which comparisons are made are not truly like the claimant or the situation of the claimant; or that, even if there has been less favourable treatment of the claimant, it was not on the ground of her sex or pregnancy. Such evidence from the respondent could, if accepted by the tribunal, be relevant as showing that, contrary to the claimant's allegations of discrimination, there is nothing in the evidence from which the tribunal could properly infer a prima facie case of discrimination on the proscribed ground. The approach of Elias J in *Laing v Manchester City Council* would be approved.

Laing v   **[2006] IRLR 748 EAT**
Manchester City Council
A tribunal should have regard to all facts at the first stage to see what proper inferences can be drawn. The onus lies on the claimant to show potentially less favourable treatment from which an inference of discrimination could properly be drawn. Typically, this will involve identifying an actual comparator treated differently or, in the absence of such a comparator, a hypothetical one who would have been treated more favourably. This involves a consideration of all material facts, as opposed to any explanation.

Brown v [2007] IRLR 259 CA
London Borough of Croydon

It is not an error of law for a tribunal not to apply the two-stage approach to the burden of proof laid down in *Igen Ltd v Wong*. There are cases in which the claimant is not prejudiced by the tribunal omitting express consideration of the first stage of the test, moving straight to the second stage of the test, the "reason why" question, and concluding that the respondent has discharged the burden on him under the second stage by proving that the treatment was not on the proscribed ground.

Maksymiuk v [2012] EqLR 917 EAT
Bar Roma Partnership

Although the guidance in *Igen v Wong* is an important template for decision-making, an employment tribunal is not required to force the facts into a constrained cordon which, in the circumstances of the particular case, they do not fit. Intelligent application of the guidance, rather than slavish obedience where it would require contorted logic, is what is required.

Amnesty International v [2009] IRLR 884 EAT
Ahmed

There would be fewer appeals in discrimination cases if more tribunals made an explicit finding as to the reason for the claimant's treatment, thereby rendering the elaborations of the *Barton/Igen* guidelines otiose, and only resorted to the provisions of [s.136(2)] where they felt unable to make positive findings on the evidence without its assistance.

Network Rail Infrastructure Ltd v [2006] IRLR 865 EAT
Griffiths-Henry

There does not have to be positive evidence that the difference in treatment is race or sex in order to establish a prima facie case.

Community Law Clinic [2011] EqLR 1048 EAT
  Solicitors Ltd v
Methuen

Where the claimant points to nothing more than his dismissal and replacement with someone of different age and sex and race that is insufficient to raise a prima facie case and to transfer the burden to the respondent of proving that they did not discriminate.

Dresdner Kleinwort Wasserstein Ltd v [2005] IRLR 514 EAT
Adebayo

In view of the statutory "like for like' requirement and the need for the relevant circumstances in the claimant's case to be the same or not materially different in the case of the comparator, in order to establish a prima facie case, a claimant in a promotion case would have to show not only that he met the stated qualifications for promotion to the post, but that he was at least as well qualified as the successful candidate.

Network Rail Infrastructure Ltd v [2006] IRLR 865 EAT
Griffiths-Henry

The suggestion in *Adebayo* that an employee would be able to establish a prima facie case if he were black, was not promoted and was at least as well qualified as the white comparator would be agreed with where there were only two candidates, but the case becomes weaker where there are a number of candidates and the black candidate is rejected with a number of equally well-qualified white candidates. There is then no distinction between all the unsuccessful candidates and the justification for inferring a prima facie case is significantly weaker.

Birmingham City Council v [2012] EqLR 910 EAT
Millwood

Although in stage one of an employment tribunal's logical analysis of the facts when applying the statutory burden of proof provisions it must ignore whether there is any adequate explanation by the respondent of its actions, that does not mean that it can and should ignore an explanation that is frankly inadequate and, in particular, one that is disbelieved. Realistically, in any case in which an employer justifies treatment that has a differential effect as between a person of one race and a person of another by putting forward a number of inconsistent explanations which are disbelieved (as opposed to not being fully accepted), there is sufficient to justify a shift of the burden of proof.

Network Rail Infrastructure Ltd v [2006] IRLR 865 EAT
Griffiths-Henry

A tribunal at the second stage is simply concerned with the reason why the employer acted as he did. The burden imposed on the employer will depend on the strength of the prima facie case. A black candidate who is better qualified than the only other candidate, who is white, and does not get the job imposes a greater burden at the second stage than would a black candidate rejected along with some others who were equally qualified.

Dresdner Kleinwort [2005] IRLR 514 EAT
  Wasserstein Ltd v
Adebayo

The shifting of the burden to employers means that tribunals are entitled to expect employers to call evidence which is sufficient to discharge the burden of proving that the explanation advanced was non-discriminatory and that it was the real reason for what occurred. Equivocal or evasive answers to legitimate queries in statutory questionnaires, failures to follow recommendations in relevant codes of practice, or the failure to call as witnesses those who were involved in the events and decisions about which complaint is made will all properly assume a greater significance in future, in cases where the burden of proving that no discrimination has occurred is found to have passed to the employer.

Pothecary Witham Weld v [2010] IRLR 572 EAT
Weld

In a case where a claimant has raised a prima facie case, it must in principle be enough to say "we were not persuaded that his explanation was right", rather than "we reject his explanation": that is what the burden of proof is about. In cases where any discriminatory motivation may well be subconscious – something notoriously difficult to prove or disprove – a tribunal may reasonably prefer to go no further than saying that the burden of proof has not been discharged.

Zafar v   **[1998] IRLR 36 HL**
Glasgow City Council
The conduct of a hypothetical reasonable employer is irrelevant to deciding whether a discrimination claimant has been treated by the alleged discriminator "less favourably" than that person treats or would have treated another. It cannot be inferred only from the fact that an employer has acted unreasonably towards one employee that he would have acted reasonably if he had been dealing with another in the same circumstances.

Eagle Place Services Ltd v   **[2010] IRLR 486 EAT**
Rudd
It is not open to an employer to say that it has not discriminated against a claimant because it would have behaved unreasonably in dismissing a comparator. It is unreasonable to suppose that it in fact would have dismissed the comparator for what amounts to an irrational reason. It is one thing to find, as in *Bahl v Law Society*, that a named individual has behaved unreasonably to both the claimant and named comparators; it is quite another to find that a corporate entity would behave unreasonably to a hypothetical comparator when it had no good reason to do so.

Rice v   **[2011] EqLR 771 NICA**
McAvoy
If an employer acts in a wholly unreasonable way, that may assist in drawing an inference that the employer's purported explanation for his actions was not in fact the true explanation and that he was covering up a discriminatory intent. However, it is not in itself determinative of the issue. Where a prima facie case is established, the onus is on the employer to negative discriminatory intent, but that question is not one that falls to be answered by determining what a reasonable employer would have done in the circumstances.

Network Rail Infrastructure Ltd v   **[2006] IRLR 865 EAT**
Griffiths-Henry
It would be inappropriate to find discrimination simply because an explanation given by the employer for the difference in treatment is not one which the tribunal considers objectively to be justified or reasonable. Unfairness is not itself sufficient to establish discrimination.

Qureshi v   **[1991] IRLR 264 CA**
London Borough of Newham
Incompetence does not, without more, become discrimination merely because the person affected by it is from an ethnic minority.

Anya v   **[2001] IRLR 377 CA**
University of Oxford
Very little direct discrimination today is overt or even deliberate. The guidance from the case law tells tribunals to look for indicators from a time before or after the particular decision which may demonstrate that an ostensibly fair-minded decision was, or equally was not, affected by racial bias.

Komeng v   **[2011] EqLR 1053 EAT**
Sandwell Metropolitan Borough Council
Employment tribunals should take care before accepting an explanation that the reason for less favourable treatment (if proven) lies merely in general poor administration. There is always the risk that poor administration masks real disadvantage to a particular group or to a particular individual on prohibited grounds.

Nelson v   **[2009] IRLR 549 NICA**
Newry and Mourne District Council
The fact that a decision could not be found to be irrational or perverse must be very relevant in deciding whether there was evidence from which it could properly be inferred that the decision-making was motivated by an improper sexually discriminatory intent.

West Midlands Passenger   **[1988] IRLR 186 CA**
  Transport Executive v
Singh
Statistical evidence may establish a discernible pattern in the treatment of a particular group: if that pattern demonstrates a regular failure of members of the group to obtain particular jobs and of underrepresentation in such jobs, it may give rise to an inference of discrimination against the group. Statistics obtained through monitoring of the workforce and of applications for recruitment and promotion are not conclusive in themselves, but if they show imbalances or disparities, they may indicate areas of discrimination.

West Midlands Passenger   **[1988] IRLR 186 CA**
  Transport Executive v
Singh
If a practice is being operated against a racial group then, in the absence of a satisfactory explanation in a particular case, it is reasonable to infer that the complainant, as a member of the group, has himself been treated less favourably on grounds of race. Evidence of discriminatory treatment against the group may be more persuasive of discrimination in a particular case than previous treatment of the complainant by the employer, which may be indicative of personal factors peculiar to the complainant and not necessarily racially motivated.

Rihal v   **[2004] IRLR 642 CA**
London Borough of Ealing
If an employer institutes an arrangement which is discriminatory, that arrangement does not cease to be so merely because the manager in charge changes. It is the employers against whom the complaint is made, not the individual manager.

Oxford v   **[1977] IRLR 225 EAT**
Department of Health and
  Social Security
Although the formal burden of proof lies upon the claimant, it would only be in exceptional or frivolous cases that it would be right for an employment tribunal to find at the end of the claimant's case that there was no case to answer and that it was not necessary to hear what the respondents had to say about it.

Scope of evidence

West Midlands Passenger Transport Executive v   **[1988] IRLR 186 CA**
Singh

As evidence from employers that both white and non-white persons hold responsible positions has been accepted as demonstrating that the employers have a policy of non-discrimination and as providing probative evidence from which an employment tribunal can decide that a particular claimant had not been discriminated against, so evidence of a discriminatory attitude on the employers' part may also have probative effect.

Chattopadhyay v   **[1981] IRLR 487 EAT**
The Headmaster of Holloway School

Evidence of events subsequent to an alleged act of discrimination is admissible where it is logically probative of a relevant fact.

Din v   **[1982] IRLR 281 EAT**
Carrington Viyella Ltd

Though no damages or other relief can be obtained relying simply on acts done outside the period of three months, it does not follow that acts done within the three months' period which are related to acts done outside the three months' period are incapable of giving rise to a cause of action.

Chattopadhyay v   **[1981] IRLR 487 EAT**
The Headmaster of Holloway School

If a person involved in an alleged act of discrimination had, before the act complained of, treated the complainant with hostility, that evidence of hostility would be admissible as showing circumstances consistent with a racialist attitude of that person, even though there might be another, innocent explanation for such hostility. There is no relevant distinction between hostility before the event and hostility after the event. Evidence of such hostility is admitted with a view to showing that the person involved was treating the complainant differently from other people, whether he was animated by racial considerations or not. In either case, it calls for an answer.

Chapman v   **[1994] IRLR 124 CA**
Simon

The jurisdiction of the employment tribunal is limited to complaints which have been made to it. If the act of which complaint is made is found to be not proven, it is not for the tribunal to find another act of discrimination of which complaint has not been made to give a remedy in respect of that other act.

United Learning Trust v   **[2012] EqLR 1077 EAT**
Rose

It must be clear by the time of the tribunal hearing which specific allegations are said to be instances of direct discrimination.

Dimtsu v   **[1991] IRLR 450 EAT**
Westminster City Council

In determining a discrimination complaint, an employment tribunal does not have an inquisitorial role to investigate generally and see that the requirements of the Act have in all respects been observed. An employment tribunal's duty is to adjudicate upon the issues before it. A tribunal is not under a duty to investigate other possible complaints, even though they arise out of the same incident, unless it is asked to do so.

VICARIOUS DISCRIMINATION

Redfearn v   **[2006] IRLR 623 CA**
Serco Ltd

Discrimination "on racial grounds" is not confined to less favourable treatment on the ground of the colour or race of the claimant. The racial characteristic of C, rather than that of B, the victim of the less favourable treatment, may be a racial ground of less favourable treatment of B by A, and therefore direct discrimination by A against B.

Showboat Entertainment Centre Ltd v   **[1984] IRLR 7 EAT**
Owens

The prohibition on direct discrimination covers all cases of discrimination "on racial grounds" whether the racial characteristics in question are those of the person treated less favourably or of some other person. Therefore, dismissal of an employee because he refused to carry out a racially discriminatory instruction to exclude blacks was "on racial grounds", notwithstanding that the employee was white.

Redfearn v   **[2006] IRLR 623 CA**
Serco Ltd

The approach in *Showboat* is not confined to cases of an employer implementing a policy of race discrimination by giving a racially discriminatory instruction to an employee, who is then treated less favourably by being dismissed for not carrying it out. White persons would also be treated less favourably than other white persons on the ground of colour in the case of a white employer who dismisses a white employee for marrying a black person, or a white publican who refuses to admit or serve a white customer on the ground that he is accompanied by a black person.

ASSOCIATIVE DISCRIMINATION

EBR Attridge Law LLP v   **[2010] IRLR 10 EAT**
Coleman (No.2)

There was nothing "impossible" about adding words to the provisions of the Disability Discrimination Act so as to cover associative discrimination. The proscription of associative discrimination is an extension of the scope of the legislation as enacted, but it is in no sense repugnant to it. On the contrary, it is an extension fully in conformity with the aims of the legislation as drafted. The Act would be interpolated so as to give effect to the reasoning of the European Court of Justice by adding a new subsection in the following terms: "A person also directly discriminates against a person if he treats him less favourably than he treats or would treat another person by reason of the disability of another person."

EBR Attridge Law LLP v   **[2010] IRLR 10 EAT**
Coleman (No.2)

Although the phrase "associative discrimination" is a convenient shorthand, the concept of association is not central to the reasoning of the European Court of Justice. What matters is that the putative victim has suffered adverse treatment on a proscribed ground, namely disability, and the fact that the disability is not his own is not of the essence.

3. INDIRECT DISCRIMINATION

(1) A person (A) discriminates against another (B) if A applies to B a provision, criterion or practice which is discriminatory in relation to a relevant protected characteristic of B's.

(2) For the purposes of subsection (1), a provision, criterion or practice is discriminatory in relation to a relevant protected characteristic of B's if –
    (a) A applies, or would apply, it to persons with whom B does not share the characteristic,
    (b) it puts, or would put, persons with whom B shares the characteristic at a particular disadvantage when compared with persons with whom B does not share it,
    (c) it puts, or would put, B at that disadvantage, and
    (d) A cannot show it to be a proportionate means of achieving a legitimate aim.

(3) The relevant protected characteristics are –
* *age;*
* *disability;*
* *gender reassignment;*
* *marriage and civil partnership;*
* *race;*
* *religion or belief;*
* *sex;*
* *sexual orientation.*

EQUALITY ACT 2010 – s.19

GENERAL PRINCIPLES

R (on the application of E) v   **[2010] IRLR 136 SC**
Governing Body of JFS
Indirect discrimination looks beyond formal equality towards a more substantive equality of results.

James v   **[1990] IRLR 288 HL**
Eastleigh Borough Council
The provisions relating to indirect discrimination cannot sensibly apply in the case of a requirement or condition which is itself gender-based.

R (on the application of E) v   **[2010] IRLR 136 SC**
Governing Body of JFS
Direct and indirect discrimination are mutually exclusive. You cannot have both at once.

R v   **[2000] IRLR 363 HL**
Secretary of State for Employment
    ex parte Seymour-Smith (No.2)
The approach adopted by the European Court is similar to that provided by the indirect discrimination provisions of the Sex Discrimination Act. A considerable disparity can be more readily established if the statistical evidence covers a long period and the figures show a persistent and relatively constant disparity. In such a case, a lesser statistical disparity may suffice to show that the disparity is considerable than if the statistics cover only a short period or if they present an uneven picture.

Clarke v   **[1982] IRLR 482 EAT**
Eley (IMI) Kynoch Ltd
The purpose of the legislature in introducing the concept of indirect discrimination was to seek to eliminate those practices which had a disproportionate impact on women and were not justifiable for other reasons. Although the policy lying behind the Act cannot be used to give the words any wider meaning than they naturally bear, it is a powerful argument against giving the words a narrower meaning thereby excluding cases which fall within the mischief with which the statute was meant to deal.

PROVISION, CRITERION OR PRACTICE

British Airways plc v   **[2005] IRLR 862 EAT**
Starmer
A discretionary management decision not applying to others can be a "provision". There is no necessity for the provision actually to apply to others. What is required in order to test whether the provision, criterion or practice is discriminatory is to extrapolate it to others.

Mather v   **[2012] EqLR 1082 EAT**
Devine
The lack of a formal application by the claimant to work part time or in a job-share on her return from maternity leave did not mean that the employer had not applied a PCP to her that she work full time. In an indirect sex discrimination claim, there is no requirement for formality in an application by the claimant as contrasted with, for example, a request for flexible working.

DISPROPORTIONATE IMPACT

Pool for comparison

Allonby v   **[2001] IRLR 364 CA**
Accrington & Rossendale College
The identification of the pool for comparison is a matter of logic rather than of discretion or fact-finding. Once the requirement or condition has been defined, there is likely to be only one pool which serves to test its effect.

Rutherford v   **[2006] IRLR 551 HL**
Secretary of State for Trade and Industry (No.2)
Since the sections of the Employment Rights Act which excluded employees over age 65 from employment rights applied to all employees over 65 and nobody under that age, there were no proportions to compare. The rule applied to the same proportion of women over age 65 as it applied to men.

Somerset County Council v   **[2009] IRLR 870 CA**
Pike
The correct ratio of *Rutherford* is that those who have no

Hacking & Paterson v Wilson [2011] EqLR 19 EAT

When choosing the appropriate pool for comparison in cases where the claimant alleges that he or she has been indirectly discriminated against by being refused access to a benefit, those who have no interest in the advantage in question should be excluded from consideration.

British Medical Association v Chaudhary [2007] IRLR 800 CA

Where the appropriate pool comprised all members who wanted the advice and support of the BMA for race discrimination claims against specific regulatory bodies, and no member of the pool could comply with the condition imposed by the BMA that it would not support such a claim, there was no comparative disadvantage for any racial group and no indirect race discrimination.

Ministry of Defence v DeBique [2010] IRLR 471 EAT

No universal principle of law dictates what the pool should be in any particular case. In reaching their decision as to the appropriate pool, an employment tribunal should consider the position in respect of different pools within the range of decisions open to them, but they are entitled to select from that range the pool which they consider will realistically and effectively test the particular allegation before them.

Proportionate comparison

Rutherford v Secretary of State for Trade and Industry (No.2) [2006] IRLR 551 HL

The question in an indirect discrimination case is whether the apparently neutral criteria or rules put one group at a comparative disadvantage to the other. The Burden of Proof Directive refers to a "substantially higher proportion of the members of one sex" being disadvantaged. This is the language of comparison. The concept is normally applied to a rule or requirement that selects people for a particular advantage or disadvantage. The disparate impact complained of is that a group of people cannot have what they want because of the rule or requirement, whereas others can.

R v Secretary of State for Employment ex parte Seymour-Smith (No.2) [2000] IRLR 363 HL

The claimants had shown that at the time of their dismissal in 1991 the two-year qualifying period to bring an unfair dismissal complaint had a disparately adverse impact on women so as to amount to indirect discrimination contrary to Article 141 in circumstances in which, from 1985 up to and including 1991, the ratio of men and women who qualified was roughly 10:9. A persistent and constant disparity of that order in respect of the entire male and female labour forces was adequate to demonstrate that the extension of the qualifying period from one to two years had a considerably greater adverse impact on women than men.

British Airways plc v Starmer [2005] IRLR 862 EAT

A tribunal is entitled to take into account, where appropriate, a more general picture than is specifically displayed by statistics put in evidence.

Coker v Lord Chancellor's Department [2002] IRLR 80 CA

Making an appointment from within a circle of family, friends and personal acquaintances is seldom likely to constitute indirect discrimination since the requirement of personal knowledge will exclude the vast proportion of the pool, be they men, women, white or another racial group.

WHETHER PARTICULAR DISADVANTAGE TO CLAIMANT

Eweida v British Airways plc [2010] IRLR 322 CA

The test of indirect discrimination requires that some identifiable section of a workforce, quite possibly a small one, must be shown to suffer a particular disadvantage which the claimant shares. Solitary disadvantage is not sufficient.

Eweida v British Airways plc [2010] IRLR 322 CA

The purpose of the phrase "would put persons ... at a particular disadvantage" is to include in the disadvantaged group not only employees to whom the condition has actually been applied but those to whom it potentially applies.

Barclays Bank plc v Kapur [1995] IRLR 87 CA

An unjustified sense of grievance cannot amount to detriment.

JUSTIFIABLE

Standard of proof

Homer v Chief Constable of West Yorkshire Police [2012] IRLR 601 UKSC / [2012] EqLR 594 UKSC

To be proportionate, a measure has to be both an appropriate means of achieving the relevant legitimate aim and reasonably necessary in order to do so. The terms "appropriate", "necessary" and "proportionate" are not equally interchangeable. A measure may be appropriate to achieving the aim but go further than is reasonably necessary in order to do so and thus be disproportionate.

Seldon v Clarkson Wright and Jakes [2012] IRLR 591 UKSC / [2012] EqLR 579 UKSC

Once the relevant legitimate aim is established, it is necessary to establish whether that is in fact the aim being pursued by the measure in question. While the aim has to be the actual objective pursued, it is not necessary that the aim was either articulated or even realised at the time: it may be an ex post facto rationalisation.

HM Land Registry v   **[2012] EqLR 300 EAT**
Benson
When considering objective justification, a tribunal should first identify the relevant PCP which had the discriminatory effect complained of. The PCP should be defined so as to focus specifically on the measures taken, ie the thing or things done by the employer which resulted in the disparate impact complained of. An employment tribunal must then identify the aim for the pursuit of which that PCP constituted the means. The distinction between means and aim is not always easy to draw.

HM Land Registry v   **[2012] EqLR 300 EAT**
Benson
An employment tribunal should then consider whether the relevant aim(s) are "legitimate" and justified. It is fundamental that not all measures with a discriminatory effect are unlawful: sometimes they have to be put up with. The task of an employment tribunal is to accept an employer's legitimate decision as to the allocation of its resources as representing a genuine "need" and to balance it against the impact complained of. An employer's decision about how to allocate resources, and specifically financial resources, will constitute a "real need" or "legitimate aim", even if it is shown that it could have afforded to make a different allocation with a lesser impact on the relevant class of employee. To say that an employer can only establish justification if it can show that it could not make the payment in question without insolvency is to adopt a test of absolute necessity, but "real need" should not be equated with absolute necessity.

R (on the application of Elias) v   **[2006] IRLR 934 CA**
Secretary of State for Defence
A three-stage test is applicable to determine whether criteria are proportionate to the aim to be achieved. First, is the objective sufficiently important to justify limiting a fundamental right? Secondly, is the measure rationally connected to the objective? Thirdly, are the means chosen no more than is necessary to accomplish the objective?

Cross v   **[2005] IRLR 423 EAT**
British Airways plc
An employer seeking to justify a discriminatory provision, criterion or practice cannot rely solely on considerations of cost. It can, however, put cost into the balance, together with other justifications if there are any. It is a matter of obvious common sense and in accordance with the principle of proportionality that economic justification, such as the saving or non-expenditure of costs (which include the avoidance of loss) must be considered in the weighing exercise. Accordingly, the costs to the employer of changing its terms and conditions could be taken into account as a justification for an indirectly discriminatory provision, criterion or practice relating to retirement.

R (on the application of Elias) v   **[2006] IRLR 934 CA**
Secretary of State for Defence
A stringent standard of scrutiny of the justification is appropriate where the discrimination, although indirect in form, is so closely related in substance to the direct form of discrimination on grounds of national origins, which can never be justified.

R v   **[2000] IRLR 363 HL**
Secretary of State for Employment
   ex parte Seymour-Smith (No.2)
The onus is on the Member State to show (1) that the allegedly discriminatory rule reflects a legitimate aim of its social policy, (2) that this aim is unrelated to any discrimination based on sex, and (3) that the Member State could reasonably consider that the means chosen were suitable for attaining that aim. Governments must be able to govern and are to be afforded a broad measure of discretion. Generalised assumptions, lacking any factual foundation, are not good enough, but national courts, acting with hindsight, are not to impose an impracticable burden on governments which are proceeding in good faith.

R v   **[2000] IRLR 363 HL**
Secretary of State for Employment
   ex parte Seymour-Smith (No.2)
If the Government introduces a measure which proves to have a disparately adverse impact, it is under a duty to take reasonable steps to monitor the working of the measure and review the position periodically. The requirements of Community law must be complied with at all relevant times. The retention of a measure having a disparately adverse impact may no longer be objectively justifiable.

Tribunal discretion

Mandla v   **[1983] IRLR 209 HL**
Lee
Whether a requirement or condition is "justifiable" is a question of fact for the tribunal to discover, and if there is evidence for which it can find the condition to be justifiable, its finding is not liable to be disturbed on appeal.

Raval v   **[1985] IRLR 370 EAT**
Department of Health and
   Social Security
The issue of justifiability, being a question of fact, is one that has been left by Parliament to the employment tribunals. Instances are bound to be rare in which a finding on justifiability is capable of being disturbed on appeal. A tribunal's finding on whether or not a requirement is justifiable cannot be disturbed if the conclusion was capable of having been reached by any reasonable tribunal, notwithstanding that another tribunal might perfectly reasonably have taken a contrary view.

4. HARASSMENT

(1) A person (A) harasses another (B) if –
    (a) A engages in unwanted conduct related to a relevant
        protected characteristic, and
    (b) the conduct has the purpose or effect of –
        (i) violating B's dignity, or
        (ii) creating an intimidating, hostile, degrading, humili-
        ating or offensive environment for B.

(2) A also harasses B if –
    (a) A engages in unwanted conduct of a sexual nature, and
    (b) the conduct has the purpose or effect referred to in sub-
        section (1)(b).

(3) A also harasses B if –
    (a) A or another person engages in unwanted conduct of a
        sexual nature or that is related to gender reassignment
        or sex,
    (b) the conduct has the purpose or effect referred to in sub-
        section (1)(b), and
    (c) because of B's rejection of or submission to the conduct,
        A treats B less favourably than A would treat B if B had
        not rejected or submitted to the conduct.

(4) In deciding whether conduct has the effect referred to in sub-
section (1)(b), each of the following must be taken into account –
    (a) the perception of B;
    (b) the other circumstances of the case;
    (c) whether it is reasonable for the conduct to have that effect.

(5) The relevant protected characteristics are –
• *age;*
• *disability;*
• *gender reassignment;*
• *race;*
• *religion or belief;*
• *sex;*
• *sexual orientation.*

EQUALITY ACT 2010 – s.26

Richmond Pharmacology Ltd v   [2009] IRLR 336 EAT
Dhaliwal
The necessary elements of liability for harassment are threefold: (1) Did the respondent engage in unwanted conduct? (2) Did the conduct in question either (a) have the purpose or (b) the effect of either (i) violating the claimant's dignity or (ii) creating an adverse environment for her – the proscribed consequences. (3) Was the conduct on a prohibited ground? However, there is substantial overlap between the questions that arise in relation to each element. Whether conduct was "unwanted" will overlap with whether it creates an adverse environment for the claimant. Many or most acts that are found to create an adverse environment for an employee will also violate her dignity.

Warby v   [2012] EqLR 536 EAT
Wunda Group plc
An employment tribunal hearing a claim of unlawful harassment is required to have regard to context. Context is everything. It is for the tribunal to decide what the context of the acts complained of is and to contextualise what has taken place. It may be a mistake to focus upon a remark

in isolation. A tribunal is entitled to take the view that a remark, however unpleasant and however unacceptable, is a remark made in a particular context; it is not simply a remark standing on its own.

Richmond Pharmacology Ltd v   [2009] IRLR 336 EAT
Dhaliwal
Reading across the case law in relation to harassment as a variety of discrimination prior to implementation of the EU Directives is likely to hinder more than it helps. Still less assistance is likely to be gained from the Protection from Harassment Act 1997 and the associated case law.

Reed and Bull Information   [1999] IRLR 299 EAT
Systems Ltd v
Stedman
The essential characteristic of sexual harassment is that it is words or conduct which are unwelcome to the recipient and it is for the recipient to decide for themselves what is acceptable to them and what they regard as offensive.

Reed and Bull Information   [1999] IRLR 299 EAT
Systems Ltd v
Stedman
Some conduct, if not expressly invited, could properly be described as unwelcome. A woman does not have to make it clear in advance that she does not want to be touched in a sexual manner. At the lower end of the scale, a woman may appear, objectively, to be unduly sensitive to what might otherwise be regarded as unexceptional behaviour. But because it is for each person to define their own levels of acceptance, the question would then be whether by words or conduct she had made it clear that she found such conduct unwelcome. Provided that any reasonable person would understand her to be rejecting the conduct of which she was complaining, continuation of the conduct would, generally, be regarded as harassment.

Conteh v   [2011] EqLR 332 EAT
Parking Partners Ltd
In considering an allegation of harassment, the employment tribunal has first to identify the "unwanted conduct" in which the employer is alleged to have engaged. "Unwanted conduct" can include inaction. If the conduct complained of is a failure to act then it has to be shown that that action was wanted. An example would be where a failure to act when an employee reasonably required that there be action had itself contributed to the atmosphere in which the employee worked, as for instance where she or he felt unsupported, to the extent that the failure to support him or her actively made the position very much worse.

Conteh v   [2011] EqLR 332 EAT
Parking Partners Ltd
In order to fall within the statutory definition, the "unwanted conduct" has to be taken on the grounds of race or ethnic or national origins. Thus, if inaction occurs for reasons that have nothing to do in themselves with race or ethnic or national origin, then the inaction is not on the grounds of race or ethnic or national origin.

Weeks v   **[2012] EqLR 788 EAT**
Newham College of Further Education

A decision of fact in a harassment case must be sensitive to all the circumstances. In a claim of harassment, the fact that unwanted conduct was not itself directed at the claimant is a relevant consideration. The timing of an individual's objection to conduct also has evidential importance. It may mean that the individual complaining of conduct after the event did not in fact perceive the conduct as having the relevant offensive qualities. However, tribunals should not place too much weight upon timing: where conduct is directed toward the sex of the victim, it may be very difficult for the victim personally, socially and, in some circumstances, culturally, to make any immediate complaint about it. While a legitimate factor to consider, the fact of there being no immediate complaint cannot prevent a complaint being justified.

Conteh v   **[2011] EqLR 332 EAT**
Parking Partners Ltd

Whether conduct had the effect of "creating" the proscribed environment is a causation question. The use of the word "creating" suggests that the focus is upon what causes the environment to begin to be as it is. What must be looked at is the environment, and how that environment was created. Creation may take place as a matter of an instant or over time. It may be that third-party behaviour has created the environment in part, but the actions of an employer, to whom those third parties are not responsible, has made it worse, in which case the environment might be said to have been created by the actions of both.

Weeks v   **[2012] EqLR 788 EAT**
Newham College of Further Education

An "environment" is a state of affairs. It may be created by an incident, but the effects are of longer duration. A tribunal must consider the relevant words spoken in context, including other words spoken and the general run of affairs within the workplace. The frequency of the use of the offending words is not irrelevant.

Insitu Cleaning Co Ltd v   **[1995] IRLR 4 EAT**
Heads

Whether a single act of verbal sexual harassment is sufficient to found a complaint is a matter of fact and degree. That the EC Code of Practice refers to "unwanted conduct" does not mean that a single act can never amount to harassment in that it cannot be said to be "unwanted" until it is done and rejected. The word "unwanted" is essentially the same as "unwelcome" or "uninvited".

Wileman v   **[1988] IRLR 144 EAT**
Minilec Engineering Ltd

A person may be happy to accept the remarks of A or B in a sexual context, and wholly upset by similar remarks made by C. Therefore, the probative value in a sexual harassment case of the fact that the complainant posed for a newspaper in a flimsy costume was almost minimal since the fact that she was upset at remarks made by a director of the employers was not vitiated in any way or inconsistent with her being willing to pose for a newspaper.

Driskel v   **[2000] IRLR 151 EAT**
Peninsula Business Services Ltd

A tribunal should not lose sight of the significance of the sex of both the complainant and the alleged discriminator. Sexual badinage of a heterosexual male by another man cannot be completely equated with like badinage by him of a woman. Prima facie the treatment is not equal, since in the latter circumstance it is the sex of the alleged discriminator that potentially adds a material element absent as between two heterosexual men.

Insitu Cleaning Co Ltd v   **[1995] IRLR 4 EAT**
Heads

A remark by a man about a woman's breasts cannot sensibly be equated with a remark by a woman about a bald head or a beard. One is sexual, the other is not.

Moonsar v   **[2005] IRLR 9 EAT**
Fiveways Express Transport Ltd

The claimant was discriminated against on grounds of her sex when on three occasions male colleagues in the same room downloaded pornographic images on to a computer. Viewed objectively, this behaviour clearly had the potential effect of causing an affront to a female employee working in a close environment, and as such would be regarded as degrading or offensive to an employee as a woman. The fact that the claimant did not complain at the time did not afford a defence where the behaviour was so obvious.

Nixon v   **[2010] EqLR 284 EAT**
Ross Coates Solicitors

Subjecting a pregnant employee to gossip about the paternity of her unborn child was unwanted conduct meeting the definition of harassment on grounds of sex in that it created an intimidating, hostile, degrading or humiliating working environment for her.

Sheffield City Council v   **[2011] IRLR 897 EAT**
Norouzi   **[2011] EqLR 1039 EAT**

Mocking a foreign accent is mocking a racial characteristic and therefore an act of harassment on grounds of race.

Wileman v   **[1988] IRLR 144 EAT**
Minilec Engineering Ltd

Evidence of how a director was alleged to have harassed other women was correctly not admitted by an employment tribunal since sexual remarks made to a number of people have to be looked at in the context of each person. All the people to whom they are made may regard them as wholly inoffensive; everyone else may regard them as offensive. Each individual has the right, if the remarks are regarded as offensive, to treat them as an offence under the Sex Discrimination Act.

British Telecommunications plc v   **[1997] IRLR 668 EAT**
Williams

An employment tribunal erred in finding that an interview by a male manager of a female employee was sexually intimidating because there was no woman present and the interview took place in a confined space. It is neither required by law nor desirable in practice that employers should see that male managers are chaperoned when dealing with female staff.

Richmond Pharmacology Ltd v Dhaliwal
[2009] IRLR 336 EAT

The broad thrust of the statutory proviso is that a respondent should not be held to be liable merely because his conduct has the effect of producing a proscribed consequence: it should be reasonable that that consequence has occurred. Whether it was reasonable for a claimant to have felt her dignity to have been violated is quintessentially a matter for the factual assessment of the tribunal, but one question that may be material is whether it should reasonably have been apparent whether the conduct was, or was not, intended to cause offence (or produce the proscribed consequences). If the perpetrator evidently did not intend to cause offence, it may not be reasonable for the claimant to have taken offence.

Prospects for People with Learning Difficulties v Harris
[2012] EqLR 781 EAT

Where an employer acts reasonably in imposing suspension with full pay, it will not amount to harassment. Suspension can be necessary for a variety of reasons. If an employer reasonably believes that it is necessary and makes it clear to an employee that the suspension is pending investigation, it would not normally constitute an act of harassment because it would not have the effect of violating the employee's dignity or creating an intimidating, hostile, degrading, humiliating or offensive environment.

Richmond Pharmacology Ltd v Dhaliwal
[2009] IRLR 336 EAT

The inquiry into the perpetrator's grounds for acting as he did is logically distinct from any issue which may arise about whether he intended to produce the proscribed consequences: a perpetrator may intend to violate a claimant's dignity for reasons other than any of the proscribed reasons. However, in some cases, the ground for the treatment is inherently discriminatory and it is not necessary to consider the respondent's mental processes.

Snowball v Gardner Merchant Ltd
[1987] IRLR 397 EAT

Evidence as to a complainant's attitude to matters of sexual behaviour was relevant and admissible for the purpose of determining the degree of injury to feelings that the complainant suffered as a result of sexual harassment. Compensation for sexual harassment must relate to the degree of detriment, and evidence as to whether she had talked freely to fellow employees about her attitude to sexual matters was relevant for determining whether the complainant was unlikely to be very upset by a degree of familiarity with a sexual connotation, so as to challenge the alleged detriment suffered and any hurt to feelings.

THIRD-PARTY HARASSMENT

(1) An employer (A) must not, in relation to employment by A, harass a person (B) –
    (a) who is an employee of A's;
    (b) who has applied to A for employment.

(2) The circumstances in which A is to be treated as harassing B under subsection (1) include those where –
    (a) a third party harasses B in the course of B's employment, and
    (b) A failed to take such steps as would have been reasonably practicable to prevent the third party from doing so.

(3) Subsection (2) does not apply unless A knows that B has been harassed in the course of B's employment on at least two other occasions by a third party; and it does not matter whether the third party is the same or a different person on each occasion.

(4) A third party is a person other than –
    (a) A, or
    (b) an employee of A's.

EQUALITY ACT 2010 – s.40

Macdonald v Advocate General for Scotland
Pearce v Governing Body of Mayfield Secondary School
[2003] IRLR 512 HL

Burton v De Vere Hotels Ltd was wrongly decided in that it treated an employer's inadvertent failure to take reasonable steps to protect employees from racial or sexual abuse by third parties as discrimination even though the failure had nothing to do with the sex or race of the employees. The employment tribunal's finding that the hotel manager's failure to protect the waitresses from the offensive content of the comedian's speech was not connected with their ethnic origin, and that, by implication, the employer would have treated white waitresses in the same way, negatived racial discrimination on the part of the employer. The approach of the EAT, that the tribunal should ask themselves whether the event in question was something which was sufficiently under the control of the employer that he could by the application of "good employment practice" have prevented the harassment or reduced the effect of it was not based on anything which is to be found in the statute.

Conteh v Parking Partners Ltd
[2011] EqLR 332 EAT

A failure to deal with third-party conduct that is inherently racist cannot be regarded as in itself inherently racist and thus on the grounds of race. However, a failure to deal adequately with a complaint of racial abuse because it was, or was perceived to be, too difficult, given its racial subject matter, could be characterised as inaction on the grounds of race in that race would be the distinction between that and other complaints.

Sheffield City Council v Norouzi
[2011] IRLR 897 EAT
[2011] EqLR 1039 EAT

Before finding that an employer is liable for third-party harassment not only must the employment tribunal identify the steps which the employer failed to take and could have taken, but also they must conclude that taking those steps could have prevented or reduced the effect complained of. There are environments – including prisons, residential homes and some schools – where employees may be subjected to a level of harassment on a proscribed ground which cannot easily be prevented or eradicated. In such cases, the employer should not too readily be held liable for conduct by third parties which is in truth a hazard of the job; and if it is to be held liable on the basis that insufficient steps were taken to protect the employee in question, a tribunal must be prepared to focus on what precisely could have been done but was not done.

Sheffield City Council v   **[2011] IRLR 897 EAT**
Norouzi   **[2011] EqLR 1039 EAT**

The respondent would be regarded as legally liable for harassment of its employee by a resident in a care home in which the employee worked, notwithstanding that the resident was not someone for whose acts it was vicariously liable under the Race Relations Act. In *R (Equal Opportunities Commission) v Secretary of State for Trade and Industry*, it was held that the Sex Discrimination Act's provisions requiring that a failure by an employer to take action against third-party harassment had to be "on the ground of" the claimant's sex did not comply with the amended Equal Treatment Directive, and Race Discrimination Directive 2000/43/EC is in substantially the same terms as the amended Equal Treatment Directive.

5. VICTIMISATION

(1) A person (A) victimises another person (B) if A subjects B to a detriment because –
(a) B does a protected act, or
(b) A believes that B has done, or may do, a protected act.

(2) Each of the following is a protected act –
(a) bringing proceedings under this Act;
(b) giving evidence or information in connection with proceedings under this Act;
(c) doing any other thing for the purposes of or in connection with this Act;
(d) making an allegation (whether or not express) that A or another person has contravened this Act.

(3) Giving false evidence or information, or making a false allegation, is not a protected act if the evidence or information is given, or the allegation is made, in bad faith.

EQUALITY ACT 2010 – s.27

GENERAL PRINCIPLES

Cornelius v   **[1987] IRLR 141 CA**
University College of Swansea
The purpose of the victimisation provisions is to protect those who seek to rely on the Act or to promote its operation by word or deed.

Parmar v   **[2011] IRLR 641 EAT**
East Leicester Medical Practice   **[2011] EqLR 564 EAT**
Judicial proceedings immunity applies to witness statements made in the context of a claim of unlawful discrimination. A claimant cannot, after the dismissal of a claim of race discrimination, later bring a claim of victimisation based on comments made in the respondent's witness statements served for the purposes of defending the original claim of race discrimination.

STANDARD OF PROOF

Nagarajan v   **[1999] IRLR 572 HL**
London Regional Transport
Conscious motivation on the part of the discriminator is not a necessary ingredient of unlawful victimisation.

St Helens Metropolitan   **[2007] IRLR 540 HL**
  Borough Council v
Derbyshire
Whether a particular act can be said to amount to victimisation must be judged primarily from the point of view of the alleged victim, whether or not they suffered any "detriment", rather than from the point of view of the alleged discriminator.

Northern Ireland Fire and   **[2012] EqLR 821 NICA**
  Rescue Service v
McNally
In determining whether or not an employer has victimised an employee for a prohibited reason, the tribunal must look at why the employer has taken the particular act from his

standpoint and whether the act has caused detriment from the point of view of the alleged victim. An unjustified sense of grievance at the act of the employer cannot amount to a detriment, but if it is the victim's opinion that the treatment was to his detriment and that was a reasonable opinion to hold, that ought to suffice to prove detriment. However, it would require positive evidence and findings to that effect. The distress has to be objectively reasonable.

Nagarajan v   **[1999] IRLR 572 HL**
London Regional Transport
If racial grounds or protected acts had a significant influence on the outcome, discrimination is made out.

Martin v   **[2011] EqLR 108 EAT**
Devonshires Solicitors
The question in any claim of victimisation is what was the "reason" that the respondent did the act complained of: if it was, wholly or in substantial part, that the claimant had done a protected act, he is liable for victimisation; and if not, not. There will, in principle, however, be cases where an employer has dismissed an employee or subjected him to some other detriment in response to the doing of a protected act but where he can, as a matter of common sense and common justice, say that the reason for the dismissal was not the complaint as such but some feature of it which can properly be treated as separable. For example, where the reason relied on is the manner of the complaint: as in the case of an employee who makes, in good faith, a complaint of discrimination but couches it in terms of violent racial abuse of the manager alleged to be responsible.

Pasab Ltd v   **[2012] EqLR 392 EAT**
Woods
While the reason why a person acted as she did is a question of fact, it is not open to a tribunal to accept the subjective reason put forward by the alleged discriminator as a matter of fact and then impute some different reason to her based on the tribunal's objective assessment of a remark and its meaning.

Villalba v   **[2006] IRLR 437 EAT**
Merrill Lynch & Co Inc
In finding that victimisation was "a very small factor, not a significant influence" in the decision to remove the claimant, the tribunal correctly applied the observations of Lord Nicholls in *Nagarajan v London Regional Transport* that discrimination is made out if the prohibited ground had a "significant influence" on the outcome. Although that wording was interpreted by the Court of Appeal in *Igen Ltd v Wong* as meaning an "influence which is more than trivial", if in relation to any particular decision a discriminatory influence is not a material influence or factor, then it is trivial.

SPECIFIC EXAMPLES

Aziz v   **[1986] IRLR 435 EAT**
Trinity Street Taxis Ltd
The statutory provisions which apply where the person victimised has given evidence or information in connec-

tion with proceedings brought under the Act are intended to cover the situation where the person victimised is not a party but is a witness or provides information in connection with the proceedings.

Kirby v   **[1980] IRLR 229 EAT**
Manpower Services Commission

Although the giving of information prior to the commencement of proceedings may fall within the Act, before an allegation of victimisation can be made it must be shown that the victimisation has occurred at a time when proceedings have actually been brought. If the proceedings had been brought, it does not matter whether the information was given before or after the commencement of proceedings so long as it is something which is relied upon by the discriminator as a reason for the victimisation.

Chief Constable of West Yorkshire   **[2001] IRLR 830 HL**
   Police v
Khan

It was not unlawful victimisation to refuse to provide a reference in respect of an employee because the employee had a pending discrimination claim against the employer and the employer needed to preserve its position in the outstanding proceedings. In such a case, the reference was not withheld "by reason that" the claimant had brought discrimination proceedings, but rather because the employer temporarily needed to preserve his position, in that the evidence established that once the litigation had concluded, the request for a reference would have been complied with.

Pasab Ltd v   **[2012] EqLR 392 EAT**
Woods

The respondent's manager, who dismissed a Muslim claimant for saying that the company was a "little Sikh club", did not dismiss her because of a protected act where the manager believed that that comment was racist rather than a complaint by the employee of discrimination on grounds of religion. If the remark was viewed by the manager as an offensive racist comment, then the reason for dismissal was not that the claimant had done a protected act, but some other feature genuinely separable from the implicit complaint of discrimination.

Waters v   **[1995] IRLR 531 EAT**
Commissioner of Police
   of the Metropolis

An employer cannot be liable for victimising an employee who alleged that she was sexually harassed by a work colleague, where the alleged harassment was not committed in the course of employment.

Bird v   **[2008] IRLR 232 CA**
Sylvester

A reasonable employee would not have concluded that a letter from her employer threatening an application for costs in respect of her tribunal claim offered any detriment beyond what was properly involved in the honest and reasonable conduct of the employer's case. The letter was a perfectly reasonable and proper act in the context of the case.

Rank Nemo (DMS) Ltd v   **[2009] IRLR 672 CA**
Coutinho

A former employee who was awarded compensation for race discrimination and unfair dismissal, and secured an order for payment in the county court, was not precluded from bringing a claim that the employer's failure to pay the judgment debt was an unlawful act of victimisation. If it was established that the reason the award had not been paid was retaliation against the claimant for having brought discrimination proceedings against the employer, there could be a link to the previous employment relationship sufficient to support a claim for post-termination discrimination.

6. EMPLOYER LIABILITY

(1) Anything done by a person (A) in the course of A's employment must be treated as also done by the employer.

(2) Anything done by an agent for a principal, with the authority of the principal, must be treated as also done by the principal.

(3) It does not matter whether that thing is done with the employer's or principal's knowledge or approval.

(4) In proceedings against A's employer (B) in respect of anything alleged to have been done by A in the course of A's employment it is a defence for B to show that B took all reasonable steps to prevent A –
  (a) from doing that thing, or
  (b) from doing anything of that description.

EQUALITY ACT 2010 – s.109

Jones v   **[1997] IRLR 168 CA**
Tower Boot Co Ltd
In determining whether conduct complained of was done by a person "in the course of employment", the words "in the course of employment" should be interpreted in the sense in which they are employed in everyday speech and not restrictively by reference to the principles laid down by case law for establishing an employer's vicarious liability for the torts committed by an employee. The application of the phrase is a question of fact for each employment tribunal to resolve.

Liversidge v   **[2002] IRLR 651 CA**
Chief Constable of Bedfordshire Police
In the ordinary employment case, where employee A makes a remark racially abusive of employee B in the course of employment, the employer may be liable for an unlawful act.

Kingston v   **[1982] IRLR 274 EAT**
British Railways Board
As a matter of law, an employer cannot say that it is not liable for the unlawful discriminatory behaviour of one employee just because the detriment flowing from that unlawful conduct involves a step taken by another, innocent employee. In such circumstances, the detriment to the complainant would flow directly from the discriminatory conduct of an employee for whom the employer was responsible.

Mahood v   **[2011] EqLR 586 EAT**
Irish Centre Housing Ltd
An employer would be liable for the discriminatory acts of an agency worker if he was exercising the employer's authority, or was controlled by them, or if he had the employer's authority to do the acts in question where those acts were done in a discriminatory manner but were just as capable of being done in a lawful manner.

Mahood v   **[2011] EqLR 586 EAT**
Irish Centre Housing Ltd
Whether vicarious liability on the part of a respondent for the acts of an agency worker could be established at common law in tort has no bearing on issues of liability under discrimination legislation.

DEFENCE

Jones v   **[1997] IRLR 168 CA**
Tower Boot Co Ltd
The policy of the statutory provisions on employer liability is to deter racial and sexual harassment in the workplace through a widening of the net of responsibility beyond the guilty employees themselves, by making all employers additionally liable for such harassment, and then supplying them with the reasonable steps defence, which will exonerate the conscientious employer who has used his best endeavours to prevent such harassment, and will encourage all employers who have not yet undertaken such endeavours to take the steps necessary to make the same defence available in their own workplace.

Croft v   **[2003] IRLR 592 CA**
Royal Mail Group plc
In considering whether an action which it is submitted the employers should have taken is reasonably practicable, it is permissible to take into account the extent of the difference, if any, which the action is likely to make. The concept of reasonable practicability entitles the employer in this context to consider whether the time, effort and expense of the suggested measures are disproportionate to the result likely to be achieved.

Canniffe v   **[2000] IRLR 555 EAT**
East Riding of Yorkshire Council
An employer does not satisfy the defence to liability for acts of their employee merely by showing that there was nothing it could have done to stop the discrimination from occurring. The proper approach to determining whether an employer has satisfied the defence is first to identify whether the employer took any steps at all to prevent the employee from doing the act or acts complained of in the course of his employment; and secondly, having identified what steps, if any, they took, to consider whether there were any further acts that they could have taken which were reasonably practicable. Whether taking any such steps would have been successful in preventing the acts of discrimination in question is not determinative. An employer will not be exculpated if it has not taken reasonably practicable steps simply because, if it had taken those steps, they would not have prevented anything from occurring.

Mahood v   **[2011] EqLR 586 EAT**
Irish Centre Housing Ltd
An employment tribunal misdirected itself as to the statutory defence in that their finding was based on what the respondent had done after the discriminatory acts. The defence is limited to matters done in order to prevent a discriminatory act and that can only have effect if steps were taken before that act.

SECONDARY LIABILITY

Bungay v [2011] EqLR 1130 EAT
Saini
In determining whether one individual has acted as the agent of another, the test of authority is whether when doing a discriminatory act the discriminator was exercising authority conferred by the principal and not whether the principal had in fact authorised the agents to discriminate.

Barlow v [2012] IRLR 898 EAT
Stone [2012] EqLR 861 EAT
It is not essential to bring a primary complaint against the employer in order to bring a complaint against the secondary party accused of aiding the unlawful act. Therefore, an employment tribunal had jurisdiction to consider a claim of victimisation brought by an employee against a fellow employee, even though no claim had been made against their mutual employer.

OTHER UNLAWFUL ACTS

Aiding unlawful acts

(1) A person (A) must not knowingly help another (B) to do anything which contravenes Part 3, 4, 5, 6 or 7 or section 108(1) or (2) or 111 (a basic contravention).
EQUALITY ACT 2010 – s.112

(1) A person (A) contravenes this section if –
(b) A does something which, by virtue of section 109(1) or (2), is treated as having been done by A's employer or principal (as the case may be), and
(c) the doing of that thing by A amounts to a contravention of this Act by the employer or principal (as the case may be).
EQUALITY ACT 2010 – s.110

Anyanwu v [2001] IRLR 305 HL
South Bank Students' Union
"Aids" is a familiar word in everyday use bearing no technical or special meaning in this context. A person aids another if he helps or assists, or co-operates or collaborates with him. He does so whether or not his help is substantial and productive, provided the help is not so insignificant as to be negligible. It does not matter who instigates or initiates the relationship, and it is not helpful to introduce "free agents" and "prime movers", which can only distract attention from the essentially simple test to be applied.

Hallam v [2001] IRLR 312 HL
Cheltenham Borough Council
The aiding provisions require more than a general attitude of helpfulness and co-operation. It is aid to another to do the unlawful act in question which must be shown.

May & Baker Ltd v [2010] IRLR 394 EAT
Okerago
The statutory definition is conditional upon a person aiding another person to do an unlawful act. A person cannot therefore aid another to do something which the second person has already done.

Allaway v [2007] IRLR 864 EAT
Reilly
If a fellow employee does an act in the course of his employment that has the effect of discriminating against the claimant and that is a result that can be concluded to have been within his knowledge at the time he carried out the act in question, the requirements of the subsection are met. Discrimination does not have to be what he intended nor does it have to have been his motive. It is enough that, on the evidence, the conclusion can be drawn that discrimination as the probable outcome was within the scope of his knowledge at the time. It would not need to be in the forefront of his mind nor would he need to have specifically addressed his mind to it.

Sinclair Roche & Temperley v [2004] IRLR 763 EAT
Heard
The element of knowledge is additional to the element of aid. Whereas discrimination can be, and very often is, unconscious, aiding cannot be.

Gilbank v [2006] IRLR 538 CA
Miles
In order to "aid" an act of unlawful discrimination, a person must have done more than merely create an environment in which discrimination can occur.

Yeboah v [2002] IRLR 634 CA
Crofton
Even if an employer is not vicariously liable because it showed that it took such steps as were reasonably practicable to prevent its employee from doing the act in question, an employee can be personally liable for "knowingly" aiding the unlawful act by the employer.

Gilbank v [2006] IRLR 538 CA
Miles
Each employee is deemed to have aided the employer to do what she herself did, and so to be personally liable for it, but she is not deemed to have aided the employer to do what fellow employees did.

Bird v [2008] IRLR 232 CA
Sylvester
The execution by a solicitor of a client's instructions is not something that is properly to be treated as aiding an unlawful act, even if the instructions involved some decision by the principal that might offend the statutory discrimination provisions. Nor can a solicitor's role as an adviser render him an aider. It is very difficult to see how a solicitor who confines himself to giving objective legal advice in good faith as to the proper protection of his client's interests, and acts strictly upon his client's instructions, could be at risk of an adverse finding.

Shepherd v [2006] IRLR 190 EAT
North Yorkshire County Council
An employer does not aid a failure by trade unions to represent their members properly merely by agreeing a

particular result in collective bargaining. It is one thing to take advantage of a failure, another altogether to aid it. Merely because an employer and a union in collective bargaining have agreed an outcome which was detrimental to a union member, it does not follow that the employer thereby aided the union to fail to represent its member properly.

Instructing, causing or inducing contraventions

(1) A person (A) must not instruct another (B) to do in relation to a third person (C) anything which contravenes Part 3, 4, 5, 6 or 7 or section 108(1) or (2) or 112(1) (a basic contravention).

(2) A person (A) must not cause another (B) to do in relation to a third person (C) anything which is a basic contravention.

(3) A person (A) must not induce another (B) to do in relation to a third person (C) anything which is a basic contravention.

(4) For the purposes of subsection (3), inducement may be direct or indirect.

(5) Proceedings for a contravention of this section may be brought —

> *(a) by B, if B is subjected to a detriment as a result of A's conduct;*
> *(b) by C, if C is subjected to a detriment as a result of A's conduct;*
> *(c) by the Commission.*

EQUALITY ACT 2010 – s.111

Commission for Racial Equality v   **[1983] IRLR 315 EAT**
Imperial Society of Teachers
  of Dancing

The word "induce" in s.31 of the Race Relations Act covers a mere request to discriminate. It does not necessarily imply an offer of some benefit or the threat of some detriment. The ordinary meaning of the word "induce" is "to persuade or to prevail upon or to bring about" and there is no reason to construe the word narrowly or in a restricted sense. Therefore, a request by the respondents' secretary to a head of careers at a school that "she would rather the school did not send anyone coloured" to fill a job vacancy constituted an attempt to induce the head of careers not to send coloured claimants for interview in contravention of s.31.

7. DISCRIMINATION BY EMPLOYERS AND NON-EMPLOYERS

(1) An employer (A) must not discriminate against a person (B) –

> *(a) in the arrangements A makes for deciding to whom to offer employment;*
> *(b) as to the terms on which A offers B employment;*
> *(c) by not offering B employment.*

(2) An employer (A) must not discriminate against an employee of A's (B) –
> *(a) as to B's terms of employment;*
> *(b) in the way A affords B access, or by not affording B access, to opportunities for promotion, transfer or training or for receiving any other benefit, facility or service;*
> *(c) by dismissing B;*
> *(d) by subjecting B to any other detriment.*

(6) Subsection (1)(b), so far as relating to sex or pregnancy and maternity, does not apply to a term that relates to pay –
> *(a) unless, were B to accept the offer, an equality clause or rule would have effect in relation to the term, or*
> *(b) if paragraph (a) does not apply, except in so far as making an offer on terms including that term amounts to a contravention of subsection (1)(b) by virtue of section 13, 14 or 18.*

(7) In subsections (2)(c) and (4)(c), the reference to dismissing B includes a reference to the termination of B's employment –
> *(a) by the expiry of a period (including a period expiring by reference to an event or circumstance);*
> *(b) by an act of B's (including giving notice) in circumstances such that B is entitled, because of A's conduct, to terminate the employment without notice.*

EQUALITY ACT 2010 – s.39

SELECTION ARRANGEMENTS

Nagarajan v   **[1999] IRLR 572 HL**
London Regional Transport
Interviewing and assessing candidates for a post can amount to making arrangements for the purpose of determining who should be offered that employment. *Brennan v J H Dewhurst Ltd* correctly held that the arrangements an employer makes encompasses more than setting up the arrangements for interviewing claimants, and also includes the manner in which the arrangements are operated.

Brennan v   **[1983] IRLR 357 EAT**
J H Dewhurst Ltd
Arrangements made for the purpose of determining who should be offered employment are unlawful if they operate so as to discriminate against a woman, even though they were not made with the purpose of so discriminating.

Cardiff Women's Aid v   **[1994] IRLR 390 EAT**
Hartup
Placing a discriminatory advertisement is not an act of discrimination by an employer in respect of which an individual can make a complaint. Only the statutory enforcement agencies can bring proceedings in respect of

causing an advertisement to be published which indicates "an intention" by a person to do an act of discrimination.

OFFER OF EMPLOYMENT

Anya v   **[2001] IRLR 377 CA**
University of Oxford
The choice between two comparably well-qualified candidates on the basis of how the panel viewed their personal and professional qualities is notoriously capable of being influenced, often not consciously, by idiosyncratic factors, especially where proper equal opportunity procedures have not been followed. If these are to any significant extent racial factors, it will in general be only from the surrounding circumstances and the previous history, not from the act of discrimination itself, that they will emerge.

Adekeye v   **[1997] IRLR 105 CA**
Post Office (No.2)
A dismissed employee seeking reinstatement by an appeal against dismissal cannot be regarded as seeking an offer of employment. On the appeal, the appellant is not seeking an offer which can be accepted or refused; the appellant is seeking the reversal of a decision to dismiss.

DETRIMENTAL TREATMENT

Shamoon v   **[2003] IRLR 285 HL**
Chief Constable of the Royal
   Ulster Constabulary
In order for a disadvantage to qualify as a "detriment", it must arise in the employment field in that the court or tribunal must find that by reason of the act or acts complained of a reasonable worker would or might take the view that he had thereby been disadvantaged in the circumstances in which he had thereafter to work.

Shamoon v   **[2003] IRLR 285 HL**
Chief Constable of the Royal
   Ulster Constabulary
An unjustified sense of grievance cannot amount to "detriment".

The Learning Trust v   **[2012] EqLR 927 EAT**
Marshall
It does not necessarily follow that a failure to investigate an allegation of discrimination, thoroughly or at all, is itself discriminatory: whether that is so or not will depend on why the failure took place.

Jiad v   **[2003] IRLR 232 CA**
Byford
Enduring physical or psychological injury can (depending on the facts) be capable of constituting detriment in the sense that a reasonable worker would regard it as a disadvantage, even though transitory hurt feelings may not (depending on the facts) suffice.

DISCRIMINATION AGAINST CONTRACT WORKERS

(1) A principal must not discriminate against a contract worker –
  (a) as to the terms on which the principal allows the worker to do the work;
  (b) by not allowing the worker to do, or to continue to do, the work;
  (c) in the way the principal affords the worker access, or by not affording the worker access, to opportunities for receiving a benefit, facility or service;
  (d) by subjecting the worker to any other detriment.

(5) A "principal" is a person who makes work available for an individual who is –
  (a) employed by another person, and
  (b) supplied by that other person in furtherance of a contract to which the principal is a party (whether or not that other person is a party to it).

(6) "Contract work" is work such as is mentioned in subsection (5).

(7) A "contract worker" is an individual supplied to a principal in furtherance of a contract such as is mentioned in subsection (5)(b).

EQUALITY ACT 2010 – s.41

Allonby v   **[2001] IRLR 364 CA**
Accrington & Rossendale College
The prohibition against discrimination against contract workers applies both between one contract worker and another and as between a contract worker and an employee so long as they are working for the same principal.

Abbey Life Assurance Co Ltd v   **[2000] IRLR 387 CA**
Tansell
The prohibition against discrimination against contract workers does not require a direct contractual relationship between the employer and the principal. It applies to a case where there is no direct contract between the person making the work available and the employer of the individual who is supplied to do that work. The statutory definition only requires the supply of the individual to be "under a contract made with 'A'." It does not expressly stipulate who is to be the party who contracts with 'A'. Although in many cases the contract with the end-user will be made by the employer who supplies the individual, the statutory definition does not require that to be the case.

Harrods Ltd v   **[1997] IRLR 583 CA**
Remick
The prohibition against discrimination against contract workers is not limited to cases where those doing the work are under the managerial power or control of the principal.

Harrods Ltd v   **[1997] IRLR 583 CA**
Remick
The prohibition against discrimination against contract workers applies if there is a contractual obligation to supply individuals to do work that can properly be described as "work for" the principal. There is no requirement that the supply of workers should be the dominant purpose of the contract made between the principal and the employer.

Leeds City Council v   **[2010] IRLR 625 CA**
Woodhouse
Where the principal and the employer of the applicant are in the relationship of contractor and subcontractor, the mere fact that the applicant does work under the subcontract from which the principal will derive some benefit is not enough to bring the case within the contract worker provisions. If the principal can exercise an element of influence or control, that may be enough to bring the case within the provisions, but control and influence are not necessary elements.

Jones v   **[2004] IRLR 783 NICA**
Friends Provident Life Office
The statutory provisions relating to contract workers were designed to prevent an employer from escaping his responsibilities under anti-discrimination legislation by bringing in workers on sub-contract, and therefore should receive a broad construction which has the effect of providing the statutory protection to a wider range of workers. The purpose of the statutory provisions is to ensure that persons who are employed to perform work for someone other than their nominal employers receive the protection of the legislation forbidding discrimination by employers.

Jones v   **[2004] IRLR 783 NICA**
Friends Provident Life Office
It is implicit in the philosophy underlying the provision that the principal must be in a position to discriminate against the contract worker. The principal must therefore be in a position to influence or control the conditions under which the employee works. It is also inherent in the concept of supplying workers under a contract that it is contemplated by the employer and the principal that the former will provide the services of employees in the course of performance of the contract. It is necessary for both these conditions to be fulfilled to bring a case within the contract worker provisions. It is not sufficient, therefore, for a claimant to show that her employer had a contract with the principal to have certain work done for the latter and that the claimant did that work as an employee of the former.

BP Chemicals Ltd v   **[1995] IRLR 128 EAT**
Gillick
The prohibition on discrimination against a contract worker is not restricted to discrimination against a contract worker who is actually working. It prohibits discrimination in the selection by the principal from among workers supplied under an agency arrangement. Therefore, a complaint could be brought by a contract worker that she had been discriminated against by a principal by not permitting her to return to work after absence due to maternity.

Abbey Life Assurance Co Ltd v   **[2000] IRLR 387 CA**
Tansell
A claimant, who was employed by a company which supplied him to an agency, which in turn supplied him to an end-user, was a "contract worker" within the meaning of

the statutory provision who could present a claim against the end-user as being a "principal".

Patefield v   [2000] IRLR 664 NICA
Belfast City Council
A council discriminated against a contract worker on grounds of sex when it replaced her with a permanent employee when she went on maternity leave, in circumstances in which there was a job available for a contract worker when she went off work for maternity reasons and she would have been kept in her post indefinitely if she had not gone off work at that time. By replacing her with a permanent employee when it knew that she wanted to return to her post after the birth of her child, the council subjected her to a detriment at that time by effectively removing the possibility of her returning to her post. In so acting, the council treated her less favourably than they would have treated a man, who would not have become unavailable for work because of pregnancy.

DISCRIMINATION BY TRADE ORGANISATIONS

(1) A trade organisation (A) must not discriminate against a person (B) –
- *(a) in the arrangements A makes for deciding to whom to offer membership of the organisation;*
- *(b) as to the terms on which it is prepared to admit B as a member;*
- *(c) by not accepting B's application for membership.*

(2) A trade organisation (A) must not discriminate against a member (B) –
- *(a) in the way it affords B access, or by not affording B access, to opportunities for receiving a benefit, facility or service;*
- *(b) by depriving B of membership;*
- *(c) by varying the terms on which B is a member;*
- *(d) by subjecting B to any other detriment.*

(7) A trade organisation is –
- *(a) an organisation of workers,*
- *(b) an organisation of employers, or*
- *(c) any other organisation whose members carry on a particular trade or profession for the purposes of which the organisation exists.*

EQUALITY ACT 2010 – s.57

Sadek v   [2005] IRLR 57 CA
Medical Protection Society
The category "any other organisation whose members carry on a particular profession … for the purposes of which the organisation exists" does not limit the category to organisations whose members are confined to a single profession.

Fire Brigades Union v   [1998] IRLR 697 CS
Fraser
An employment tribunal erred in finding that a union discriminated against a member on grounds of sex by refusing

to afford him access to representation or legal assistance for the purpose of disciplinary proceedings by his employer following a complaint of sexual harassment made against him by a woman member. Although the union might have treated those complaining of sexual harassment more favourably than alleged harassers, there was no material on which the tribunal could draw the inference that the decision not to provide representation was gender-related, rather than conduct-related. Therefore, the tribunal was not entitled to find that a woman accused of sexual harassment would have been treated differently.

National Federation of Self-Employed   [1997] IRLR 340 EAT
    and Small Businesses Ltd v
Philpott
The expression "organisation of employers" has to be given its ordinary and natural meaning in the context in which it appears, having regard to the characteristics of the organisation in question. On that basis, the National Federation of Self-Employed and Small Businesses is an "organisation of employers", notwithstanding that not all of its members are employers, since it represents its members, who are predominantly employers, specific-ally as employers, as well as across a range of other matters.

DISCRIMINATION BY QUALIFICATIONS BODIES

(1) A qualifications body (A) must not discriminate against a person (B) –
- *(a) in the arrangements A makes for deciding upon whom to confer a relevant qualification;*
- *(b) as to the terms on which it is prepared to confer a relevant qualification on B;*
- *(c) by not conferring a relevant qualification on B.*

(2) A qualifications body (A) must not discriminate against a person (B) upon whom A has conferred a relevant qualification –
- *(a) by withdrawing the qualification from B;*
- *(b) by varying the terms on which B holds the qualification;*
- *(c) by subjecting B to any other detriment.*

EQUALITY ACT 2010 – s.53

(1) This section applies for the purposes of section 53.

(2) A qualifications body is an authority or body which can confer a relevant qualification.

(3) A relevant qualification is an authorisation, qualification, recognition, registration, enrolment, approval or certification which is needed for, or facilitates engagement in, a particular trade or profession.

EQUALITY ACT 2010 – s.54

Ahsan v   [2008] IRLR 243 HL
Watt
An "authorisation or qualification" suggests some kind of objective standard which the qualifying body applies, an even-handed test which people may pass or fail.

British Judo Association v   [1981] IRLR 484 EAT
Petty

The prohibition on discrimination by qualifying bodies covers all cases where a qualification in fact facilitates a woman's employment, whether or not it is intended by the authority or body which confers the authorisation or qualification so to do.

British Judo Association v   [1981] IRLR 484 EAT
Petty

The prohibition on discrimination by qualifying bodies renders unlawful all discriminatory conditions attached to qualifications affecting employment. There is no requirement that the discriminatory term (as opposed to the qualification itself) has any impact on the employment prospects of the person discriminated against or that they must show proof of actual damage. A complainant must show simply that the qualification facilitates his or her job prospects and that attached to such qualification is a term which is discriminatory against the sex or race of the complainant.

Tattari v   [1997] IRLR 586 CA
Private Patients Plan

The prohibition on discrimination by qualifying bodies applies to a body which has the power or authority to confer on a person a professional qualification or other approval needed to enable them to practice a profession, exercise a calling or take part in some other activity. It does not refer to a body like PPP which is not authorised to or empowered to confer such qualification or permission but which stipulates that a particular qualification is required for the purpose of its commercial agreements. Therefore, the claimant could not bring a complaint that PPP's failure to include her on their list of specialists because it did not recognise her EC certificate of higher specialist training was racially discriminatory.

King v   [2012] EqLR 852 EAT
Health Professions Council

The statutory language deals with a situation where less than the full benefits of registration are conferred by the qualifications body rather than with the process of applying for registration. The words "in the terms upon which it is prepared to confer" an authorisation do not cover either facilitating or hindering the process of application. They relate to those terms which govern the extent of enjoyment of the authorisation or qualification once conferred – effectively, qualification subject to a condition. Therefore, an indication in advance of any application to the effect that a would-be applicant's qualifications would not be acceptable did not amount to unlawful discrimination by a qualifications body.

Ahsan v   [2008] IRLR 243 HL
Watt

A political party, such as the Labour Party, is not a "qualifying body" because the main criteria for selection as a candidate are not objective.

Patterson v   [2004] IRLR 153 CA
Legal Services Commission

When the Legal Services Commission grants a franchise to a solicitor, it is conferring an authorisation on the franchisee to perform publicly funded legal services for its clients. The franchise "facilitates" engagement in the profession of solicitor, in that it makes it easier or less difficult to carry on the profession.

Jooste v   [2012] EqLR 1048 EAT
General Medical Council

An appeal within the meaning of s.120(7) of the Equality Act 2010, which excludes complaints of discrimination by qualification bodies from the jurisdiction of the employment tribunal in relation to acts which may, by virtue of an enactment, be the subject of an appeal or proceedings in the nature of an appeal, is simply the opportunity to have a decision considered again by a different body of people with power to overturn it. The right to claim judicial review of an act arises under an enactment. Thus the right of the claimant to apply for judicial review of decisions of the GMC is by virtue of an enactment which provides for proceedings in the nature of an appeal.

Iteshi v   [2012] EqLR 553 EAT
General Council of the Bar

The requirement that barristers' chambers must fund all pupillages to a minimum extent did not indirectly discriminate on grounds of race against those seeking pupillage or who apply for a practising certificate at the end of pupillage, and therefore was not covered by the prohibition on discrimination by qualification bodies.

8. INDIVIDUAL REMEDIES

(1) This section applies if an employment tribunal finds that there has been a contravention of a provision referred to in section 120(1).

(2) The tribunal may –
  (a) make a declaration as to the rights of the complainant and the respondent in relation to the matters to which the proceedings relate;
  (b) order the respondent to pay compensation to the complainant;
  (c) make an appropriate recommendation.

(3) An appropriate recommendation is a recommendation that within a specified period the respondent takes specified steps for the purpose of obviating or reducing the adverse effect of any matter to which the proceedings relate –
  (a) on the complainant;
  (b) on any other person.

(4) Subsection (5) applies if the tribunal –
  (a) finds that a contravention is established by virtue of section 19, but
  (b) is satisfied that the provision, criterion or practice was not applied with the intention of discriminating against the complainant.

(5) It must not make an order under subsection (2)(b) unless it first considers whether to act under subsection (2)(a) or (c).

(6) The amount of compensation which may be awarded under subsection (2)(b) corresponds to the amount which could be awarded by a county court or the sheriff under section 119.

(7) If a respondent fails, without reasonable excuse, to comply with an appropriate recommendation in so far as it relates to the complainant, the tribunal may –
  (a) if an order was made under subsection (2)(b), increase the amount of compensation to be paid;
  (b) if no such order was made, make one.

EQUALITY ACT 2010 – s.124

(4) An award of damages may include compensation for injured feelings (whether or not it includes compensation on any other basis).

(5) Subsection (6) applies if the county court or sheriff –
  (a) finds that a contravention of a provision referred to in section 114(1) is established by virtue of section 19, but
  (b) is satisfied that the provision, criterion or practice was not applied with the intention of discriminating against the claimant or pursuer.

EQUALITY ACT 2010 – s.119

COMPENSATION

General principles

Ministry of Defence v   **[1998] IRLR 23 CA**
Wheeler
The general principle in assessing compensation is that, as far as possible, complainants should be placed in the same position as they would have been in but for the unlawful act.

Chagger v   **[2010] IRLR 47 CA**
Abbey National plc
The employment tribunal's task is to put the employee in the position he would have been in had there been no discrimination. That is not necessarily the same as asking what would have happened to the particular employment relationship had there been no discrimination. The reason is that the features of the labour market are not necessarily equivalent in the two cases. Where there has been a discriminatory dismissal, the employee is on the labour market at a time and in circumstances which are not of his own choosing. It does not follow therefore that his prospects of obtaining a new job are the same as they would have been had he not been dismissed. It is generally easier to obtain employment from a current job than from the status of being unemployed. It may also be that the labour market is more difficult in one case compared with another. In addition, the claimant may have been stigmatised by taking proceedings and that may have some effect on his chances of obtaining future employment.

Wardle v   **[2011] IRLR 694 CA**
Credit Agricole Corporate and   **[2011] EqLR 787 CA**
   Investment Bank
It is generally only in rare cases that it is appropriate for a court to assess an individual's loss over a career lifetime because in most cases assessing the loss up to the point where the employee would be likely to obtain an equivalent job fairly assesses the loss. In the normal case, if a tribunal assesses that the employee is likely to get an equivalent job by a specific date, that will encompass the possibility that he might secure the job earlier or later than predicted. A tribunal should only assess loss on the basis that it will continue for the course of the claimant's working life where it is entitled to take the view on the evidence before it that there is no real prospect of the employee ever obtaining an equivalent job.

Ministry of Defence v   **[1994] IRLR 509 EAT**
Cannock
There is no separate head of damage for loss of career prospects. The financial consequences of being deprived of the opportunity of promotion should be compensated for under damages for loss of employment. The award for injury to feelings should include a sum for the injury to feelings sustained as a result of the loss of chosen career.

Coleman v   **[1981] IRLR 398 CA**
Skyrail Oceanic Ltd
Compensation is to be awarded for foreseeable damage arising directly from an unlawful act of discrimination. It follows that a claimant can claim for any pecuniary loss properly attributable to an unlawful act of discrimination.

Chief Constable of West Midlands   **[2012] EqLR 20 EAT**
   Police v
Gardner
When calculating pension loss in a claim of discrimination, an employment tribunal should calculate compensation by applying the principles applicable to the calculation of damages in claims of tort. The tribunal is entitled to address the question of what is full and fair compensation such as would be awarded in a claim in tort in any way which properly answers

that question. It is not bound, as a matter of law, to adopt the methodology usually used in personal injury litigation in the civil courts, namely the "Ogden" tables – or, alternatively, the "substantial" or "simplified" approach set out in the 2003 booklet, *Compensation for loss of pension rights.* However, if a tribunal does depart from either the Ogden approach or that set out in the 2003 booklet and adopts a mixed approach, it must do so for good, cogent, intelligent and appropriate reasons and it must state what those reasons are.

Sheriff v   **[1999] IRLR 481 CA**
Klyne Tugs (Lowestoft) Ltd
An employment tribunal has jurisdiction to award compensation by way of damages for personal injury, including both physical and psychiatric injury, caused by the statutory tort of unlawful discrimination.

Essa v   **[2004] IRLR 313 CA**
Laing Ltd
A claimant who is the victim of direct discrimination in the form of racial abuse is entitled to be compensated for the loss which arises naturally and directly from the wrong. It is not necessary for the claimant to show that the particular type of loss was reasonably foreseeable.

London Borough of Hackney v   **[2011] IRLR 740 EAT**
Sivanandan   **[2011] EqLR 670 EAT**
In awarding compensation for unlawful discrimination, where the same, indivisible, damage is done to a claimant by two or more respondents who either are jointly liable for the same act or have separately contributed to the same damage, each is liable for the whole of that damage. A tribunal has no power to apportion damages as between the claimant and any particular respondent. The claimant can recover in full against whichever respondent he chooses, and that respondent bears the burden of recovery of any contribution from the others, and the risk that they may not be solvent.

Brennan v   **[2012] EqLR 771 EAT**
Sunderland City Council
An employment tribunal has no jurisdiction to entertain a claim under the Civil Liability (Contribution) Act 1978 by one of two or more people who either are jointly or concurrently liable for damage caused by an act of unlawful discrimination, for a contribution from the other towards the financial liability of the first to the claimant.

Thaine v   **[2010] EqLR 268 EAT**
London School of Economics
Where a tribunal finds that the loss that has been sustained by the claimant has more than one concurrent cause, one or more of which amounted to unlawful discrimination for which the employer is liable, and others which were not the legal responsibility of the employer, it is legally open to it to discount an award of compensation by such percentage as would reflect its apportionment of that responsibility.

HM Prison Service v   **[2005] IRLR 568 CA**
Beart (No.2)
An unfair dismissal does not break the chain of causation, thereby terminating the liability for the earlier wrong of dis-

ability discrimination so that all further losses have to be assessed under the unfair dismissal regime with its statutory cap on compensation. That would be contrary to the principle that a defendant cannot rely on its own further wrong to break the chain of causation.

Chagger v   **[2010] IRLR 47 CA**
Abbey National plc
The original dismissing employer is liable for stigma loss. It is one of the difficulties facing an employee on the labour market. The mere fact that third-party employers are the immediate cause of the loss does not free the original wrongdoer from liability. The fact that the direct cause is their decision not to recruit does not of itself break the chain of causation.

Chagger v   **[2010] IRLR 47 CA**
Abbey National plc
It would be wrong for a tribunal to infer that the employee will in future suffer from widespread stigma simply from his assertion to that effect, or because he is suspicious that this might be the case. If he is unwilling to make good his suspicions by taking proceedings against the alleged wrongdoing employers, he cannot expect the tribunal to put much weight on what is little more than conjecture. However, where there is very extensive evidence of attempted mitigation failing to result in a job, a tribunal is entitled to conclude that, whatever the reason, the employee is unlikely to obtain future employment in the industry.

Bullimore v   **[2010] EqLR 260 EAT**
Pothecary Witham Weld   **[2011] IRLR 18 EAT**
  Solicitors (No.2)
Where a claimant's former employer sent a reference concerning the claimant, which amounted to post-employment victimisation, the unlawful act of the recipient of the reference in withdrawing a job offer because of its contents did not break the chain of causation of loss. Accordingly, the former employer was still liable for any loss of earnings resulting from the post-employment victimisation. It would be most unsatisfactory if a claimant who lost the opportunity of employment as a result of such a reference were unable to recover substantial damages from the person giving it.

Alexander v   **[1988] IRLR 190 CA**
The Home Office
The mere fact that a defendant is guilty of discrimination is not in itself a factor affecting damages. Although in the substantial majority of discrimination cases the unlawful conduct will cause personal hurt, in the sense of injury to feelings, or of preventing the complainant from obtaining a better, more remunerative job, the court must feel it right to draw an inference that the discrimination will cause a plaintiff "hurt" of a particular kind.

Coleman v   **[1981] IRLR 398 CA**
Skyrail Oceanic Ltd
An appellate court is entitled to interfere with the assessment of compensation by an employment tribunal where the tribunal has acted on a wrong principle of law or has misapprehended the facts, or for other reasons has made a wholly erroneous estimate of the damage suffered.

Aggravated damages

Alexander v   [1988] IRLR 190 CA
The Home Office
Compensatory damages may, and in some instances should, include an element of aggravated damages where, for example, the defendant may have behaved in a high-handed, malicious, insulting or oppressive manner in committing the act of discrimination.

Scott v   [2004] IRLR 713 CA
Commissioners of Inland Revenue
Aggravated damages are intended to deal with cases where the injury was inflicted by conduct which was high-handed, malicious, insulting or oppressive. Aggravated damages, therefore, should not be aggregated with and treated as part of the damages for injury to feelings.

Ministry of Defence v   [1995] IRLR 539 EAT
Meredith
In order for aggravated damages to be granted, there must be a causal connection between the exceptional or contumelious conduct or motive in committing the wrong and the intangible loss, such as injury to feelings, suffered by the plaintiff. Thus, in order for the plaintiff's feelings to have suffered an aggravated hurt, he or she must have had some knowledge or suspicion of the conduct or motive which caused that increase.

Bungay v   [2011] EqLR 1130 EAT
Saini
There is no justification for refusing to award aggravated damages where a campaign of discrimination was continued after the employment ceased.

Zaiwalla & Co v   [2002] IRLR 697 EAT
Walia
There is no reason in law why aggravated damages should not be awarded by reference to conduct in the defence of proceedings in a discrimination case.

Governing Body of St Andrew's   [2010] EqLR 156 EAT
   Catholic Primary School v
Blundell
It was open to an employment tribunal to award aggravated damages in respect of the way the employers conducted a remedies hearing at the tribunal and, in particular, the bringing of a battery of evidence effectively to undermine the claimant's capability. This had the effect of causing further offence to the claimant, which aggravated her injury to feelings.

City of Bradford Metropolitan   [1989] IRLR 442 EAT
   Council v
Arora
In considering an award of aggravated damages for injury to feelings, an employment tribunal is entitled to take into account unsatisfactory answers to a statutory questionnaire. The answers to a statutory questionnaire are part of the conduct of the proceedings and may in some cases merit consideration.

HM Prison Service v   [2001] IRLR 425 EAT
Salmon
An employment tribunal did not err in awarding aggravated damages to reflect its view that the manner in which the employers dealt with an incident in which offensive and sexually degrading comments were written about the claimant by one of her colleagues suggested that the employers perceived the entire incident as trivial and that the way the incident was dealt with communicated that perception to the claimant. The tribunal was entitled to find that conduct aggravated the injury to the claimant's feelings.

British Telecommunications plc v   [2004] IRLR 327 CA
Reid
A complainant having to undergo a totally unjustified disciplinary investigation into his own conduct could be an indignity which exacerbates his wounded feelings arising from the act of discrimination itself.

Ministry of Defence v   [2010] IRLR 25 EAT
Fletcher
It is open to an employment tribunal to award aggravated damages in respect of oppressive use of disciplinary procedures against a claimant and for failure properly to investigate and provide redress for her complaints of discrimination.

Exemplary damages

London Borough of Hackney v   [2011] IRLR 740 EAT
Sivanandan   [2011] EqLR 670 EAT
Exemplary damages should be awarded if, but only if, the public authority has been shown to be guilty of oppressive, arbitrary or unconstitutional action and if the award otherwise payable would not suffice by way of punishment and deterrence.

Ministry of Defence v   [2010] IRLR 25 EAT
Fletcher
Exemplary damages are to be reserved for the very worst cases of oppressive use of power by public authorities. To merit an award of exemplary damages the conduct of the wrongdoer must be conscious and contumelious.

Psychiatric injury

HM Prison Service v   [2001] IRLR 425 EAT
Salmon
The assessment of damages for psychiatric injury caused by an act of unlawful discrimination is a matter of fact to be determined by the employment tribunal, which can only be overturned on appeal if the tribunal has made an error of principle or arrived at a figure which is so high or so low as to be perverse.

HM Prison Service v   [2001] IRLR 425 EAT
Salmon
In principle, injury to feelings and psychiatric injury are distinct. In practice, however, the two types of injury are

not always easily separable, giving rise to a risk of double recovery. In a given case, it may be impossible to say with any certainty or precision when the distress and humiliation that may be inflicted on the victim of discrimination becomes a recognised psychiatric illness such as depression. Injury to feelings can cover a very wide range. At the lower end are comparatively minor instances of upset or distress, typically caused by one-off acts or episodes of discrimination. At the upper end, the victim is likely to be suffering from serious and prolonged feelings of humiliation, low self-esteem and depression; and in these cases it may be fairly arbitrary whether the symptoms are put before the tribunal as a psychiatric illness, supported by a formal diagnosis and/or expert evidence.

Injury to feelings

(1) Armitage, (2) Marsden and   **[1997] IRLR 162 EAT**
(3) HM Prison Service v
Johnson

The relevant principles for assessing awards for injury to feelings for unlawful discrimination can be summarised as follows:

(i) Awards for injury to feelings are compensatory. They should be just to both parties. They should compensate fully without punishing the tortfeasor. Feelings of indignation at the tortfeasor's conduct should not be allowed to inflate the award.

(ii) Awards should not be too low as that would diminish respect for the policy of the anti-discrimination legislation. Society has condemned discrimination and awards must ensure that it is seen to be wrong. On the other hand, awards should be restrained, as excessive awards could be seen as the way to untaxed riches.

(iii) Awards should bear some broad general similarity to the range of awards in personal injury cases. This should be done by reference to the whole range of such awards, rather than to any particular type of award.

(iv) In exercising their discretion in assessing a sum, tribunals should remind themselves of the value in everyday life of the sum they have in mind. This may be done by reference to purchasing power or by reference to earnings.

(v) Tribunals should bear in mind the need for public respect for the level of awards made.

Vento v   **[2003] IRLR 102 CA**
Chief Constable of West Yorkshire
    Police (No.2)

Three broad bands of compensation for injury to feelings, as distinct from compensation for psychiatric or similar personal injury, can be identified:

1. The top band should normally be between £15,000 and £25,000. Sums in this range should be awarded in the most serious cases, such as where there has been a lengthy campaign of discriminatory harassment on the ground of sex or race. Only in the most exceptional case should an award of compensation for injury to feelings exceed £25,000.

2. The middle band of between £5,000 and £15,000 should be used for serious cases, which do not merit an award in the highest band.

3. Awards of between £500 and £5,000 are appropriate for less serious cases, such as where the act of discrimination is an isolated or one off occurrence. In general, awards of less than £500 are to be avoided altogether, as they risk being regarded as so low as not to be a proper recognition of injury to feelings.

Da'bell v   **[2010] IRLR 19 EAT**
NSPCC

The guidelines for awarding compensation for injury to feelings set out by the Court of Appeal in *Vento v Chief Constable of West Yorkshire Police* would be updated in line with inflation so that the bottom band would be increased from £5,000 to £6,000; the top of the middle band would be increased from £15,000 to £18,000; and the top of the higher band would be increased from £25,000 to £30,000.

Da'bell v   **[2010] IRLR 19 EAT**
NSPCC

Disputes about the placement within a band of an award are likely to be about fact and impression. They are more likely to raise questions of law if they are about placement in the wrong band or at the extremes.

Vento v   **[2003] IRLR 102 CA**
Chief Constable of West Yorkshire
    Police (No.2)

Subjective feelings of upset, frustration, worry, anxiety, mental distress, fear, grief, anguish, humiliation, stress, depression etc and the degree of their intensity are incapable of objective proof or of measurement in monetary terms. Translating hurt feelings into hard currency is bound to be an artificial exercise. Nevertheless, employment tribunals have to do the best they can on the available material to make a sensible assessment. In carrying out this exercise, they should have in mind the summary of the general principles on compensation for non-pecuniary loss by Smith J in *Armitage v Johnson*.

R (on the application of Elias) v   **[2006] IRLR 934 CA**
Secretary of State for Defence

Quantifying injury to feelings is more a broad brush exercise of estimation than of calculation, comparison with precedents or cold logic. A trial judge's assessment of damages for injury to feelings will only be interfered with on appeal if the award is so much out of line as to amount to an error of law, because the trial judge has misdirected himself in principle or reached a decision which was for some other reason, such as an erroneous evaluation of the facts, plainly wrong. The court is not entitled to interfere simply on the ground that it would have awarded a higher amount, if it had been trying the case.

Ministry of Defence v   **[1994] IRLR 509 EAT**
Cannock

An award for injury to feelings is not automatically to be made whenever unlawful discrimination is proved or admitted. Injury must be proved, though it will often be easy to prove in the sense that no tribunal will take much persuasion that the anger, distress and affront caused by the act of discrimination has injured the claimant's feelings.

Murray v   **[1992] IRLR 257 EAT**
Powertech (Scotland) Ltd

A claim for hurt feelings is so fundamental to a sex discrimination case that it is almost inevitable. All that is
required is that the matter of hurt feelings be simply stated.
It is then for the employment tribunal to consider what
degree of hurt feelings had been sustained and to make an
award accordingly.

Alexander v   **[1988] IRLR 190 CA**
The Home Office

The injury to feelings for which compensation is sought
must have resulted from knowledge of the discrimination.
If the plaintiff knows of the discrimination and that he has
thereby been held up to "hatred, ridicule or contempt",
then the injury to his feelings will be an important element
in the damages.

Moyhing v   **[2006] IRLR 860 EAT**
Barts and London NHS Trust

Harbouring a legitimate and principled sense of grievance
is not to be confused with suffering an injury to feelings.

ICTS (UK) Ltd v   **[2000] IRLR 643 EAT**
Tchoula

A global approach to assessing compensation for injury to
feelings is preferable to making separate awards in respect
of each of three acts of discrimination, since it would be
unrealistic to seek to ascribe to each act of discrimination a
proportion of the overall injury to feelings suffered.

Al Jumard v   **[2008] IRLR 345 EAT**
Clywd Leisure Ltd

Where more than one form of discrimination arises out
of the same facts, such as race and disability discrimination, it can be artificial and unreal to ask to what extent
each discrete head of discrimination has contributed to the
injured feelings, and there will be no error of law where
the tribunal fails to do that. However, where certain acts of
discrimination fall only into one category or another, then
the injury to feelings should be considered separately with
respect to those acts. Each is a separate wrong for which
damages should be provided.

O'Donoghue v   **[2001] IRLR 615 CA**
Redcar & Cleveland Borough Council

That a claimant would notionally have been fairly dismissed within a relatively short period is properly to be
taken into account as a cut-off point in respect of any claim
based on future loss of earnings in respect of a discriminatory dismissal but is not grounds for discounting an award
for injury to feelings.

Alexander v   **[1988] IRLR 190 CA**
The Home Office

Damages for injury to feelings, humiliation and insult in
respect of unlawful discrimination should not be minimal
since this would tend to trivialise or diminish respect for
the public policy to which the statute gives effect. On the
other hand, awards should be restrained. To award sums
which are generally felt to be excessive would do almost as
much harm to the policy, and the results which it seeks to
achieve, as nominal awards.

Voith Turbo Ltd v   **[2005] IRLR 228 EAT**
Stowe

Compensation for injury to feelings caused by dismissal
found to be on grounds of race was correctly assessed in
accordance with the middle band set out by the Court of
Appeal in *Vento (No.2)*, rather than the lowest band applicable to a one-off occurrence. Dismissal on grounds of
race discrimination is a very serious incident and cannot be
described as one-off or isolated.

Orlando v   **[1996] IRLR 262 EAT**
Didcot Power Station Sports &
   Social Club

In assessing injury to feelings, the willingness of the
employer to admit that it has acted in breach of the discrimination legislation may help to reduce the hurt which
is felt, in that it can spare the complainant the indignity and
further hurt of having to rehearse the nature of her treatment.

Orlando v   **[1996] IRLR 262 EAT**
Didcot Power Station Sports &
   Social Club

The nature of lost employment, including the fact that the
position was part time, is relevant in making an award
for injury to feelings. A person who unlawfully loses an
evening job may be expected to be less hurt and humiliated
by the discriminatory treatment than a person who loses
their entire professional career.

Ministry of Defence v   **[1994] IRLR 509 EAT**
Cannock

There is sufficient overlap between compensation for
injury to feelings and loss of congenial employment due to
discrimination for employment tribunals to confine themselves to making an award for injury to feelings, where
such has been proved, which will include compensation for
the hurt caused by the loss of a chosen career which gave
job satisfaction.

HM Prison Service v   **[2001] IRLR 425 EAT**
Salmon

There is nothing wrong in principle in a tribunal treating
"stress and depression" as part of the injury to be compensated for under the heading "injury to feelings", provided
it clearly identifies the main elements in the victim's condition which the award is intended to reflect (including
any psychiatric injury) and the findings in relation to
them. But where separate awards are made, tribunals must
be alert to the risk that what is essentially the same suffering may be being compensated twice under different
heads.

Orthet Ltd v   **[2004] IRLR 857 EAT**
Vince-Cain

An award of compensation for injury to feelings should be
made without regard to the tax implications of the award,
and therefore should not be grossed-up.

Unintentional indirect discrimination

J H Walker Ltd v   **[1996] IRLR 11 EAT**
Hussain

"Intention" is concerned with the state of mind of the respondent in relation to the consequences of his acts. He intended those consequences to follow from his acts if he knew when he did them that those consequences would follow and if he wanted those consequences to follow. Accordingly, a requirement or condition resulting in indirect discrimination is applied with the "intention of treating the claimant unfavourably on racial grounds" if, at the time the relevant act is done, the person (a) wants to bring about the state of affairs which constitutes the prohibited result of unfavourable treatment on racial grounds; and (b) knows that that prohibited result will follow from his acts. The provisions are not concerned with the motivation of a respondent, ie the reason why he did what he did.

British Medical Association v   **[2007] IRLR 800 CA**
Chaudhary

For the respondent to intend to treat the claimant unfavourably on racial grounds, he would have to have actual knowledge or conscious realisation that the condition he had imposed would have disparate impact on one racial group and that he positively wished to have that effect. It is doubtful that constructive knowledge of the discriminatory consequences would be sufficient to satisfy the first limb of the test in *Hussain*.

J H Walker Ltd v   **[1996] IRLR 11 EAT**
Hussain

A tribunal may infer that a person wanted to produce certain consequences from the fact that he acted knowing what those consequences would be. For example, if an employer continued to apply an indirectly discriminatory requirement or condition after it had been declared unlawful, it would not be difficult for a tribunal to infer that he intended to treat an employee unfavourably on racial grounds, even though his reason or motive for persisting in the action was business efficiency.

British Medical Association v   **[2007] IRLR 800 CA**
Chaudhary

The burden on the respondent to show that he did not intend to treat the claimant less favourably on racial grounds is a lesser hurdle for him to cross than simply to show that he had not treated the claimant less favourably on racial grounds. One may act on racial grounds subconsciously but one cannot intend to discriminate subconsciously.

Mitigation

Ministry of Defence v   **[1996] IRLR 139 EAT**
Hunt

The burden of proving a failure to mitigate loss is on the person who asserts it. If a tribunal is to be invited to con-sider whether or not there has been a failure to mitigate or, if there has been such a failure, the quantification of any reduction in the value of the claim, it must be provided with the evidence with which to perform its task, either arising from cross-examination or from evidence called. It is not for the employment tribunal, as an industrial jury, to fill an evidential vacuum itself.

Ministry of Defence v   **[1996] IRLR 139 EAT**
Hunt

In a case where an employment tribunal has assessed a percentage chance of completing a certain number of years service and has also found some failure to mitigate on the part of the claimant, in the final calculation of compensation the tribunal should deduct the failure to mitigate figure before, rather than after, applying the percentage chance figure.

ACTION RECOMMENDATION

Lycée Français Charles de Gaulle v   **[2011] EqLR 948 EAT**
Delambre

An employment tribunal can only require an employer to take action which appears to that tribunal to be practicable. The requirement of practicability is met when the employment tribunal focuses upon what was practicable in terms of its effect on the complainant, although the practicability of a recommendation also has to be seen from the perspective of an employer. Only a recommendation which is completely impracticable would constitute an error of law.

Lycée Français Charles de Gaulle v   **[2011] EqLR 948 EAT**
Delambre

An employment tribunal was entitled to make a recommendation that the tribunal's judgments be circulated to the respondent's governing body and senior management team; that an HR professional be recruited to review and redraft the respondent's employment policies and procedures; and that the respondent undertake a programme of formal equality and diversity training.

REMEDIES UNDER EU LAW

In order to carry out their task and in accordance with the provisions of this Treaty, the European Parliament acting jointly with the Council, the Council and the Commission shall make regulations and issue directives, take decisions, make recommendations or deliver opinions.

   A regulation shall have general application. It shall be binding in its entirety and directly applicable in all Member States.

   A directive shall be binding, as to the result to be achieved, upon each Member State to which it is addressed, but shall leave to the national authorities the choice of form and methods.

   A decision shall be binding in its entirety upon those to whom it is addressed.

   Recommendations and opinions shall have no binding force.

EU TREATY – Article 189

Direct enforcement

Marshall v   **[1986] IRLR 140 ECJ**
Southampton and South-West
  Hampshire Area Health Authority

A Directive may not of itself impose obligations on an individual, as opposed to a State authority, and a provision of a Directive may not be relied upon as against an individual. According to Article 189 of the EU Treaty, the binding nature of a Directive, which constitutes the basis for the possibility of relying on the Directive before a national court, exists only in relation to "each Member State to which it is addressed". Whether a respondent must be regarded as having acted as an individual is for the national court to determine according to the circumstances of each case.

Marshall v   **[1986] IRLR 140 ECJ**
Southampton and South-West
  Hampshire Area Health Authority

Wherever the provisions of an EU Directive appear, as far as their subject-matter is concerned, to be unconditional and sufficiently precise, those provisions may be relied upon by an individual against the State where that State fails to implement the Directive in national law by the end of the period prescribed, or where it fails to implement the Directive correctly.

Verholen v   **[1992] IRLR 38 ECJ**
Sociale Verzekeringsbank Amsterdam

Community law does not preclude a national court from examining of its own motion whether national legal rules comply with the precise and unconditional provisions of a Directive, the period for whose implementation has elapsed.

Marshall v   **[1986] IRLR 140 ECJ**
Southampton and South-West
  Hampshire Area Health Authority

Where a person involved in legal proceedings is able to rely on a Directive as against the State, he may do so regardless of the capacity in which the latter is acting, whether employer or public authority.

Foster v   **[1990] IRLR 354 ECJ**
British Gas plc

Unconditional and sufficiently precise provisions of a Directive can be relied on against an organisation, whatever its legal form, which is subject to the authority or control of the State or which has been made responsible, pursuant to a measure adopted by the State, for providing a public service under the control of the State and has for that purpose special powers beyond those which result from the normal rules applicable in relations between individuals.

Foster v   **[1991] IRLR 268 HL**
British Gas plc

The sole questions under the test laid down by the European Court are whether the employer, pursuant to a measure adopted by the State, provides a public service under the control of the State and exercises special powers. That the employer engages in commercial activities, does not perform any of the traditional functions of the State and is not the agent of the State is not relevant to this test.

Foster v   **[1991] IRLR 268 HL**
British Gas plc

The principle laid down by the European Court of Justice was that the State must not be allowed to take advantage of its own failure to comply with Community law. There is no justification for a narrow or strained construction of the ruling of the European Court, which was couched in terms of broad principle and purposive language.

Doughty v   **[1992] IRLR 126 CA**
Rolls-Royce plc

The three criteria formulated by the European Court in *Foster* for determining whether a particular entity is such that the provisions of a Directive are directly enforceable against it are cumulative requirements rather than alternative. The power of control is only one of the cumulative criteria.

Webb v   **[1993] IRLR 27 HL**
EMO Air Cargo (UK) Ltd

Although an EU Directive does not have direct effect upon the relationship between a worker and an employer who is not an emanation of the State, it is for a United Kingdom court to construe domestic legislation in any field covered by a Community Directive so as to accord with the interpretation of the Directive as laid down by the European Court, if that can be done without distorting the meaning of the domestic legislation. That is so whether the domestic legislation came after or preceded the Directive. However, as the European Court said in the Marleasing case, a national court must construe a domestic law to accord with the terms of a Directive in the same field only if it is possible to do so. That means that the domestic law must be open to an interpretation consistent with the Directive.

Ministry of Defence v   **[2011] EqLR 388 CA**
Wallis

A claimant who had directly effective rights conferred by the Equal Treatment Directive against her employer, an emanation of the state, was entitled to effective judicial protection of those rights, even though as a matter of domestic law she could not bring herself within the scope of the Sex Discrimination Act. Accordingly, words would be read into the Act to cover the case of a person who is employed to work wholly at an establishment outside Great Britain, but whose employment has a sufficient connection with Great Britain to entitle her to the protection of employment law in the courts and tribunals in Great Britain.

Secretary of State for Scotland v   **[1991] IRLR 187 EAT**
Wright

An employment tribunal has jurisdiction to hear a claim brought under directly applicable provisions of the Equal Treatment Directive in circumstances where the claimant has no remedy under domestic legislation. Accordingly, the tribunal had jurisdiction to hear the employees' complaint that their exclusion from the right to a contractual redundancy payment contravened the Equal Treatment Directive.

Blaik v   **[1994] IRLR 280 EAT**
Post Office

If there is a sufficient remedy given by domestic law, it is unnecessary and impermissible to explore the same complaint under the equivalent provisions in a Directive. It is only if there is a disparity between the two that it becomes necessary to consider whether the provisions in EC law are directly enforceable by the complainant in his proceedings against the respondent.

Sanctions

Member States shall introduce into their national legal systems such measures as are necessary to ensure real and effective compensation or reparation as the Member States so determine for the loss and damage sustained by a person injured as a result of discrimination contrary to Article 3, in a way which is dissuasive and proportionate to the damage suffered; such compensation or reparation may not be restricted by the fixing of a prior upper limit, except in cases where the employer can prove that the only damage suffered by a claimant as a result of discrimination within the meaning of this Directive is the refusal to take his/her job application into consideration.

EQUAL TREATMENT DIRECTIVE 2006/54 – Article 18

Coote v   **[1998] IRLR 656 ECJ**
Granada Hospitality Ltd

By virtue of [Article 18], all persons have the right to obtain an effective remedy in a competent court against measures which they consider interfere with the equal treatment for men and women laid down in the Directive. It is for the Member States to ensure effective judicial control of compliance with the applicable provisions of Community law and of national legislation intended to give effect to the rights for which the Directive provides.

Marshall v   **[1993] IRLR 445 ECJ**
Southampton and South-West Hampshire
  Area Health Authority (No.2)

The Equal Treatment Directive must be interpreted as meaning that compensation for the loss and damage sustained by a victim of discrimination may not be limited by national law to an upper limit fixed a priori or by excluding an award of interest to compensate for the loss sustained by the recipient as a result of the effluxion of time until the capital sum awarded is actually paid. Financial compensation must be adequate, in that it must enable the loss and damage actually sustained as a result of discrimination to be made good in full in accordance with the applicable national rules.

Marshall v   **[1993] IRLR 445 ECJ**
Southampton and South-West Hampshire
  Area Health Authority (No.2)

[Article 18] of the Equal Treatment Directive may be relied upon by individuals before the national courts as against an authority of the State acting in its capacity as an employer in order to set aside a national provision which imposes limits on the amount of compensation recoverable by way of reparation.

Dekker v   **[1991] IRLR 27 ECJ**
VJV-Centrum

The Equal Treatment Directive does not make the liability of the discriminator in any way dependent upon evidence of fault on the part of the employer, nor require that it be established that there are no grounds for justification which he can take advantage of. Accordingly, where a Member State chooses a civil law sanction, any breach of the prohibition of discrimination must in itself be sufficient to impose full liability on the discriminator and no account can be taken of grounds for justification provided for under national law.

Dræhmpæhl v   **[1997] IRLR 538 ECJ**
Urania Immobilenservice ohG

The Equal Treatment Directive precludes provisions of domestic law which, unlike other provisions of domestic civil and labour law, place an upper limit of three months' salary for the job in question as the amount of compensation which may be claimed by a claimant discriminated against on grounds of sex in the making of an appointment, where that claimant would have obtained the vacant position if the selection process had been carried out without discrimination. A Member State must ensure that infringements of Community law are penalised under procedural and substantive conditions which are analogous to those applicable to infringements of domestic law of a similar nature and importance.

Time limits

Emmott v   **[1991] IRLR 387 ECJ**
Minister for Social Welfare

In the absence of Community rules on the subject, it is for the domestic legal system of each Member State to determine the procedural conditions governing actions at law intended to ensure the protection of rights which individuals derive from the direct effect of Community law, provided that such conditions are not less favourable than those relating to similar actions of a domestic nature, nor framed so as to render virtually impossible the exercise of rights conferred by Community law. The laying down of reasonable time limits, which if unobserved bar proceedings, in principle satisfies these two conditions.

Emmott v   **[1991] IRLR 387 ECJ**
Minister for Social Welfare

Until such time as a Directive has been properly transposed into domestic law, a defaulting Member State may not rely on an individual's delay in initiating proceedings against it in order to protect rights conferred upon him by the provisions of the Directive, and a period laid down by national law within which proceedings must be initiated cannot begin to run before that time.

Bulicke v   [2010] EqLR 105 ECJ
Deutsche Büro Service GmbH
The fixing of a period of two months for submitting a
claim did not appear liable to render practically impossible
or excessively difficult the exercise of rights conferred by
EU law because the starting point for the time limit was at
the point at which the worker has knowledge of the alleged
discrimination.

Setiya v   [1995] IRLR 348 EAT
East Yorkshire Health Authority
The principle laid down in *Emmott* relates only to time
limits for initiating proceedings, and has no application to
national time limits for appealing against a decision.

9. PROTECTED CHARACTERISTICS

The following characteristics are protected characteristics –
- *age*
- *disability;*
- *gender reassignment;*
- *marriage and civil partnership;*
- *pregnancy and maternity;*
- *race;*
- *religion or belief;*
- *sex;*
- *sexual orientation.*

EQUALITY ACT 2010 – s.4

AGE

EU AGE DISCRIMINATION LAW

(1) For the purposes of this Directive, the "principle of equal treatment" shall mean that there shall be no direct or indirect discrimination whatsoever on any of the grounds referred to in Article 1.

**FRAMEWORK EMPLOYMENT EQUALITY
DIRECTIVE 2000/78 – Article 2**

Within the limits of the areas of competence conferred on the Community, this Directive shall apply to all persons, as regards both the public and private sectors, including public bodies, in relation to:

(a) conditions for access to employment, to self-employment or to occupation, including selection criteria and recruitment conditions, whatever the branch of activity and at all levels of the professional hierarchy, including promotion;

(b) access to all types and to all levels of vocational guidance, vocational training, advanced vocational training and retraining, including practical work experience;

(c) employment and working conditions, including dismissals and pay;

(d) membership of, and involvement in, an organisation of workers or employers, or any organisation whose members carry on a particular profession, including the benefits provided for by such organisations.

**FRAMEWORK EMPLOYMENT EQUALITY
DIRECTIVE 2000/78 – Article 3**

(1) Notwithstanding Article 2(2), Member States may provide that differences of treatment on grounds of age shall not constitute discrimination, if, within the context of national law, they are objectively and reasonably justified by a legitimate aim, including legitimate employment policy, labour market and vocational training objectives, and if the means of achieving that aim are appropriate and necessary.

Such differences of treatment may include, among others:

(a) the setting of special conditions on access to employment and vocational training, employment and occupation, including dismissal and remuneration conditions, for young people, older workers and persons with caring responsibilities in order to promote their vocational integration or ensure their protection;

(b) the fixing of minimum conditions of age, professional experience or seniority in service for access to employment or to certain advantages linked to employment;

(c) the fixing of a maximum age for recruitment which is based on the training requirements of the post in question or the need for a reasonable period of employment before retirement.

**FRAMEWORK EMPLOYMENT EQUALITY
DIRECTIVE 2000/78 – Article 6**

GUIDE TO DISCRIMINATION LAW

Kücüdeveci v **[2010] IRLR 346 ECJ**
Swedex GmbH & Co LG
The principle of non-discrimination on grounds of age is a general principle of EU law. The Framework Employment Equality Directive 2000/78 merely gives expression to, but does not lay down, the principle of equal treatment in employment and occupation. Accordingly, it is for the national court, faced with a national provision falling within the scope of EU law which it considers to be incompatible with that principle, and which cannot be interpreted in conformity with that principle, to disapply that provision.

OCCUPATIONAL REQUIREMENTS

(1) Notwithstanding Article 2(1) and (2), member states may provide that a difference of treatment which is based on a characteristic related to any of the grounds referred to in Article 1 shall not constitute discrimination where, by reason of the nature of the particular occupational activities concerned or of the context in which they are carried out, such a characteristic constitutes a genuine and determining occupational requirement, provided that the objective is legitimate and the requirement is proportionate.

FRAMEWORK EMPLOYMENT EQUALITY DIRECTIVE 2000/78 – Article 4

Wolf v **[2010] IRLR 244 ECJ**
Stadt Frankfurt am Main
German national legislation which sets a maximum age of 30 for recruitment to intermediate career posts in the fire service was justifiable as a genuine and determining occupational requirement under Article 4(1) of the Framework Employment Equality Directive 2000/78. The maximum age was appropriate to the objective of ensuring the operational capacity and proper functioning of the fire service and did not go beyond what was necessary to achieve that objective. Possession of especially high physical capacities is a genuine and determining occupational requirement for such a post in the fire service. This need is related to age in that some of the tasks, such as fighting fires or rescuing persons, can be performed only by young employees. Scientific data shows that respiratory capacity, musculature and endurance diminish with age. Very few employees over age 45 have sufficient physical capacity to perform fire-fighting duties. Accordingly, recruitment at an older age than 30 would have the consequence that too large a number of employees could not be assigned to the most physically demanding duties. Similarly, such recruitment would not allow the employees thus recruited to be assigned to those duties for a sufficiently long period.

Prigge v **[2011] IRLR 1052 CJEU**
Deutsche Lufthansa AG **[2011] EqLR 1175 CJEU**
Although possessing particular physical capabilities may be a genuine and determining occupational requirement for acting as an airline pilot and possession of those physical capabilities is related to age, since both national and inter-

national legislation provide that between the ages of 60 and 65 years of age an individual may carry out the profession of airline pilot, with restrictions, a collective agreement which terminated the claimants' employment at age 60 imposed a disproportionate requirement on pilots covered by it.

R (on the application of the **[2009] IRLR 373 ECJ**
National Council on Ageing) v
Secretary of State for Business, Enterprise and Regulatory Reform
The scope of the Framework Employment Equality Directive 2000/78 extends to national rules, such as those in the Age Discrimination Regulations, which permit employers to dismiss employees aged 65 or over by reason of retirement.

MEASURES TO PROTECT PUBLIC SECURITY AND HEALTH

5. This Directive shall be without prejudice to measures laid down by national law which, in a democratic society, are necessary for public security, for the maintenance of public order and the prevention of criminal offences, for the protection of health and for the protection of the rights and freedoms of others.

FRAMEWORK EMPLOYMENT EQUALITY DIRECTIVE 2000/78 – Article 2

Prigge v **[2011] IRLR 1052 CJEU**
Deutsche Lufthansa AG **[2011] EqLR 1175 CJEU**
A measure which fixes the age limit from which pilots may no longer carry out their professional activities at 60 whereas national and international legislation fixes that age at 65, is not a measure that is necessary for public security and protection of health, within the meaning of the Article 2(5) of the Framework Employment Equality Directive 2000/78. Measures that aim to avoid aeronautical accidents by monitoring pilots' aptitude and physical capabilities with the aim of ensuring that human failure does not cause accidents are undeniably measures of a nature to ensure public security within the meaning of Article 2(5). However, a measure such as the collective agreement in the present case, which operates to terminate the employment of airline pilots when they reach 60 years of age, is not necessary for the achievement of that objective.

Petersen v **[2010] IRLR 254 ECJ**
Berufungsausschuss für Zahnärzte für den Bezirk Westfalen-Lippe
A national measure setting a maximum age of 68 for practising as a panel dentist does not fall within the scope of Article 2(5) of the Framework Employment Equality Directive 2000/78, which provides that the Directive is without prejudice to measures which are "necessary ... for the protection of health", notwithstanding that the aim of the measure was to protect the health of patients against the decline in performance of those dentists after that age, in circumstances in which the age limit did not apply to dentists practising outside the panel system.

DIRECT DISCRIMINATION

Palacios de la Villa v   **[2007] IRLR 989 ECJ**
Cortefiel Servicios SA

National legislation under which the fact that a worker has reached the retirement age laid down by the legislation leads to automatic termination of his employment contract must be regarded as directly imposing less favourable treatment for all workers who have reached that age as compared with all other persons in the labour force. Such legislation therefore establishes a difference in treatment directly based on age within the meaning of Article 2 of Directive 2000/78.

JUSTIFICATION

General principles

Prigge v   **[2011] IRLR 1052 CJEU**
Deutsche Lufthansa AG   **[2011] EqLR 1175 CJEU**

While the list of legitimate aims that might justify a measure that was discriminatory on grounds of age within the meaning of Article 6(1) is not exhaustive, the legitimate aims set out in that provision are related to employment policy, labour market and vocational training. The stated aim of the measure in question in the present case (to safeguard air traffic safety) was not a social policy objective and therefore did not constitute a legitimate aim within the meaning of Article 6(1).

R (on the application of the   **[2009] IRLR 373 ECJ**
   National Council on Ageing) v
Secretary of State for Business, Enterprise
   and Regulatory Reform

Article 6(1) of Directive 2000/78 does not require a member state to draw up, in their measures of transposition, a specific list of the differences in treatment which may be justified by a legitimate aim. However, Article 6(1) offers the option to derogate from the principle of prohibiting discrimination on grounds of age only in respect of measures justified by legitimate social policy objectives, such as those related to employment policy, the labour market or vocational training. By their public interest nature, those legitimate aims are distinguishable from purely individual reasons particular to the employer's situation, such as cost reduction or improving competitiveness, although it cannot be ruled out that a national rule may recognise, in the pursuit of those legitimate aims, a certain degree of flexibility for employers.

R (on the application of the   **[2009] IRLR 373 ECJ**
   National Council on Ageing) v
Secretary of State for Business, Enterprise
   and Regulatory Reform

In choosing the means capable of achieving their social policy objectives, member states enjoy broad discretion. However, that discretion cannot have the effect of frustrating the implementation of the principle of non-discrimination on grounds of age. Mere generalisations concerning the capacity of a specific measure to contribute to employment policy, labour market or vocational training objectives are not enough to show that the aim of that measure is capable of justifying derogation from that principle and do not constitute evidence on the basis of which it could reasonably be considered that the means chosen are suitable for achieving that aim. Article 6(1) imposes on member states, notwithstanding their broad discretion in matters of social policy, the burden of establishing to a high standard of proof the legitimacy of the aim pursued.

R (on the application of Age UK) v   **[2009] IRLR 1017 HC**
Secretary of State for Business,
   Innovation & Skills

In a challenge to the legality and sufficiency of a transposition of EU legislation, the question is principally determined by reference to the social policy aims identified by the Government at the time of transposition. Subsequent developments may show that the Government is required to review those aims and their impact upon the class who suffer equal treatment, but just as there is a broad measure of discretion as to the adoption of social policy aims, and the best means of giving effect to them, so there is a broad measure of discretion afforded to governments as to when those aims and the methods of giving effect to them need to be reviewed.

Fuchs v   **[2011] IRLR 1052 CJEU**
Land Hessen   **[2011] EqLR 990 CJEU**

A change in the context of a law leading to an alteration of the aim pursued by that law does not, of itself, preclude that law from pursuing a legitimate aim within the meaning of Article 6(1) because circumstances may change and a law may nevertheless be preserved for other reasons. Nor does the co-existence of a number of aims preclude the existence of a legitimate aim.

Fuchs v   **[2011] IRLR 1052 CJEU**
Land Hessen   **[2011] EqLR 990 CJEU**

Although budgetary considerations cannot in themselves constitute a legitimate aim within the meaning of Article 6, EU law does not preclude a Member State from taking account of budgetary considerations which may underpin its chosen social policy and influence the nature or extent of the measures which that Member State wishes to adopt.

Fuchs v   **[2011] IRLR 1052 CJEU**
Land Hessen   **[2011] EqLR 990 CJEU**

In deciding whether a particular measure is appropriate and necessary to achieve a legitimate aim, it is for the national court to assess, according to the rules of national law, the probative value of the evidence adduced, which may include statistical evidence. The measure must not appear unreasonable in the light of the aim pursued and must be supported by evidence rather than mere generalisations. However, the Member State's choice of an appropriate measure may be based on economic, social, demographic and/or budgetary considerations which include forecasts which, by their nature, may prove to be inaccurate and are thus to some extent inherently uncertain.

Hörnfeldt v   **[2012] IRLR 785 CJEU**
Posten Meddelande AB   **[2012] EqLR 892 CJEU**
The prohibition of discrimination on grounds of age set out in Directive 2000/78 must be read in the light of the right to engage in work recognised in Article 15(1) of the Charter of Fundamental Rights of the European Union. Consequently, particular attention must be paid to the participation of older workers in the labour force, and thus in economic, cultural and social life. Keeping older workers in the labour force promotes diversity in the workforce and contributes to the realisation of their potential and to the quality of the life of the workers concerned.

Retirement

Hörnfeldt v   **[2012] IRLR 785 CJEU**
Posten Meddelande AB   **[2012] EqLR 892 CJEU**
EU law did not preclude a national provision pursuant to which employees had an unconditional right to work until age 67 but whose employment contracts could be terminated by their employer once they reached that age without it being treated as age discrimination. The aims of the rule – to avoid termination in situations which are humiliating for workers by reason of their advanced age; to enable retirement pension regimes to be adjusted on the basis of the principle that income received over the full course of a career must be taken into account; to reduce obstacles for those who wish to work beyond their 65th birthday; to adapt to demographic developments and to anticipate the risk of labour shortages; to establish a right, and not an obligation, to work until the age of 67; and to make it easier for young people to enter the labour market – in principle objectively justified a difference of treatment on grounds of age. It was not unreasonable for the social partners to take the view that the 67-year rule was appropriate to achieve those aims and the rule did not unduly prejudice the interests of workers who reach age 67, even though it did not specifically take account of the level of pension received by the individual worker since the rule took effect after the statutory retirement age and took account of the fact that the worker is entitled to a replacement income in the form of a retirement pension.

Fuchs v   **[2011] IRLR 1052 CJEU**
Land Hessen   **[2011] EqLR 990 CJEU**
The Framework Employment Equality Directive did not preclude a national law which sets a compulsory retirement age of 65 for civil servants employed as prosecutors where the law had the aim of establishing a balanced age structure between younger and older civil servants, encouraging the recruitment and promotion of young people, and improving personnel management thereby preventing possible disputes concerning employees' fitness to work beyond a certain age, whilst at the same time seeking to provide a high-quality justice service that was in the public interest, so long as that aim was achieved by appropriate and necessary means.

Georgiev v   **[2011] EqLR 84 CJEU**
Tehnicheski universitet – Sofia, filial Plovdiv
Article 6(1) of the Framework Employment Equality Directive does not preclude national legislation under which university professors are compulsorily retired when they reached the age of 68 and may continue working from the age of 65 only by means of fixed-term one-year contracts, renewable at most twice, provided that that legislation pursues a legitimate aim linked to employment and labour policy and that the means used to achieve that aim are appropriate and necessary. Encouragement of recruitment undoubtedly constitutes a legitimate aim, particularly where the promotion of access of young people to a profession is involved. Furthermore, the mix of different generations of teaching staff and researchers promotes an exchange of experiences and innovation, and thereby enhances the development of the quality of teaching and research at universities.

Petersen v   **[2010] IRLR 254 ECJ**
Berufungsausschuss für Zahnärzte für
   den Bezirk Westfalen-Lippe
Article 6(1) of the Framework Employment Equality Directive 2000/78 does not preclude a national measure in Germany setting a maximum age of 68 for practising as a panel dentist where its aim was to share out employment opportunities among the generations, if, taking into account the situation in the labour market concerned, the measure was appropriate and necessary for achieving that aim. The difference in treatment on grounds of age resulting from such an aim may be regarded as objectively and reasonably justified by that aim, and the means of achieving that aim as appropriate and necessary, provided that there was a situation in which there was an excessive number of panel dentists or a latent risk that such a situation would occur.

Rosenbladt v   **[2010] EqLR 365 CJEU**
Gebäudereinigungsges mbH   **[2011] IRLR 51 CJEU**
Article 6(1) of the Framework Employment Equality Directive 2000/78 does not preclude legislation covering the cleaning industry in Germany which provides for automatic termination of employment contracts at age 65, the age at which an employee is eligible to retire and claim a retirement pension. The aims described by the German Government, based on the notion of sharing employment between generations, must, in principle, be regarded as "objectively and reasonably justifying" a difference in treatment on grounds of age such as that in this case. Those aims included the fact that the automatic termination of the employment contracts on reaching retirement age directly benefits young workers by making it easier for them to find work. The rights of older workers are adequately protected as most of them wish to stop working as soon as they are able to retire and the pension they receive serves as a replacement income once they lose their salary. The automatic termination of employment contracts also has the advantage of not requiring employers to dismiss employees on the ground that they are no longer capable of working, which may be humiliating for those who have reached an advanced age. It was not

unreasonable for the German Government to take the view that the measure was appropriate and necessary to achieve these legitimate aims.

Palacios de la Villa v   [2007] IRLR 989 ECJ
Cortefiel Servicios SA

The aim of Spanish legislation providing for compulsory retirement at age 65 – to create opportunities for persons seeking employment – was a legitimate aim of social policy which, in principle, must be regarded as objectively and reasonably justifying a difference in treatment on grounds of age.

Palacios de la Villa v   [2007] IRLR 989 ECJ
Cortefiel Servicios SA

It could not reasonably be maintained that national legislation providing for compulsory retirement at age 65 was incompatible with the requirements of Directive 2000/78, where the member state reasonably took the view that the measure was appropriate and necessary in order to achieve a legitimate aim in the context of national employment policy, consisting of the promotion of full employment by facilitating access to the labour market, the legislation took account of the fact that the persons concerned were entitled to a retirement pension, and the legislation had the flexibility of allowing the social partners to opt by way of collective agreement to apply the compulsory retirement mechanism to take account of the specific features of the jobs in question.

Terms and conditions

Kücüdeveci v   [2010] IRLR 346 ECJ
Swedex GmbH & Co LG

EU law precludes national legislation which provides that periods of employment completed by an employee before reaching the age of 25 are not taken into account in calculating the notice period for dismissal. Although the aim of the legislation is to afford employers greater flexibility in dismissing young workers, the legislation is not appropriate for achieving that aim since it applies to all employees who joined the undertaking before the age of 24, whatever their age at the time of dismissal.

Ingeniørforeningen i Danmark   [2010] EqLR 345 ECJ
(acting for Andersen) v
Region Syddanmark

A national law which excluded workers from receipt of a severance allowance on dismissal in circumstances where they were entitled to claim a pension was incompatible with the Framework Employment Equality Directive 2000/78 because it entailed an unjustifiable difference of treatment directly on grounds of age. Although the aim pursued by the severance allowance of protecting workers with many years of service and helping them to find new employment fell within the category of legitimate labour market objectives, the measure went beyond what is necessary to attain the objective pursued in that it treated those who will actually receive an old-age pension from their employer in the same way as those who are eligible

for such a pension. The measure actually made it more difficult for workers who are eligible for an old-age pension to exercise their right to work because they are not entitled to the severance allowance when seeking new employment.

Hennigs v   [2011] EqLR 1175 CJEU
Eisenbahn-Bundesamt
Land Berlin v
Mai

The principle of non-discrimination on grounds of age set out in the Framework Employment Equality Directive, and which is also a general principle of EU law, precludes a measure set out in a collective agreement which provided that the basic pay step of a public sector employee within a salary group was determined on appointment by reference solely to that employee's age. Such a provision constituted an unjustifiable difference of treatment on grounds of age.

Hennigs v   [2011] EqLR 1175 CJEU
Eisenbahn-Bundesamt
Land Berlin v
Mai

Where a discriminatory pay system had been replaced by a new system but, because of transitional arrangements, employees received a payment that equated to their pay under the previous discriminatory system, the difference in treatment on the sole ground of the age of the employee when appointed, which was thereby perpetuated, was nonetheless justified. The protection of the established rights of a category of persons constitutes an overriding reason in the public interest which justifies that restriction, provided that the restrictive measure does not go beyond what is necessary for that protection. In the present case, the maintenance of earlier pay and consequently of a system that discriminated according to age, had the aim of avoiding losses of pay and was a decisive factor in enabling the social partners to implement the new pay system.

Tyrolean Airways Tiroler   [2012] IRLR 781 CJEU
Luftfahrt Gesellschaft mbH v   [2012] EqLR 834 CJEU
Betriebsrat Bord der Tyrolean Airways
Tiroler Luftfahrt Gesellschaft mbH

Article 2(2)(b) of Directive 2000/78 does not preclude a provision in a collective agreement which only takes into account professional experience acquired as a cabin crew member while working for a specific airline, and excludes substantively identical experience acquired in the service of another airline belonging to the same group of companies, for the purposes of grading staff between employment categories and establishing the level of pay to which they were entitled. Such a provision does not entail a difference of treatment either directly or indirectly based on age. It is neither inextricably, nor indirectly, linked to the age of employees concerned, even if it is conceivable that as a result of its application, some cabin crew members will advance from a lower to a higher pay category at a later age than they would have done had their experience been with the specific airline.

DIRECT DISCRIMINATION

(1) A person (A) discriminates against another (B) if, because of a protected characteristic, A treats B less favourably than A treats or would treat others.

(2) If the protected characteristic is age, A does not discriminate against B if A can show A's treatment of B to be a proportionate means of achieving a legitimate aim.

EQUALITY ACT 2010 – s.13

James v   **[2012] EqLR 314 EAT**
Gina Shoes Ltd
A rhetorical question by the respondent's managing director as to whether the claimant's age might have been the reason why he could not perform as the respondent wanted, that had he been younger it might have been possible to train him, and that "you can't teach an old dog new tricks" plainly raised a prima facie case of direct age discrimination.

Justification

Seldon v   **[2012] IRLR 591 UKSC**
Clarkson Wright and Jakes   **[2012] EqLR 579 UKSC**
The correct approach to justification of direct age discrimination cannot be identical to that applicable to justification of indirect discrimination. Section 13(2) of the Equality Act 2010 must be read accordingly.

Seldon v   **[2012] IRLR 591 UKSC**
Clarkson Wright and Jakes   **[2012] EqLR 579 UKSC**
Direct age discrimination may only be justified if it seeks to achieve a legitimate aim of a public interest nature, such as one related to employment policy, the labour market and vocational training. It is for Member States, rather than individual employers, to establish the legitimacy of such social policy objectives: the evolving case law of the Court of Justice demonstrates that a distinction must be drawn between those types of social policy objectives and purely individual reasons that are specific to the situation of a particular employer, such as cost-reduction or improving competitiveness, which would not be legitimate. The UK legislature has, however, chosen to give employers and partnerships the flexibility to choose which objectives to pursue, provided always that (i) those objectives can count as legitimate objectives of a public interest nature within the meaning of the Directive; (ii) they are consistent with the social policy aims of the state; and (iii) the means used to achieve the objective are proportionate, that is both appropriate to the aim and reasonably necessary to achieve it.

Seldon v   **[2012] IRLR 591 UKSC**
Clarkson Wright and Jakes   **[2012] EqLR 579 UKSC**
The European Court of Justice has identified two different kinds of legitimate objectives in the context of direct age discrimination. The first is intergenerational fairness, which can mean facilitating access to employment for young people; or enabling older people to remain in the workforce; or sharing limited opportunities to work in a particular profession fairly between the generations; or it can mean promoting diversity and the interchange of ideas between younger and older workers. The second kind of legitimate objective may be described as dignity, which has been put as avoiding the need to dismiss older workers on the grounds of incapacity or underperformance, thus preserving their dignity and avoiding humiliation and the need for costly and divisive disputes about capacity or underperformance. The Court of Justice has held that the avoidance of unseemly debates about capacity is capable of being a legitimate aim.

Seldon v   **[2012] IRLR 591 UKSC**
Clarkson Wright and Jakes   **[2012] EqLR 579 UKSC**
To determine whether direct age discrimination is justified, it is necessary to examine whether the aim identified is legitimate in the particular circumstances of the employment concerned, and that the means chosen are both appropriate and necessary. For example, improving the recruitment of young people, in order to achieve a balanced and diverse workforce, is in principle a legitimate aim, but if there is in fact no problem in recruiting the young and the problem is in retaining the older and more experienced workers then it may not be a legitimate aim for the business concerned. Avoiding the need for performance management may be a legitimate aim, but if in fact the business already has sophisticated management measures in place, it may not be legitimate to avoid them for only one section of the workforce. The means chosen also have to be carefully scrutinised in the context of the particular business concerned in order to see whether they do meet the relevant objective and there are not other, less discriminatory, measures which would do so.

Seldon v   **[2012] IRLR 591 UKSC**
Clarkson Wright and Jakes   **[2012] EqLR 579 UKSC**
If it is justified to have a general rule, then the existence of that rule will usually justify the treatment which results from it without the need to establish that it is justified to apply the rule to a particular individual.

London Borough of Tower Hamlets v   **[2009] IRLR 980 EAT**
Wooster
In a case of alleged direct discrimination (where the act complained of is not inherently discriminatory), the tribunal is required in principle to consider the "mental processes" of the relevant decision-maker(s). It is accordingly necessary to identify who the decision-maker(s) was or were.

Pulham v   **[2010] IRLR 184 EAT**
London Borough of Barking & Dagenham
It would be wrong in principle to exclude a defence of justification on the basis that the employer had not himself articulated or recognised the matters relied on at the time that he did the act complained of. The fact that a justification is produced long after the event may entitle a tribunal to treat it with some scepticism, but that depends on the circumstances of the particular case.

Woodcock v   **[2012] IRLR 491 CA**
Cumbria Primary Care Trust   **[2012] EqLR 463 CA**
The guidance of the Court of Justice of the European

Union is that an employer cannot justify discriminatory treatment "solely" because the elimination of such treatment would involve increased costs. That means no more than that the saving or avoidance of costs will not, without more, amount to the achieving of a "legitimate aim".

Loxley v   **[2008] IRLR 853 EAT**
BAE Systems (Munitions & Ordnance) Ltd
The fact that an agreement is made with a trade union does not render an otherwise unlawful scheme lawful, but in determining whether treatment is proportionate, it is right to attach some significance to the fact that the collective parties have agreed a scheme which they consider to be fair.

Pulham v   **[2010] IRLR 184 EAT**
London Borough of Barking & Dagenham
While a tribunal is entitled to have regard, in assessing the justifiability of a discriminatory measure, to the fact that it has been negotiated with the representatives of the workforce, it cannot abdicate the responsibility of itself carrying out the necessary proportionality exercise.

Canadian Imperial Bank   **[2010] EqLR 120 EAT**
   of Commerce v
Beck
The deliberate adoption by the employers in a briefing document to a recruitment consultant of the description of the person being sought for a new role replacing the claimant as "younger" was a flagrant instance of potential age discrimination that shifted the burden of proof to the respondent bank, and the respondents had not discharged the burden of showing that a decision to dismiss was not significantly influenced by the claimant's age.

Pulham v   **[2010] IRLR 184 EAT**
London Borough of Barking & Dagenham
Pay protection arrangements following withdrawal of an incremental pay scheme based on age and length of service are capable in principle of being justified notwithstanding that they perpetuate age discrimination.

DISCRIMINATION BY EMPLOYERS

(1) An employer (A) must not discriminate against a person (B) –
   (a) in the arrangements A makes for deciding to whom to offer employment;
   (b) as to the terms on which A offers B employment;
   (c) by not offering B employment.

(2) An employer (A) must not discriminate against an employee of A's (B) –
   (a) as to B's terms of employment;
   (b) in the way A affords B access, or by not affording B access, to opportunities for promotion, transfer or training or for receiving any other benefit, facility or service;
   (c) by dismissing B;
   (d) by subjecting B to any other detriment.

EQUALITY ACT 2010 – s.39

Dismissal

Seldon v   **[2012] IRLR 591 UKSC**
Clarkson Wright and Jakes   **[2012] EqLR 579 UKSC**
All businesses will have to give careful consideration to what, if any, mandatory retirement rules can be justified.

Seldon v   **[2012] IRLR 591 UKSC**
Clarkson Wright and Jakes   **[2012] EqLR 579 UKSC**
The aims which the provisions in a law firm's partnership deed requiring retirement at age 65 sought to achieve – staff retention and workforce planning, and limiting the need to expel partners by way of performance management – were legitimate aims. However, when considering whether the measure was proportionate, the tribunal did not sufficiently analyse the specific retirement age of 65 which was chosen and discuss it in relation to each of those objectives.

London Borough of Tower Hamlets v **[2009] IRLR 980 EAT**
Wooster
It is plainly a legitimate aim for an employer to dismiss employees who are genuinely redundant. Where an employer no longer has work for an employee, he is not obliged to postpone the dismissal for however long is necessary in order to entitle the employee to qualify for an age-related benefit which has not yet accrued.

London Borough of Tower Hamlets v **[2009] IRLR 980 EAT**
Wooster
A local authority unlawfully discriminated on grounds of age when it dismissed an employee instead of redeploying him or extending his employment because it was motivated by a desire to terminate his employment before he reached age 50 and became eligible for an early retirement pension, which the authority would have had to fund.

Rolls-Royce plc v   **[2009] IRLR 576 EAT**
Unite the Union
Length of service as one of the criteria for redundancy selection is a proportionate means of achieving a legitimate aim. The legitimate aim is the reward of loyalty, and the overall desirability of achieving a stable workforce in the context of a fair process of redundancy selection. Proportionate means was amply demonstrated where length of service was only one of a substantial number of criteria for measuring employee suitability for redundancy and was by no means determinative.

Woodcock v   **[2012] IRLR 491 CA**
Cumbria Primary Care Trust   **[2012] EqLR 463 CA**
The respondent's decision to terminate the claimant's employment on grounds of redundancy and to time the giving of notice of termination so as to ensure that the claimant was not employed by them when he reached his 50th birthday did not constitute unlawful direct age discrimination. Had the claimant remained in the respondent's employment on his 50th birthday, he would have been entitled to take early retirement on enhanced terms with significantly increased costs to the respondent. The dismissal of an employee who has become redundant is a legitimate aim and does not cease to be a legitimate aim simply because, if there is no dismissal, the employer will continue to incur costs that such dismissal is directed at

saving. It was also legitimate for the employer to ensure that, in giving effect to the dismissal, it saved the additional element of costs. The respondent was entitled to have regard to that consideration and would have been irresponsible not to do so.

INDIRECT DISCRIMINATION

Homer v   **[2012] IRLR 601 UKSC**
Chief Constable of West   **[2012] EqLR 594 UKSC**
  Yorkshire Police
The claimant was subjected to prima facie indirect discrimination on grounds of age when he was not permitted to progress to the highest threshold of the respondent's new pay scale unless he held a law degree, in circumstances where because he was age 62 at the relevant time, he could not obtain that qualification before he was due to retire at age 65. The employment tribunal correctly concluded that, for the purposes of the claim of indirect discrimination, the appropriate age group was people aged 60–65 who would not be able to obtain a law degree before they retired; that that group was put at a particular disadvantage compared with younger people because they were prevented from reaching the highest threshold on the pay scale; and that the claimant was put at a disadvantage because he could not achieve that qualification before he retired.

Homer v   **[2012] IRLR 601 UKSC**
Chief Constable of West   **[2012] EqLR 594 UKSC**
  Yorkshire Police
There is unreality in differentiating between age and retirement. It was inappropriate to conclude, as the EAT and Court of Appeal had done, that what put the claimant at a disadvantage was not his age but his impending retirement. That argument involved taking the particular disadvantage suffered by a particular age group for a reason related to their age and equating it with a similar disadvantage suffered by others for a different reason, unrelated to their age.

HM Land Registry v   **[2012] EqLR 300 EAT**
Benson
Selecting applicants for voluntary early retirement or voluntary redundancy on the basis of whose benefits would cost less to fund had a disparate impact on employees aged between 50 and 54 because their benefits were more expensive to fund, but was objectively justified having regard to the respondent's legitimate aim of reducing its staffing costs within its set budget and the fact that there were no other practicable criteria which the respondent could have used to select between applicants.

Benefits based on length of service

(1) It is not an age contravention for a person (A) to put a person (B) at a disadvantage when compared with another (C), in relation to the provision of a benefit, facility or service in so far as the disadvantage is because B has a shorter period of service than C.

EQUALITY ACT 2010 – Sch.9, para 10

Rolls-Royce plc v   **[2009] IRLR 576 EAT**
Unite the Union
Length of service as a criterion for redundancy selection is capable of constituting a "benefit", in the absence of any statutory definition which inhibits the word from otherwise having its wide dictionary definition.

Contractual redundancy scheme

MacCulloch v   **[2008] IRLR 846 EAT**
Imperial Chemical Industries plc
In a contractual redundancy scheme, where there is a standard set of rules identifying the amount of redundancy payment to be paid, and no discretion in the amount of payment, it would be an error to examine the application of the scheme to the individual as though the scheme was irrelevant to his or her position. The reason for the individual's treatment is linked inextricably to the aims of the scheme. Accordingly, whilst the proportionality test must focus on the extent of the disadvantage to the individual, the balancing exercise must have regard to the impact which a different scheme would have on the whole range of employees.

MacCulloch v   **[2008] IRLR 846 EAT**
Imperial Chemical Industries plc
It cannot be assumed that because a scheme in broad terms achieves certain business objectives that this necessarily establishes the justification for differentials in pay linked to age. The reasonable needs of the business must be balanced with the discriminatory effects on the claimant.

Loxley v   **[2008] IRLR 853 EAT**
BAE Systems (Munitions & Ordnance) Ltd
It may be justified to exclude those who are entitled to immediate benefits from their pension fund from the scope of a contractual redundancy scheme since preventing a windfall can be a legitimate feature of a scheme. However, such an exclusion is not inevitably and in all cases justified. Ultimately, it must depend upon the nature of both schemes. The tribunal must ask whether the treatment of the claimant achieves a legitimate objective and is proportional to any disadvantage which he suffers.

Kraft Foods UK Ltd v   **[2010] EqLR 18 EAT**
Hastie
A cap on awards made pursuant to a voluntary redundancy scheme was justified, notwithstanding that it disproportionately adversely affected employees closer to retirement. The cap prevented employees from recovering more than they would have earned if they had remained in employment until retirement age, thereby preventing a windfall. A provision which prevents an employee recovering more than they would have been entitled to earn is necessarily justifiable whether the amount of the windfall is large or small.

DISABILITY

Chacon Navas v   **[2006] IRLR 706 ECJ**
Eurest Colectividades SA
The concept of "disability" for the purpose of Directive 2000/78 must be understood as referring to a limitation which results in particular from physical, mental or psychological impairments and which hinders the participation of the person concerned in professional life.

Chacon Navas v   **[2006] IRLR 706 ECJ**
Eurest Colectividades SA
A person who has been dismissed by his employer solely on account of sickness is not protected by the prohibition against discrimination on grounds of disability in Framework Employment Equality Directive 2000/78.

Coleman v   **[2008] IRLR 722 ECJ**
Attridge Law
The prohibition of direct discrimination laid down by Framework Employment Equality Directive 2000/78 is not limited only to people who are themselves disabled. Where an employer treats an employee who is not himself disabled less favourably than another employee is, has been or would be treated in a comparable situation, and it is established that the less favourable treatment of that employee is based on the disability of his child, whose care is provided primarily by that employee, such treatment is contrary to the prohibition of direct discrimination laid down by Article 2(2)(a).

MEANING OF DISABILITY

(1) A person (P) has a disability if –
    (a) P has a physical or mental impairment, and
    (b) the impairment has a substantial and long-term adverse effect on P's ability to carry out normal day-to-day activities.

(2) A reference to a disabled person is a reference to a person who has a disability.

EQUALITY ACT 2010 – s.6

General approach

Goodwin v   **[1999] IRLR 4 EAT**
The Patent Office
When faced with an issue as to whether a person has a disability within the meaning of the Act, the tribunal should adopt an inquisitorial or interventionist role. There is a risk

of a "Catch 22" situation, in that some disabled persons may be unable or unwilling to accept that they have a disability. Without the direct assistance of the tribunal at the hearing, there may be cases where the claimant, for a reason related to his disability, is unwilling to support the claim.

Rugamer v   **[2001] IRLR 644 EAT**
Sony Music Entertainment UK Ltd
McNicol v
Balfour Beatty Rail Maintenance
An employment tribunal is not an inquisitorial body in the same sense as a medical or other tribunal dealing with a disablement issue as part of the statutory machinery for determining benefit claims. The observations of Morison J in *Goodwin v Patent Office* that the role of tribunals in a disability discrimination case contains "an inquisitorial element" mean no more than that the tribunal is obliged to conduct the hearing in a fair and balanced manner, intervening and making its own inquiries in the course of the hearing of such persons appearing before it and such witnesses as are called before it as it considers appropriate, so as to ensure due consideration of the issues raised by, or necessarily implicit in, the complaint being made. The role of the tribunal is not thereby extended so as to place on it the duty to conduct a freestanding inquiry of its own, or to require it to attempt to obtain further evidence beyond that placed in front of it on the issues raised by the parties, or to cause the parties to raise additional issues they have not sought to rely on at all.

Goodwin v   **[1999] IRLR 4 EAT**
The Patent Office
The tribunal should adopt a purposive approach to construction, construing the statutory language in a way which gives effect to the stated or presumed intention of Parliament, but with due regard to the ordinary and natural meaning of the words in question. Explicit reference should always be made to any relevant provision of the Guidance issued by the Secretary of State or of the Code of Practice, which the tribunal has taken into account. However, the Guidance should not be used as an extra hurdle over which the claimant must jump.

Ministry of Defence v   **[2008] IRLR 928 EAT**
Hay
The statutory approach is self-evidently a functional one directed towards what a claimant cannot, or can no longer, do at a practical level.

Meaning of impairment

McNicol v   **[2002] IRLR 711 CA**
Balfour Beatty Rail Maintenance Ltd
The term "impairment" bears its ordinary and natural meaning. Impairment may result from an illness or it may consist of an illness. The essential question in each case is whether, on a sensible interpretation of the relevant evidence, including the expert medical evidence and reasonable inferences which can be made from all the evidence, the claimant can fairly be described as having a physical or mental impairment. Such a decision can and should be

made without substituting for the statutory language a different word or form of words in an attempt to describe or define the concept of "impairment".

Ministry of Defence v   **[2008] IRLR 928 EAT**
Hay
A "disability" is not the same as an "impairment".

McNicol v   **[2002] IRLR 711 CA**
Balfour Beatty Rail Maintenance Ltd
The onus is on the claimant to prove the impairment on the conventional balance of probabilities.

Millar v   **[2006] IRLR 112 CS**
Inland Revenue Commissioners
Physical impairment can be established without reference to causation, and, in particular, without reference to any form of "illness". Many forms of physical impairment result from conditions that cannot be described as "illness".

Hospice of St Mary of Furness v   **[2007] IRLR 944 EAT**
Howard
It is not necessary for a claimant to establish the cause of an alleged physical impairment, but where there is an issue as to the existence of a physical impairment, it is open to a respondent to seek to disprove the existence of such impairment, including by seeking to prove that the impairment is not genuine or is a mental and not a physical impairment.

J v   **[2010] IRLR 936 EAT**
DLA Piper UK LLP   **[2010] EqLR 164 EAT**
It is good practice in every case for a tribunal to state conclusions separately on the questions of impairment and of adverse effect, and in the case of adverse effect, the questions of substantiality and long-term effect arising under it.

J v   **[2010] IRLR 936 EAT**
DLA Piper UK LLP   **[2010] EqLR 164 EAT**
There are sometimes cases where identifying the nature of the impairment from which a claimant may be suffering involves difficult medical questions. In cases where there may be a dispute about the existence of an impairment, it will make sense to start by making findings about whether the claimant's ability to carry out normal day-to-day activities is adversely affected (on a long-term basis), and to consider the question of impairment in the light of those findings. If the tribunal finds that the claimant's ability to carry out normal day-to-day activities has been adversely affected on a long-term basis, it will in many or most cases follow as a matter of common-sense inference that the claimant is suffering from a condition which has produced that adverse effect – ie, an "impairment". If that inference can be drawn, it will be unnecessary for the tribunal to try to resolve difficult medical issues.

J v   **[2010] IRLR 936 EAT**
DLA Piper UK LLP   **[2010] EqLR 164 EAT**
If a tribunal finds that the claimant's ability to carry out normal day-to-day activities has been substantially impaired by symptoms characteristic of depression for 12

months or more, it would in most cases be likely to conclude that he or she was suffering "clinical depression" rather than simply a reaction to adverse circumstances.

Morgan v   **[2002] IRLR 190 EAT**
Staffordshire University
Medical notes which refer to "anxiety", "stress" and "depression" do not amount to proof of a mental impairment.

Dunham v   **[2005] IRLR 608 EAT**
Ashford Windows
A tribunal hearing a mental impairment case based on learning difficulties should look for expert evidence as to the nature and degree of the impairment claimed and for evidence of a particular identified condition (which may have a specific or a generalised effect on function). It is unlikely to be sufficient for a claimant to put his case only on the basis that he had difficulties at school or is "not very bright".

Dunham v   **[2005] IRLR 608 EAT**
Ashford Windows
In a case of learning difficulties, there is no reason why the essential evidence which establishes the nature of the claimant's condition should not be provided by a suitably qualified psychologist. What is important is that there should be evidence from a suitably qualified expert who can speak, on the basis of their experience and expertise, as to the relevant condition.

J v   **[2010] IRLR 936 EAT**
DLA Piper UK LLP   **[2010] EqLR 164 EAT**
A GP is fully qualified to express an opinion on whether a patient is suffering from depression, and on any associated questions arising under the disability discrimination legislation. Depression is a condition very often encountered in general practice.

Leonard v   **[2001] IRLR 19 EAT**
Southern Derbyshire Chamber
   of Commerce
An employment tribunal misdirected themselves as to the manner in which the Guidance on the definition of disability should be applied by taking examples from the Guidance of what the claimant could do, such as being able to eat and drink, and catch a ball and then weighing that against what she could not do, such as negotiate pavement edges safely. This was inappropriate, since her ability to catch a ball did not diminish her inability to negotiate pavement edges safely.

Excluded conditions

(1) Subject to para. (2) below, addiction to alcohol, nicotine or any other substance is to be treated as not amounting to an impairment for the purposes of the Act.

(2) Para. (1) above does not apply to addiction which was originally the result of administration of medically prescribed drugs or other medical treatment.

EQUALITY ACT 2010 (DISABILITY)
REGULATIONS 2010 – reg. 3

Power v [2003] IRLR 151 EAT
Panasonic UK Ltd

It is not material to a decision as to whether a person has a disability within the meaning of the Act to consider how the impairment which they have was caused. What is material is to ascertain whether the disability which they have at the material time is a disability within the meaning of the Act or whether, where it is relevant, it is an impairment which is excluded by reason of the Regulations from being treated as such a disability. In this case, the tribunal erred in not considering whether the claimant's depression had a substantial and long-term adverse effect on her ability to carry out normal day-to-day activities, but by considering instead whether alcoholism caused her depression, and concluding that her case fell within reg.3(1), which provides that "addiction to alcohol ... is to be treated as not amounting to an impairment for the purposes of the Act."

(1) For the purposes of the Act the following conditions are to be treated as not amounting to impairments –
    (a) a tendency to set fires,
    (b) a tendency to steal,
    (c) a tendency to physical or sexual abuse of other persons,
    (d) exhibitionism, and
    (e) voyeurism.

**EQUALITY ACT 2010 (DISABILITY)
REGULATIONS 2010 – reg. 4**

Governing Body of X Endowed [2009] IRLR 1007 HC
  Primary School v
Special Educational Needs and Disability Tribunal

The exclusion in respect of a "condition" within the meaning of para. 4(1) includes both an independent, free-standing condition and symptoms or manifestations of an underlying impairment.

Long-term effects

2. (1) The effect of an impairment is long-term if –
    (a) it has lasted for at least 12 months,
    (b) it is likely to last for at least 12 months, or
    (c) it is likely to last for the rest of the life of the person affected.

EQUALITY ACT 2010 – Sch.1

Richmond Adult Community College v [2008] IRLR 227 CA
McDougall

The point in time for determining whether the effect of an impairment is likely to last for at least 12 months is the time of the decision complained of. The tribunal should make its judgment on the basis of evidence as to the circumstances prevailing at the time of that decision.

Patel v [2010] IRLR 280 EAT
Oldham Metropolitan Borough Council

The effect of an illness or condition likely to develop or which has developed from another illness or condition forms part of the assessment of whether the effect of the original impairment is likely to last or has lasted at least 12 months.

Normal day-to-day activities

Goodwin v [1999] IRLR 4 EAT
The Patent Office

The Act is concerned with a person's ability to carry out activities. The fact that a person can carry out such activities does not mean that his ability to carry them out has not been impaired. The focus of the Act is on the things that the claimant either cannot do or can only do with difficulty, rather than on the things that the person can do.

Ahmed v [2011] EqLR 464 EAT
Metroline Travel Ltd

As a matter of principle, it is impermissible for an employment tribunal to seek to weigh what a claimant can do against what he or she cannot do, and then determine whether or not the claimant has a disability by weighing those matters in the balance. The tribunal must focus upon what a claimant cannot do. However, where there is a factual dispute as to what a claimant is asserting that he cannot do, findings of fact as to what a claimant actually can do may throw significant light on the disputed question of what he cannot do.

Ekpe v [2001] IRLR 605 EAT
Commissioner of Police of the Metropolis

What is "normal" for the purposes of the Act may be best understood by defining it as anything which is not abnormal or unusual (or, in the words of the Guidance issued by the Secretary of State, "particular" to the individual claimant). What is normal cannot sensibly depend on whether the majority of people do it. The antithesis for the purposes of the Act is between that which is "normal" and that which is "abnormal" or "unusual" as a regular activity, judged by an objective population standard.

Ekpe v [2001] IRLR 605 EAT
Commissioner of Police of the Metropolis

Anything done by most women, or most men, is a normal day-to-day activity. Therefore, an employment tribunal erred in discounting the fact that the claimant could not put rollers in her hair and that she could not always use her right hand to apply make-up on grounds that neither was a "normal day-to-day activity" because they are activities carried out almost exclusively by women.

Law Hospital NHS Trust v [2001] IRLR 611 CS
Rush

Evidence of the nature of a claimant's duties at work, and the way in which they are performed, particularly if they include "normal day-to-day activities, can be relevant to the assessment which the tribunal has to make of the claimant's case.

Chief Constable of Dumfries & [2009] IRLR 612 EAT
  Galloway Constabulary v
Adams

The European Court of Justice's use of the term "participation in professional life" in *Chacon Navas* means that when assessing whether a person is limited in their normal day-to-day activities, it is relevant to consider whether they are limited in an activity which is to be found across a range of employment situations. Although work of a particular form is not a "normal day-to-day activity", something that a person does only at work may be classed as normal if it is common to different types of employment.

Sussex Partnership NHS   **[2012] EqLR 1068 EAT**
Foundation Trust v
Norris

Although there must be a causal link between the impairment and a substantial and long-term adverse effect in the ability to carry out day-to-day activities, that causal link does not have to be direct. If, on the evidence, the impairment causes the substantial adverse effect on the claimant's ability to carry out day-to-day activities, it is not material that there is an intermediate step between the impairment and its effect, provided that there is a causal link between the two.

Paterson v   **[2007] IRLR 763 EAT**
Commissioner of Police of the Metropolis

The Act can be read in a way which gives effect to EU law by giving a meaning to day-to-day activities that encompasses the activities that are relevant to participation in professional life. Where it is not disputed that the employee is suffering a substantial disadvantage because of the effects of his or her disability in the procedures adopted for deciding between candidates for promotion, the only proper inference is that those effects must involve more than a trivial effect on his ability to undertake normal day-to-day activities.

Paterson v   **[2007] IRLR 763 EAT**
Commissioner of Police of the Metropolis

Carrying out an assessment or examination is properly to be described as a normal day-to-day activity.

Chief Constable of Lothian and   **[2010] IRLR 109 EAT**
Borders Police v
Cumming

Paterson and *Chacon* are not authority for the broad proposition that being afforded general participation in or access to professional life is a day-to-day activity. The status of disability for the purposes of the statute cannot be dependent on the decision of the employer as to how to react to the employee's impairment.

Chief Constable of Dumfries &   **[2009] IRLR 612 EAT**
Galloway Constabulary v
Adams

There are enough people working on night shifts for it to be a normal day-to-day activity.

Cruickshank v   **[2002] IRLR 24 EAT**
VAW Motorcast Ltd

In a case where, as a result of a medical condition, the effects of an impairment on ability to carry out normal day-to-day activities fluctuate and may be exacerbated by conditions at work, the tribunal should consider whether the impairment has a substantial and long-term adverse effect on the employee's ability to perform normal day-to-day activities both while actually at work and while not at work. If, while at work, a claimant's symptoms are such as to have a significant and long-term effect on his ability to perform day-to-day tasks, such symptoms are not to be ignored simply because the work itself may be specialised and unusual, so long as the disability and its consequences can be measured in terms of the ability of a claimant to undertake day-to-day tasks.

Vicary v   **[1999] IRLR 680 EAT**
British Telecommunications plc

It is not for a doctor to express an opinion as to what is a normal day-to-day activity. Nor is it for the medical expert to tell the tribunal whether the impairments which had been found proved were or were not substantial. Those are matters for the employment tribunal to arrive at its own assessment.

Ekpe v   **[2001] IRLR 605 EAT**
Commissioner of Police
of the Metropolis

An employment tribunal is entitled to have regard to its own observation of the claimant in determining the extent of a claimant's disability. A decision as to whether a disability has an adverse impact on normal day-to-day activities and whether that impact is substantial may properly be influenced by the behaviour of a claimant as demonstrated before the tribunal, although any tribunal considering whether to draw any conclusion from such behaviour would be expected to raise that possibility at the hearing.

Kapadia v   **[2000] IRLR 699 CA**
London Borough of Lambeth

An employment tribunal was obliged to conclude that a claimant's mental impairment had a substantial adverse effect on his normal day-to-day activities, in circumstances in which there was direct medical evidence that his anxiety, neuroses and depression would have had such an effect but for the fact that he had received medical treatment, and there was no contrary expert medical evidence or challenge to the factual bases of those opinions.

Recurring conditions

(2) If an impairment ceases to have a substantial adverse effect on a person's ability to carry out normal day-to-day activities, it is to be treated as continuing to have that effect if that effect is likely to recur.

EQUALITY ACT 2010 – Sch.1, para.2

Swift v   **[2004] IRLR 540 EAT**
Chief Constable of Wiltshire Constabulary

In considering the application of para.2(2), a tribunal should ask itself the following questions: first, was there at some stage an impairment which had a substantial adverse effect on the claimant's ability to carry out normal day-to-day activities? Secondly, did the impairment cease to have a substantial adverse effect on the claimant's ability to carry out normal day-to-day activities, and if so when? Thirdly, what was the substantial adverse effect? Fourthly, is that substantial adverse effect likely to recur. The tribunal must be satisfied that the same effect is likely to recur and will again amount to a substantial adverse effect on the claimant's ability to carry out normal day-to-day activities.

Swift v [2004] IRLR 540 EAT
Chief Constable of Wiltshire Constabulary
Although the tribunal must be satisfied that the substantial adverse effect is likely to recur, it need not be satisfied that the recurrence is likely to last for at least 12 months. The effect of para.2(2) is that the impairment is treated as continuing for as long as its substantial adverse effect is likely to recur. Even if the impairment has ceased to have a substantial adverse effect, it "lasts" for as long as its substantial adverse effect is likely to recur.

Swift v [2004] IRLR 540 EAT
Chief Constable of Wiltshire Constabulary
The question for the tribunal is whether the substantial adverse effect is likely to recur, not whether the illness is likely to recur. The Act contemplates that an illness may run its course to a conclusion but leave behind an impairment.

J v [2010] IRLR 936 EAT
DLA Piper UK LLP [2010] EqLR 164 EAT
If a woman over a five-year period suffers several short episodes of depression which have a substantial adverse impact on her ability to carry out normal day-to-day activities but who between those episodes is symptom-free and does not require treatment, it may be appropriate to regard her as suffering from a mental impairment throughout the period in question, ie even between episodes. The model would be of a single condition producing recurrent symptomatic episodes.

Substantial adverse effect

Goodwin v [1999] IRLR 4 EAT
The Patent Office
"Substantial" means "more than minor or trivial" rather than "very large". The tribunal may take into account how the claimant appears to the tribunal to "manage", although it should be slow to regard a person's capabilities in the relatively strange adversarial environment as an entirely reliable guide to the level of ability to perform normal day-to-day activities.

Paterson v [2007] IRLR 763 EAT
Commissioner of Police of the Metropolis
In the population at large there will be differences in such things as manual dexterity, ability to lift objects or to concentrate. In order to be substantial, the effect must fall outwith the normal range of effects that one might expect from a cross-section of the population. However, when assessing the effect, the comparison is not with the population at large. What is required is to compare the difference between the way in which the individual in fact carries out the activity in question and how he would carry it out if not impaired.

Abadeh v [2001] IRLR 23 EAT
British Telecommunications plc
It is not the task of the medical expert to tell the tribunal whether an impairment was or was not substantial. That is a

question which the tribunal itself has to answer. The medical report should deal with the doctor's diagnosis of the impairment, the doctor's observation of the claimant carrying out day-to-day activities and the ease with which he was able to perform those functions, together with any relevant opinion as to prognosis and the effect of medication.

Vicary v [1999] IRLR 680 EAT
British Telecommunications plc
Having concluded that the ability of the claimant to do a number of activities was impaired, the tribunal should have concluded that she had a disability within the meaning of the Act.

Paterson v [2007] IRLR 763 EAT
Commissioner of Police of the Metropolis
In some cases, coping strategies will prevent the impairment having adverse effects, but only where they can be relied on in all circumstances.

Abadeh v [2001] IRLR 23 EAT
British Telecommunications plc
An assessment of disability by a Medical Appeal Tribunal is clearly relevant evidence for an employment tribunal to take into account as part of the evidence before them on the issue of disability.

Goodwin v [1999] IRLR 4 EAT
The Patent Office
An employment tribunal erred in finding that a paranoid schizophrenic who was dismissed after complaints relating to his behaviour, was not a "disabled person" because the adverse effect of the impairment on his ability to carry out normal day-to-day activities was not "substantial". The claimant was unable to carry on a normal day-to-day conversation with work colleagues, which was good evidence that his capacity to concentrate and communicate had been adversely affected in a significant manner.

Severe disfigurement

3(1) An impairment which consists of a severe disfigurement is to be treated as having a substantial adverse effect on the ability of the person concerned to carry out normal day-to-day activities.

EQUALITY ACT 2010 – Sch. 1

Cosgrove v [2007] IRLR 397 NICA
Northern Ireland Ambulance Service
An impairment "consisting of" disfigurement means that the impairment relates solely to the cosmetic aspect of the condition, and not to a condition, one aspect of which is disfigurement. Therefore, the severe disfigurement provisions did not protect a claimant with psoriasis, where the reason he was not employed as an ambulance worker was not as a result of his disfigurement but because it was judged that he was at risk of infection and that his condition carried the danger that he would infect others.

Effect of medical treatment

5(1) An impairment is to be treated as having a substantial adverse effect on the ability of the person concerned to carry out normal day-to-day activities if –
  (a) measures are being taken to treat or correct it, and
  (b) but for that, it would be likely to have that effect.

(2) "Measures" includes, in particular, medical treatment and the use of a prosthesis or other aid.

(3) Sub-paragraph (1) does not apply –
  (a) in relation to the impairment of a person's sight, to the extent that the impairment is, in the person's case, correctable by spectacles or contact lenses or in such other ways as may be prescribed;
  (b) in relation to such other impairments as may be prescribed, in such circumstances as are prescribed.

EQUALITY ACT 2010 – Sch.1

SCA Packaging Ltd v **[2009] IRLR 746 HL**
Boyle
The word "likely" is used in the sense of "could well happen" rather than whether it is more probable than not.

SCA Packaging Ltd v **[2009] IRLR 746 HL**
Boyle
The provision on the effect of medical treatment is far-reaching. Where it applies, the individual's actual situation with the benefit of the course of treatment must be ignored, and she must be considered as if she was not having the treatment and the impairment was completely unchecked.

Woodrup v **[2003] IRLR 111 CA**
London Borough of Southwark
The question to be asked is whether, if treatment were stopped at the relevant date, would the person then, notwithstanding such benefit as had been obtained from prior treatment, have an impairment which would have the relevant adverse effect?

Abadeh v **[2001] IRLR 23 EAT**
British Telecommunications plc
The provision on the effect of medical treatment applies only to continuing medical treatment, ie to measures that "are being taken" and not to concluded treatment where the effects of such treatment may be more readily ascertained. Where treatment has ceased, the effects of that treatment should be taken into account in order to assess the disability.

Abadeh v **[2001] IRLR 23 EAT**
British Telecommunications plc
Where the medical evidence satisfies the tribunal that the effect of continuing medical treatment is to create a permanent improvement, the effects of that treatment should be taken into account in order to assess the disability as measures are no longer needed to treat or correct it once the permanent improvement has been established.

Kapadia v **[2000] IRLR 14 EAT**
London Borough of Lambeth
Counselling sessions with a consultant clinical psychologist constitute "medical treatment".

Carden v **[2005] IRLR 720 EAT**
Pickerings Europe Ltd
A plate and pins surgically inserted in the claimant's ankle and requiring no further treatment could be regarded as an "other aid" within the definition of "measures", which includes "in particular, medical treatment and the use of a prosthesis or other aid" so as to fall within the deduced effects provisions, so long as there was continuing support or assistance being given by the pins and plate to the functioning of the claimant's ankle.

Progressive conditions

6(1) Cancer, HIV infection and multiple sclerosis are each a disability.

(2) HIV infection is infection by a virus capable of causing the Acquired Immune Deficiency Syndrome.

8(1) This paragraph applies to a person (P) if –
  (a) P has a progressive condition,
  (b) as a result of that condition P has an impairment which has (or had) an effect on P's ability to carry out normal day-to-day activities, but
  (c) the effect is not (or was not) a substantial adverse effect.

(2) P is to be taken to have an impairment which has a substantial adverse effect if the condition is likely to result in P having such an impairment.

EQUALITY ACT 2010 – Sch.1

Mowat-Brown v **[2002] IRLR 235 EAT**
University of Surrey
It is not enough simply for a claimant to establish that he has a progressive condition and that it has or has had an effect on his ability to carry out normal day-to-day activities. He must go on and show that it is more likely than not that at some stage in the future he will have an impairment which will have a substantial adverse effect on his ability to carry out normal day-to-day activities. In some cases it may be possible to produce medical evidence of his likely prognosis. In other cases it may be possible to discharge the onus of proof by statistical evidence.

Kirton v **[2003] IRLR 353 CA**
Tetrosyl Ltd
The words "as a result of that condition" should not be so narrowly construed as to exclude an impairment which results from a standard and common form of operative procedure for cancer. Impairment in this context also includes the ordinary consequences of an operation to relieve the disease. Therefore, a claimant who had an operation for prostate cancer which led to urinary incontinence fell within the definition of disability relating to a "progressive condition", notwithstanding that his incontinence was not a direct result of the progressive condition, but was a result of the surgery by which the progressive condition was treated.

EMPLOYMENT DISCRIMINATION

Direct discrimination

(1) A person (A) discriminates against another (B) if, because of a protected characteristic, A treats B less favourably than A treats or would treat others.

(3) If the protected characteristic is disability, and B is not a disabled person, A does not discriminate against B only because A treats or would treat disabled persons more favourably than A treats B.

EQUALITY ACT 2010 – s.13

(1) On a comparison of cases for the purposes of section 13, 14, or 19 there must be no material difference between the circumstances relating to each case.

(2) The circumstances relating to a case include a person's abilities if –
> *(a) on a comparison for the purposes of section 13, the protected characteristic is disability;*
> *(b) on a comparison for the purposes of section 14, one of the protected characteristics in the combination is disability.*

EQUALITY ACT 2010 – s.23

Cordell v   **[2011] EqLR 1210 EAT**
Foreign and Commonwealth Office
Whether there is direct discrimination requires the Tribunal to consider two questions: "the less favourable treatment question" and "the reason why question". Those two questions are two sides of the same coin, and the answer to the one should in most cases give the answer to the other. As between the two questions, however, it is the "reason why" question that is in truth fundamental. Where there is an actual comparator, asking the less favourable treatment question may be the most direct route to the answer to both questions; but, where there is none, it will usually be better to focus on the reason why question than to get bogged down in the often arid and confusing task of constructing a hypothetical comparator.

High Quality Lifestyles Ltd v   **[2006] IRLR 850 EAT**
Watts
In order to establish direct discrimination, it is not sufficient for the claimant to show that his treatment was on the grounds of his disability. It also has to be established that the treatment was less favourable than the treatment which would be afforded to a hypothetical comparator in circumstances that are "not materially different".

Aylott v   **[2010] IRLR 994 CA**
Stockton on Tees Borough Council   **[2010] EqLR 69 CA**
There are dangers in attaching too much importance to constructing a hypothetical comparator and to less favourable treatment as a separate issue. If a claimant was dismissed on the ground of disability, then it is likely that he was treated less favourably than a hypothetical comparator

not having the particular disability would have been treated in the same relevant circumstances. The finding of the reason for the dismissal supplies the answer to the question whether he received less favourable treatment.

JP Morgan Europe Ltd v   **[2011] IRLR 673 CA**
Chweidan   **[2011] EqLR 779 CA**
An employment tribunal erred in holding that the claimant had been subjected to direct disability discrimination in respect of his dismissal and the level of bonus he was paid where it had also concluded that his claims of disability-related discrimination failed because the respondent had established that a non-disabled employee in the same circumstances would have been treated in the same way.

Duty to make reasonable adjustment

(1) Where this Act imposes a duty to make reasonable adjustments on a person, this section, sections 21 and 22 and the applicable Schedule apply; and for those purposes, a person on whom the duty is imposed is referred to as A.

(2) The duty comprises the following three requirements.

(3) The first requirement is a requirement, where a provision, criterion or practice of A's puts a disabled person at a substantial disadvantage in relation to a relevant matter in comparison with persons who are not disabled, to take such steps as it is reasonable to have to take to avoid the disadvantage.

(4) The second requirement is a requirement, where a physical feature puts a disabled person at a substantial disadvantage in relation to a relevant matter in comparison with persons who are not disabled, to take such steps as it is reasonable to have to take to avoid the disadvantage.

(5) The third requirement is a requirement, where a disabled person would, but for the provision of an auxiliary aid, be put at a substantial disadvantage in relation to a relevant matter in comparison with persons who are not disabled, to take such steps as it is reasonable to have to take to provide the auxiliary aid.

(6) Where the first or third requirement relates to the provision of information, the steps which it is reasonable for A to have to take include steps for ensuring that in the circumstances concerned the information is provided in an accessible format.

(7) A person (A) who is subject to a duty to make reasonable adjustments is not (subject to express provision to the contrary) entitled to require a disabled person, in relation to whom A is required to comply with the duty, to pay to any extent A's costs of complying with the duty.

(9) In relation to the second requirement, a reference in this section or an applicable Schedule to avoiding a substantial disadvantage includes a reference to –
> *(a) removing the physical feature in question,*
> *(b) altering it, or*
> *(c) providing a reasonable means of avoiding it.*

EQUALITY ACT 2010 – s.20

20(1) A is not subject to a duty to make reasonable adjustments if A does not know, and could not reasonably be expected to know –

> *(a) in the case of an applicant or potential applicant, that an interested disabled person is or may be an applicant for the work in question;*
> *(b) in any other case referred to in this Part of this Schedule, that an interested disabled person has a disability and is likely to be placed at the disadvantage referred to in the first, second or third requirement.*

EQUALITY ACT 2010 – Sch 8

Provision, criterion or practice

Archibald v   **[2004] IRLR 651 HL**
Fife Council
The duty to make an adjustment is triggered where an employee becomes so disabled that she can no longer meet the requirements of her job description. The duty applies to the job description for a post and the liability of anyone who becomes incapable of fulfilling the job description to be dismissed, as much as it applies to an employer's arrangements for deciding who gets what job or how much each is paid.

O'Hanlon v   **[2006] IRLR 840 EAT**
Commissioners for HM Revenue and Customs
The whole premise of the reasonable adjustment provisions is that the disabled employee may be disadvantaged by the application of common rules.

Roberts v   **[2012] EqLR 196 EAT**
North West Ambulance Service
Tribunals should not ask whether a PCP was "applied" to a disabled person, but instead should ask whether the PCP placed the disabled person at a substantial disadvantage. There will sometimes be cases where PCPs that are applied to others at work, place a disabled person at a substantial disadvantage even if they are not applied directly to the disabled person.

Smith v   **[2006] IRLR 41 CS**
Churchills Stairlifts plc
The proper comparator is readily identified by reference to the disadvantage caused by the relevant arrangements. It is not with the population generally who do not have a disability.

Kenny v   **[1999] IRLR 76 EAT**
Hampshire Constabulary
An employer's duty to make a reasonable adjustment to arrangements on which employment is offered or afforded is restricted to "job related" matters. Not every failure to make an arrangement which deprives an employee of a chance to be employed is unlawful.

When duty applies

Archibald v   **[2004] IRLR 651 HL**
Fife Council
A claimant was placed "at a substantial disadvantage in comparison with persons who are not disabled" where her job description required her to be physically fit, which she was no longer able to meet, and that exposed her to a con-dition that if she was physically unable to do the job she was employed to do, she was liable to be dismissed.

Paul v   **[2004] IRLR 190 EAT**
National Probation Service
The existence of a disability does not of itself substantially disadvantage a disabled person who is subject to a general requirement of clearance from an occupational health adviser. In many cases, having a disability does not adversely affect an individual's general health and an occupational health assessment will not lead to a refusal of employment unless the disability affects the claimant's ability to do the work and no reasonable adjustments can be made.

Chief Constable of West Midlands   **[2012] EqLR 20 EAT**
Police v
Gardner
Without showing what it is about a disability that gives rise to the substantial disadvantage, and therefore what it is that requires to be remedied by adjustment, no assessment of what is, or what is not, reasonable by way of adjustment can be made.

Newcastle upon Tyne Hospitals   **[2012] EqLR 634 EAT**
NHS Foundation Trust v
Bagley
The mere fact that a particular rule affects more disabled than non-disabled people means that it may be indirectly discriminatory, but it does not mean that the duty to make reasonable adjustments arises.

Archibald v   **[2004] IRLR 651 HL**
Fife Council
The duty to make adjustments may require the employer to treat a disabled person more favourably to remove the disadvantage which is attributable to the disability. This necessarily entails a measure of positive discrimination.

Chief Constable of South   **[2010] IRLR 744 EAT**
Yorkshire Police v
Jelic
Employers are required to take reasonable steps to help disabled people, which they are not required to take for others, in order to achieve for them substantive equality and to assist their integration in the working environment.

Archibald v   **[2004] IRLR 651 HL**
Fife Council
The comparison with persons who are not disabled is not confined to non-disabled people doing the same job. Therefore, the steps which the employer might have to take in order to prevent the arrangements placing a disabled employee at a substantial disadvantage in comparison with non-disabled persons include transferring her to another job.

Newcastle upon Tyne Hospitals   **[2012] EqLR 634 EAT**
NHS Foundation Trust v
Bagley
The substantial disadvantage of the disabled person in comparison with persons who are not disabled has to be because of the disability.

Fareham College Corporation v   **[2009] IRLR 991 EAT**
Walters

It is not necessary for a claimant in a reasonable adjustment case to satisfy the tribunal that someone who did not have a disability but whose circumstances were otherwise the same as hers would have been treated differently. The more general comparative exercise required in a reasonable adjustment claim, involving a class or group of non-disabled comparators, differs from the individual, like-for-like comparison required in cases of direct discrimination. In many cases the facts will speak for themselves and the identity of the non-disabled comparators will be clearly discernible from the provision, criterion or practice found to be in play.

Archibald v   **[2004] IRLR 651 HL**
Fife Council

The duty to take such steps as it is reasonable in all the circumstances for the employer to have to take could include transferring without competitive interview a disabled employee from a post she can no longer do to a post which she can do. The employer's duty may require moving the disabled person to a post at a slightly higher grade. A transfer can be upwards as well as sideways or downwards.

Chief Constable of South   **[2010] IRLR 744 EAT**
   Yorkshire Police v
Jelic

A tribunal is not precluded as a matter of law from holding that it would be a reasonable adjustment to create a new job for a disabled employee, if the particular facts of the case support such a finding.

Tarbuck v   **[2006] IRLR 664 EAT**
Sainsbury's Supermarkets Ltd

There is no obligation on an employer to create a post specifically, which is not otherwise necessary, merely to create a job for a disabled person.

Beart v   **[2003] IRLR 238 CA**
HM Prison Service

The test of reasonableness is directed to the steps to be taken to prevent the employment from having a detrimental effect on the disabled employee.

British Gas Services Ltd v   **[2001] IRLR 60 EAT**
McCaull

The test is an objective one: did the employer take such steps as it is reasonable in all the circumstances of the case for him to have to take in order to prevent the arrangements made by the employer from placing the disabled person at a substantial disadvantage in comparison with those who are not disabled? The test of whether it was reasonable for an employer to have to take a particular step does not relate to what the employer considered but to what he did and did not do. That is for the tribunal to consider. If Parliament had intended an employer to be in breach of statutory duty because he failed to consider what steps he might reasonably take, it would have so provided in the Act.

Wilcox v   **[2011] EqLR 810 EAT**
Birmingham CAB Services Ltd

An employer is not under any duty to make reasonable adjustments unless he knows, actually or constructively, both that the employee is disabled and that the employee is disadvantaged by the disability compared to non-disabled persons. Logically, the second of those two elements, knowledge of the relevant disadvantage, will not come into play unless the first is satisfied and the employer knew or should have known that the employee was disabled.

Wilcox v   **[2011] EqLR 810 EAT**
Birmingham CAB Services Ltd

If the employer knew, or could reasonably be expected to have known, that the claimant had an impairment within the meaning of the Act, it does not matter that it had no precise diagnosis. It is, however, a requirement that the employer should know, actually or constructively, that the claimant had an impairment the adverse effects of which were both substantial and long term.

Gallop v   **[2012] EqLR 998 EAT**
Newport City Council

An employer did not have actual or constructive knowledge of the claimant's disability because it was entitled to rely upon advice it had received from its external occupational health advisers that, despite suffering from a stress-related illness, the claimant was not disabled within the meaning of the statutory definition.

Matuszowicz v   **[2009] IRLR 288 CA**
Kingston upon Hull City Council

There may be inadvertent and non-deliberate omissions on the part of the employer which are breaches of the duty to make reasonable adjustments.

Nottinghamshire County Council v   **[2004] IRLR 703 CA**
Meikle

Payment of full sick pay by an employer can be an adjustment falling within the scope of [s.4A].

O'Hanlon v   **[2006] IRLR 840 EAT**
Commissioners for HM Revenue and Customs

It will be a very rare case where giving higher sick pay than would be payable to a non-disabled person who in general does not suffer the same disability-related absence would be considered necessary as a reasonable adjustment.

O'Hanlon v   **[2007] IRLR 404 CA**
Commissioners for HM Revenue and Customs

The employers did not have a duty as a reasonable adjustment to disaggregate entitlement for disability-related absence and absence for a non-disability-related reason, and not count disability-related absence against entitlement to full pay under the employers' sick pay rules.

Kenny v   **[1999] IRLR 76 EAT**
Hampshire Constabulary

Employers are not under a statutory duty to provide carers to attend to their employees' personal needs, such as assistance in going to the toilet. A line has to be drawn on the extent of the employer's responsibilities in providing adjustments to accommodate a disabled employee.

Burke v   **[2011] EqLR 454 EAT**
College of Law
A requirement that a candidate take his LPC examinations within particular time periods was a "competence standard" such that no duty to make adjustments arose.

Failure to make reasonable adjustment

(1) A failure to comply with the first, second or third requirement is a failure to comply with a duty to make reasonable adjustments.

(2) A discriminates against a disabled person if A fails to comply with that duty in relation to that person.

EQUALITY ACT 2010 – s.21

Clark v   **[1999] IRLR 318 CA**
TDG Ltd t/a Novacold
A claim for a breach of a duty of reasonable adjustment is not dependent on successfully establishing a claim for less favourable treatment for a reason related to disability.

Environment Agency v   **[2008] IRLR 20 EAT**
Rowan
An employment tribunal considering a claim that an employer has discriminated against an employee by failing to comply with the duty of reasonable adjustment must identify: (a) the provision, criterion or practice applied by or on behalf of an employer, or (b) the physical feature of premises occupied by the employer, (c) the identity of non-disabled comparators (where appropriate) and (d) the nature and extent of the substantial disadvantage suffered by the claimant. Identification of the substantial disadvantage suffered by the claimant may involve a consideration of the cumulative effect of both the "provision, criterion or practice applied by or on behalf of an employer" and the "physical feature of premises". Unless the tribunal has gone through that process, it cannot go on to judge if any proposed adjustment is reasonable because it will be unable to say what adjustments were reasonable to prevent the provision, criterion or practice, or feature, placing the disabled person concerned at a substantial disadvantage.

Salford NHS Primary Care Trust v   **[2011] EqLR 1119 EAT**
Smith
Reasonable adjustments are limited to those that prevent a provision, criterion or practice or feature of premises from placing a disabled person at a substantial disadvantage in comparison with persons who are not disabled. They are primarily concerned with enabling the disabled person to remain in or return to work with the employer. Any proposed reasonable adjustment must be judged against the criteria that it must prevent the PCP from placing the disabled person at the relevant substantial disadvantage. If the adjustment does not alleviate the disabled person's substantial disadvantage, it is not a reasonable adjustment within the meaning of disability discrimination legislation.

Project Management Institute v   **[2007] IRLR 579 EAT**
Latif
The claimant must not only establish that the duty of reasonable adjustment has arisen, but that there are facts from which it could reasonably be inferred, absent an explanation, that it has been breached. By the time the case is heard by the tribunal, there must be evidence of some apparently reasonable adjustment that could be made, even though the claimant does not have to identify the proposed adjustment until after the alleged failure to implement it. Although the claimant does not have to provide the detailed adjustment that would need to be made, it is necessary for the respondent to understand the broad nature of the adjustment proposed and to be given sufficient detail to enable him to engage with the question of whether or not it could reasonably be achieved. It would be an impossible burden to place on a respondent to prove a negative, that there is no adjustment that could reasonably be made.

Leeds Teaching Hospital   **[2011] EqLR 1075 EAT**
   NHS Trust v
Foster
When considering whether an adjustment is reasonable, it is sufficient for an employment tribunal to find that there would be a prospect of the adjustment removing the disabled person's disadvantage; it does not have to be satisfied that there is a "good" or "real" prospect of that occurring.

Salford NHS Primary Care Trust v   **[2011] EqLR 1119 EAT**
Smith
A career break is incapable of being a reasonable adjustment because it does not enable the claimant to return to work.

Noor v   **[2011] EqLR 448 EAT**
Foreign & Commonwealth Office
Although the purpose of a reasonable adjustment is to prevent a disabled person from being at a substantial disadvantage, it is certainly not the law that an adjustment will be reasonable only if it is completely effective.

Cordell v   **[2011] EqLR 1210 EAT**
Foreign and Commonwealth Office
Financial cost is one of the central considerations in the assessment of reasonableness. A decision about whether a particular adjustment is a reasonable one, or specifically how much it is reasonable to expect an employer to spend, cannot be a product of nice analysis. There is no objective measure by which the distinct considerations of the disadvantage to an employee if the adjustments are not made and the cost of making them, can be balanced. Ultimately, a Tribunal must determine in its capacity as an industrial jury what it considers is right and just. That judgment of what cost it is reasonable to expect an employer to bear may be informed by a variety of considerations which may enable the Tribunal to see the expenditure in context and in proportion. In addition to the points made in the Code of Practice and the degree to which the employee would benefit from the adjustment, other relevant considerations include the size of any budget dedicated to reasonable

adjustments; what the employer has already spent in comparable situations; what other employers are prepared to spend; and any collective agreement or other indication of what level of expenditure is regarded as appropriate by representative organisations.

Tarbuck v   **[2006] IRLR 664 EAT**
Sainsbury's Supermarkets Ltd

There is no separate and distinct duty of reasonable adjustment on an employer to consult the disabled employee about what adjustment might be made. The reasoning to this effect in *Mid Staffordshire General Hospitals NHS Trust v Cambridge* was incorrect. The only question is, objectively, whether the employer has complied with his obligations or not (even though it will always be good practice for the employer to consult and it will potentially jeopardise the employer's legal position if he does not do so, because the employer cannot use the lack of knowledge that would have resulted from consultation as a shield to defend a complaint that he has not made reasonable adjustments). If the employer does what is required of him, then the fact that he failed to consult about it or did not know that the obligation existed is irrelevant. It may be an entirely fortuitous and unconsidered compliance, but that is enough. Conversely, if he fails to do what is reasonably required, it avails him nothing that he has consulted the employee.

HM Prison Service v   **[2007] IRLR 951 EAT**
Johnson

That the disability from which the claimant was suffering was caused, at least in substantial part, by the employer's failings is potentially relevant to the assessment of reasonableness. It may require an employer to do more by way of reasonable adjustment than would be necessary in other circumstances, but it cannot give rise to an unlimited obligation to accommodate the employee's needs.

Fareham College Corporation v   **[2009] IRLR 991 EAT**
Walters

Dismissing the claimant was itself an unlawful act of disability discrimination by reason of a failure to make reasonable adjustments allowing her to return to work.

Eagle Place Services Ltd v   **[2010] IRLR 486 EAT**
Rudd

Once adjustments have been considered to be reasonable, an employer cannot then assert that because of their perceived financial implications he is entitled to dismiss the employee because he would dismiss any employee who was not disabled whose adjustments gave rise to the same financial implications. Such an argument would give the employer a "second bite of the cherry" and drive a coach and horses through the statutory protection given to disabled employees. An employer could always disregard the need to make reasonable adjustments with impunity by dismissing the employee and asserting that he would have dismissed a non-disabled employee requiring the same adjustments, on financial grounds, notwithstanding that the adjustments had been adjudged to be "reasonable".

VICTIMISATION

Veitch v   **[2011] EqLR 181 NICA**
Red Sky Group Ltd

Whether or not a person is disabled within the statutory definition, they are entitled to the statutory protection from victimisation if they are treated less favourably by reason of doing a protected act.

DISABILITY DISCRIMINATION BY EMPLOYERS

Dismissal

H J Heinz Co Ltd v   **[2000] IRLR 144 EAT**
Kenrick

An employer who does not adequately consider alternative employment or shorter hours may find that the dismissal is held not to be justified, on the basis that a reason for the dismissal such as continuing incapability would not be material to the circumstances so long as part-time or lighter duties might have fitted the bill.

Kent County Council v   **[2000] IRLR 90 EAT**
Mingo

The employers unlawfully discriminated against the claimant when, notwithstanding his disability, they treated him less favourably for the purposes of redeployment than employees at risk of redundancy. A redeployment policy of giving preferential treatment to redundant or potentially redundant employees does not adequately reflect the statutory duty on employers under the Disability Discrimination Act, since it means that those with disabilities are relatively handicapped in the redeployment system.

REMEDIES

Compensation

Buxton v   **[1999] IRLR 158 EAT**
Equinox Design Ltd

An employment tribunal's finding that the period of loss should be one year for an employee with multiple sclerosis who was dismissed lacked a sufficient evidential basis, since it involved making a finding as to the outcome of a risk assessment in the context of a disease which has variable effects. Without medical evidence, the tribunal was not in a position to say what the outcome would be.

Sheffield Forgemasters v   **[2009] IRLR 192 EAT**
    International Ltd
Fox

Receipt of incapacity benefit does not preclude a claimant from obtaining compensation for loss of earnings in respect of the same period, since the fact that they have obtained incapacity benefit does not in itself show that they were not able to work and earn money during that period.

Al Jumard v   [2008] IRLR 345 EAT
Clywd Leisure Ltd
It would not necessarily be wrong in an appropriate case for a tribunal to fix a separate sum for the injury to feelings flowing from acts of direct disability discrimination and the failure to make reasonable adjustments respectively.

.

GENDER REASSIGNMENT

(1) A person has the protected characteristic of gender reassignment if the person is proposing to undergo, is undergoing or has undergone a process (or part of a process) for the purpose of reassigning the person's sex by changing physiological or other attributes of sex.

(2) A reference to a transsexual person is a reference to a person who has the protected characteristic of gender reassignment.

(3) In relation to the protected characteristic of gender reassignment –
>   *(a) a reference to a person who has a particular protected characteristic is a reference to a transsexual person;*
>   *(b) a reference to persons who share a protected characteristic is a reference to transsexual persons.*

EQUALITY ACT 2010 – s.7

A v   [2004] IRLR 573 HL
Chief Constable of West Yorkshire Police
In gender reassignment cases, it is necessary to compare the claimant's treatment with that afforded to a member of the sex to which he or she used to belong. Thus, for the purposes of discrimination between men and women in the fields covered by the Equal Treatment Directive, a trans person is to be regarded as having the sexual identity of the gender to which he or she has been reassigned.

Croft v   [2003] IRLR 592 CA
Royal Mail Group plc
Acquiring the status of transsexual does not carry with it the right to choose which toilet to use. Conversely, it does not follow that, until the final stage is reached, an employee can necessarily be required, in relation to lavatories, to behave as if they were not undergoing gender reassignment. A judgment has to be made as to when a male to female transsexual employee becomes a woman and is entitled to the same facilities as other women. The moment at which a person at the "real life test" stage is entitled to use female toilets depends on all the circumstances. The employer must take into account the stage reached in treatment, including the employee's own assessment and presentation, although the employer is not bound by the employee's self-definition when making a judgment as to when the changes occurred. The employer is also entitled to take into account, though not to be governed by, the susceptibilities of other members of the workforce. Regard should also be had to the particular difficulties which arise with respect to toilet facilities, and the need for separate facilities for men and women. It is inherent in a situation in which two sets of facilities, male and female, are required and in which a category of persons changing from one sex to another is recognised, that there must be a period during which the employer is entitled to make separate arrangements for those undergoing the change.

MARRIAGE AND CIVIL PARTNERSHIP

Hawkins v   **[2012] IRLR 807 EAT**
Atex Group Ltd   **[2012] EqLR 397 EAT**
Where an employee complains that they have been dismissed or treated less favourably on grounds that they are married to a particular person, that complaint only fell within s.3 of the Sex Discrimination Act 1975 if the fact that they are married, rather than in a close relationship which happens to take the form of marriage, is part of the ground for the employer's action.

Hawkins v   **[2012] IRLR 807 EAT**
Atex Group Ltd   **[2012] EqLR 397 EAT**
The characteristic that is protected by the legislation is the fact of being married (or of being in a civil partnership). The behaviour that is proscribed is less favourable treatment on the ground that a person is married. The relevant comparator is thus a person who is not married. Since in any comparison for the purpose of the section the relevant circumstances, apart from the protected characteristic, must be the same, the appropriate comparator will usually be someone in a relationship akin to marriage but who is not actually married. If the ground for the employer's action is not the fact that the claimant and her husband are married but simply the closeness of their relationship and the problems to which that is perceived to give rise, the claimant will not have been treated less favourably than a comparator if a common-law spouse would have been treated in the same way.

PREGNANCY AND MATERNITY

2. For the purposes of this Directive, discrimination includes:...
    (c) any less favourable treatment of a woman related to pregnancy or maternity leave within the meaning of Directive 92/85/EEC.

EQUAL TREATMENT DIRECTIVE 2006/54 – Article 2

PREGNANCY AND SEX DISCRIMINATION

Dekker v   **[1991] IRLR 27 ECJ**
VJV-Centrum
Whether a refusal to employ results in direct discrimination on grounds of sex depends on whether the most important reason is one which applies without distinction to employees of both sexes or whether it exclusively applies to one sex. As employment can only be refused because of pregnancy to women, such a refusal is direct discrimination on grounds of sex. Therefore, an employer is acting in direct contravention of the principle of equal treatment embodied in the EC Equal Treatment Directive if he refuses to enter into a contract of employment with a female claimant, found suitable by him for the post in question, because of the possible adverse consequences to him of employing a pregnant woman.

Handels- og Kontorfunktionærernes   **[1991] IRLR 31 ECJ**
   Forbund i Danmark (acting for Hertz) v
Dansk Arbejdsgiverforening
   (acting for Aldi Marked K/S)
The dismissal of a female worker because of her pregnancy constitutes direct discrimination on grounds of sex, in the same way as does the refusal to recruit a pregnant woman. Therefore, a woman is protected from dismissal because of her absence during the maternity leave from which she benefits under national law.

Webb v   **[1994] IRLR 482 ECJ**
EMO Air Cargo (UK) Ltd
Dismissal of a woman on grounds of pregnancy constitutes direct discrimination on grounds of sex. In determining whether there is discrimination on grounds of sex contrary to the Directive, the situation of a woman who finds herself incapable by reason of pregnancy of performing the task for which she was recruited cannot be compared with that of a man similarly incapable for medical or other reasons.

Mayr v   **[2008] IRLR 387 ECJ**
Bäckerei und Konditorei Gerhard
   Flöckner OHG

The prohibition of dismissal of pregnant workers provided for in the Pregnant Workers Directive 92/85 does not extend to a female worker who is undergoing in vitro fertilisation treatment where, on the date she is given notice of her dismissal, her ova have already been fertilised by her partner's sperm cells, so that in vitro fertilised ova exist, but they have not yet been transferred into her uterus. However, dismissal of a female worker essentially because she is at an advanced stage of in vitro fertilisation treatment, between the follicular puncture and the immediate transfer of the in vitro fertilised ova into her uterus, constitutes direct discrimination on grounds of sex contrary to the Equal Treatment Directive since such treatment directly affects only women.

Dekker v   **[1991] IRLR 27 ECJ**
VJV-Centrum

A refusal to employ because of the financial consequences of absence connected with pregnancy must be deemed to be based principally on the fact of the pregnancy. Such discrimination cannot be justified by the financial detriment that would be suffered by the employer during the woman's maternity leave.

Dekker v   **[1991] IRLR 27 ECJ**
VJV-Centrum

If the reason a woman is not selected is because she is pregnant, the decision is directly related to the claimant's sex and it is not important that there were no male claimants.

Mahlburg v   **[2000] IRLR 276 ECJ**
Land Mecklenburg-Vorpommern

It is contrary to the Equal Treatment Directive for an employer to refuse to appoint a pregnant woman to a post of an unlimited duration on the ground that a statutory prohibition on employment arising on account of her pregnancy would prevent her from being employed in that post from the outset and for the duration of the pregnancy.

Sarkatzis Herrero v   **[2006] IRLR 296 ECJ**
Instituto Madrileño de la Salud

When a female employee is on maternity leave at the time of her appointment, deferring the start of her career, for the purposes of calculating her seniority, to the date on which she actually took up the post constitutes discrimination on grounds of sex contrary to European Community law.

Busch v   **[2003] IRLR 625 ECJ**
Klinikum Neustadt GmbH & Co Betriebs-KG

It is contrary to the Equal Treatment Directive to require an employee who wishes to return to work before the end of parental leave to inform her employer that she is pregnant, even though she will be unable to carry out all of her duties because of legislative provisions. Such discrimination cannot be justified by the fact that a woman is temporarily prevented from performing all of her duties by a legislative prohibition imposed because of pregnancy. That would

be contrary to the objective of protection pursued by the Equal Treatment Directive and the Pregnant Workers Directive and would rob them of any practical effect.

Pregnancy and working conditions

CNAVTS v   **[1998] IRLR 399 ECJ**
Thibault

The principle of non-discrimination on grounds of sex in working conditions requires that a woman who continues to be bound to her employer by her contract of employment during maternity leave should not be deprived of the benefit of working conditions which apply to both men and women and are the result of that employment relationship. The exercise by women of pregnancy and maternity rights cannot be the subject of unfavourable treatment regarding their access to employment or their working conditions.

Land Brandenburg v   **[2005] IRLR 147 ECJ**
Sass

A woman who is treated unfavourably because of absence on maternity leave suffers discrimination on the ground of her pregnancy and of that leave. Community law requires that taking such statutory protective leave should interrupt neither the employment relationship of the woman concerned nor the application of the rights derived from it and cannot lead to discrimination against that woman.

Álvarez v   **[2010] EqLR 238 ECJ**
Sesa Start España ETT SA

The Equal Treatment Directive precludes a Spanish national law which provides that female workers who are mothers and whose status is that of an employed person are entitled to time off to feed an unweaned child whereas male workers who are fathers with that same status are not entitled to the same leave unless the child's mother is also an employed person. The fact that the leave might be taken by the employed father or the employed mother without distinction meant that feeding and devoting time to the child could be carried out just as well by the father as by the mother. Since their positions were comparable with regard to their possible need to reduce their daily working time in order to look after their child, this precluded a finding that the measure ensured the protection of a woman's biological condition following pregnancy. To hold that only a mother whose status is that of an employed person is the holder of the right to qualify for such leave, whereas a father with the same status could only enjoy this right but not be the holder of it, would be liable to perpetuate a traditional distribution of the roles of men and women by keeping men in a role subsidiary to that of women in relation to the exercise of their parental duties.

CNAVTS v   **[1998] IRLR 399 ECJ**
Thibault

It is contrary to the Equal Treatment Directive for a woman to be accorded unfavourable treatment regarding her working conditions by being deprived of the right to an annual assessment of her performance and, therefore, of the opportunity of qualifying for promotion to a higher pay grade as a result of her absence on account of maternity leave.

Boyle v   **[1998] IRLR 717 ECJ**
Equal Opportunities Commission
A contractual term according to which a worker who does not return to work after childbirth is required to repay the difference between the pay received by her during her maternity leave and the Statutory Maternity Pay to which she was entitled does not constitute discrimination on grounds of sex contrary to EC law, notwithstanding that for other forms of paid leave, such as sick leave, workers are entitled to their salary without having to undertake to return to work at the end of their leave. The situation of a pregnant woman cannot be compared to that of a man or a woman on sick leave.

Boyle v   **[1998] IRLR 717 ECJ**
Equal Opportunities Commission
EC law does not preclude a clause in a contract of employment which requires a woman who is on sick leave with a pregnancy-related illness to take paid maternity leave if the period of sick leave occurs within six weeks of the expected date of childbirth, notwithstanding that any other worker who is sick is entitled to exercise their right to unconditional paid sick leave.

Boyle v   **[1998] IRLR 717 ECJ**
Equal Opportunities Commission
EC law does not preclude a clause in a contract of employment which limits the period during which annual holiday accrues to the statutory minimum 14 weeks' maternity leave period and which provides that annual holiday ceases to accrue during any period of supplementary maternity leave granted by the employer.

Land Brandenburg v   **[2005] IRLR 147 ECJ**
Sass
The fact that legislation grants women maternity leave of more than the minimum period of 14 weeks laid down by the Pregnant Workers Directive does not preclude that leave from being considered to be maternity leave as referred to in Article 8 of that Directive and, therefore, a period during which the rights connected with the employment contract must be ensured. The decision in *Boyle v Equal Opportunities Commission* did not prejudge this since *Boyle* concerned additional leave granted by an employer rather than statutory leave.

Pregnancy and dismissal

Brown v   **[1998] IRLR 445 ECJ**
Rentokil Ltd
Dismissal of a woman at any time during her pregnancy for absences due to incapacity for work caused by an illness resulting from that pregnancy is direct discrimination on grounds of sex contrary to the EC Equal Treatment Directive.

Webb v   **[1994] IRLR 482 ECJ**
EMO Air Cargo (UK) Ltd
It is contrary to the Equal Treatment Directive to dismiss a woman employed for an unlimited term who, shortly after her recruitment is found to be pregnant, even though she was recruited initially to replace another employee during the latter's maternity leave and notwithstanding that the employer would have dismissed a male employee engaged for this purpose who required leave of absence at the relevant time for medical or other reasons.

Webb v   **[1994] IRLR 482 ECJ**
EMO Air Cargo (UK) Ltd
Dismissal of a pregnant woman recruited for an indefinite period cannot be justified on grounds relating to her inability to fulfil a fundamental condition of her contract of employment.

Tele Danmark v   **[2001] IRLR 853 ECJ**
HK (acting on behalf of Brandt-Nielsen)
[Article 2] of the Equal Treatment Directive and Article 10 of the Pregnant Workers Directive preclude a worker from being dismissed on the ground of pregnancy, notwithstanding that she was recruited for a fixed period, failed to inform the employer that she was pregnant even though she was aware of this when the contract of employment was concluded, and because of her pregnancy was unable to work during a substantial part of the term of that contract. Dismissal of a worker on account of pregnancy constitutes direct discrimination on grounds of sex, whatever the nature and extent of the economic loss incurred by the employer as a result of her absence because of pregnancy. Whether the contract was concluded for a fixed or an indefinite period has no bearing on the discriminatory character of the dismissal. In either case the employee's inability to perform her contract of employment is due to pregnancy.

Brown v   **[1998] IRLR 445 ECJ**
Rentokil Ltd
It is direct discrimination on grounds of sex to dismiss a pregnant woman because of absences resulting from pregnancy in accordance with a contractual term providing that an employer may dismiss workers of either sex after a stipulated number of weeks of continuous absence.

Brown v   **[1998] IRLR 445 ECJ**
Rentokil Ltd
The Equal Treatment Directive affords a woman protection against dismissal on grounds of her absence throughout the period of pregnancy and during the maternity leave accorded to her under national law. Where a woman is absent owing to illness resulting from pregnancy or childbirth, and that illness arose during pregnancy and persisted during and after maternity leave, her absence not only during maternity leave but also during the period extending from the start of her pregnancy to the start of her maternity leave cannot be taken into account for computation of the period justifying her dismissal under national law. Absence after maternity leave may be taken into account under the same conditions as a man's absence through incapacity for work of the same duration.

Habermann-Beltermann v Arbeiterwohlfahrt, Bezirksverband Ndb/Opf eV [1994] IRLR 364 ECJ

Termination of a contract without a fixed term on account of a woman's pregnancy cannot be justified on the ground that a statutory prohibition, imposed because of pregnancy, temporarily prevents the employee from performing night work.

Jiménez Melgar v Ayuntamiento de Los Barrios [2001] IRLR 848 ECJ

Non-renewal of a fixed-term contract is a refusal of employment and, where non-renewal of a fixed-term contract is based on the worker's pregnancy, it constitutes direct discrimination on grounds of sex contrary to Articles 2(1) and 3(1) of the Equal Treatment Directive.

Handels- og Kontorfunktionærernes Forbund i Danmark (acting for Hertz) v Dansk Arbejdsgiverforening (acting for Aldi Marked K/S) [1991] IRLR 31 ECJ

The Equal Treatment Directive does not preclude dismissals resulting from absence due to an illness which originated in pregnancy or confinement and which appears after maternity leave.

Danosa v LKB Līzings SIA [2011] EqLR 48 CJEU

A pregnant worker falls within Article 2(a) of the Pregnant Workers Directive only if they have informed their employer of their condition in accordance with national legislation and/or national practice. However, that procedural requirement cannot remove the special protection for women provided for in Article 10 of the Directive, which prohibits the dismissal of pregnant workers and workers who have recently given birth or are breastfeeding, save in exceptional cases for reasons unrelated to the condition of the worker. If, without having been formally informed by the worker in person, the employer learns of her pregnancy, it would be contrary to the spirit and purpose of the Pregnant Workers Directive to interpret the provisions of Article 2(a) restrictively and to deny the worker the protection against dismissal provided for under Article 10.

Danosa v LKB Līzings SIA [2011] EqLR 48 CJEU

The objective to protect women before and after they give birth would not be achieved if the protection against dismissal granted to pregnant women under European law were to depend on the formal categorisation of their employment relationship under national law or on the choice made at the time of their appointment between one type of contract and another. If the claimant was dismissed essentially because of her pregnancy it does not matter whether the Pregnant Workers Directive or the Equal Treatment Directive applied. Whichever Directive applied, it is important to ensure the protection granted under EU law to pregnant women where the legal relationship linking her to another person has been severed on account of her pregnancy.

(1) This section has effect for the purposes of the application of Part 5 (work) to the protected characteristic of pregnancy and maternity.

(2) A person (A) discriminates against a woman if, in the protected period in relation to a pregnancy of hers, A treats her unfavourably –
- *(a) because of the pregnancy, or*
- *(b) because of illness suffered by her as a result of it.*

(3) A person (A) discriminates against a woman if A treats her unfavourably because she is on compulsory maternity leave.

(4) A person (A) discriminates against a woman if A treats her unfavourably because she is exercising or seeking to exercise, or has exercised or sought to exercise, the right to ordinary or additional maternity leave.

(5) For the purposes of subsection (2), if the treatment of a woman is in implementation of a decision taken in the protected period, the treatment is to be regarded as occurring in that period (even if the implementation is not until after the end of that period).

(6) The protected period, in relation to a woman's pregnancy, begins when the pregnancy begins, and ends –
- *(a) if she has the right to ordinary and additional maternity leave, at the end of the additional maternity leave period or (if earlier) when she returns to work after the pregnancy;*
- *(b) if she does not have that right, at the end of the period of 2 weeks beginning with the end of the pregnancy.*

(7) Section 13, so far as relating to sex discrimination, does not apply to treatment of a woman in so far as –
- *(a) it is in the protected period in relation to her and is for a reason mentioned in paragraph (a) or (b) of subsection (2), or*
- *(b) it is for a reason mentioned in subsection (3) or (4).*

EQUALITY ACT 2010 – s.18

Webb v EMO Air Cargo (UK) Ltd [1993] IRLR 27 HL

To dismiss a woman because she is pregnant or to refuse to employ a woman of child-bearing age because she may become pregnant is unlawful direct discrimination since child-bearing and the capacity for child-bearing are characteristics of the female sex.

Webb v EMO Air Cargo (UK) Ltd (No.2) [1995] IRLR 645 HL

To dismiss a woman because she was found to be pregnant, in circumstances in which she had been recruited for an unlimited term with a view, initially, to replacing another employee during the latter's maternity leave and would not be available for work at the time when the task for which she was recruited fell to be performed, is unlawful discrimination.

Fletcher v   **[2005] IRLR 689 EAT**
Blackpool Fylde & Wyre Hospitals NHS Trust

A complaint of discrimination by a pregnant woman cannot be defended by saying that all employees are treated in the same way. Treating pregnant women or women on maternity leave during the "protected period" in the same way as other employees, in circumstances in which they are disadvantaged because of their pregnancy or maternity, is applying the same treatment to different situations and is therefore discrimination.

Fletcher v   **[2005] IRLR 689 EAT**
Blackpool Fylde & Wyre Hospitals NHS Trust

Whilst it is not necessary for the pregnant woman to compare her treatment with that of a sick man in order to succeed in her claim of discrimination, and whilst an employer dismissing a woman on grounds of pregnancy cannot defend her complaint of sex discrimination by stating that he would have treated a sick man in the same way, the purpose of the *Webb* principle is to protect pregnant women. It is not to prevent them from comparing their treatment with more favourable treatment afforded to sick men, where appropriate, in order to demonstrate that a different rule is being applied in comparable circumstances and that discrimination has occurred.

O'Neill v   **[1996] IRLR 372 EAT**
Governors of St Thomas More
  RCVA Upper School

The distinction between pregnancy per se and pregnancy in the circumstances of the case as motives is legally erroneous. The critical question is whether, on an objective consideration of all the surrounding circumstances, the dismissal or other treatment complained of is on the ground of pregnancy, or on some other ground. This must be determined by an objective test of causal connection. The event or factor alleged to be causative of the matter complained of need not be the only or even the main cause of the result complained of. It is enough if it is an effective cause. The concept of pregnancy per se is misleading, because it suggests pregnancy as the sole ground for dismissal. Pregnancy always has surrounding circumstances.

O'Neill v   **[1996] IRLR 372 EAT**
Governors of St Thomas More
  RCVA Upper School

A religious education teacher who was dismissed after it became known that she had become pregnant by a Roman Catholic priest was dismissed on grounds of pregnancy. The factors surrounding the pregnancy – the paternity of the child, the publicity of that fact and the consequent untenability of the appellant's position as a religious education teacher – were all causally related to the fact that she was pregnant. Her pregnancy precipitated and permeated the decision to dismiss her. Therefore, it was not possible to say that the ground for dismissal was anything other than pregnancy.

O'Neill v   **[2010] IRLR 384 EAT**
Buckinghamshire County Council

There is no general obligation to carry out a risk assessment on pregnant employees. Therefore, failure to carry out such a risk assessment is not discrimination per se. The obligation to carry out a risk assessment of a pregnant worker is only triggered where (a) the employee notifies the employer that she is pregnant in writing; (b) the work is of a kind which could involve a risk of harm or danger to the health and safety of a new expectant mother or her baby; (c) the risk arises from either processes or working conditions or physical biological chemical agents in the workplace at the time specified in the list in Pregnant Workers Directive 92/85/EEC.

Hoyland v   **[2005] IRLR 438 EAT**
ASDA Stores Ltd

A worker who takes maternity leave during a bonus year must be paid bonus in respect of the periods when she is at work and the two weeks of compulsory maternity leave. However, a proportionate reduction to reflect absence on ordinary maternity leave is permitted.

GUS Home Shopping Ltd v   **[2001] IRLR 75 EAT**
Green

An employer unlawfully discriminated against the claimants when it treated them as disqualified from receiving payment under a loyalty bonus scheme because they were absent from work during the relevant period because of pregnancy-related illness or maternity leave.

Eversheds Legal Services Ltd v   **[2011] IRLR 448 EAT**
De Belin   **[2011] EqLR 436 EAT**

An obligation on employers to afford special protection to employees who are pregnant or on maternity leave cannot extend to favouring them beyond what is reasonably necessary to compensate them for the disadvantages occasioned by their condition. Such special treatment would be reasonably necessary if it complied with the proportionality principle. If a benefit granted to a woman who is pregnant or on maternity leave is disproportionate then a colleague who is correspondingly disadvantaged is entitled to claim for sex discrimination. Accordingly, construing s. 2(2) of the Sex Discrimination Act as far as possible so as to conform to the underlying principles of EU law, it is necessary to read the words "special treatment afforded to women in connection with pregnancy or childbirth" as referring only to treatment accorded to a woman so far as it constitutes a proportionate means of achieving the legitimate aim of compensating her for the disadvantages occasioned by her pregnancy or her maternity leave, rather than as applying to any more favourable treatment of a woman which was in fact – however unreasonably or excessively – accorded to her because she was pregnant or had given birth.

Eversheds Legal Services Ltd v   **[2011] IRLR 448 EAT**
De Belin   **[2011] EqLR 436 EAT**

The employer unlawfully discriminated against the claimant on the grounds of his sex by giving a woman on maternity leave a notional maximum score on one factor during a redundancy selection exercise while confining the claimant to his own actual score. The means chosen by the employer to compensate the woman for the disadvantage caused to her by her absence on maternity leave were not proportionate. The attribution to the woman of a maximum score for the criterion measured as at a date at which she was on maternity leave caused a real injustice to the claimant.

COMPENSATION

Ministry of Defence v   **[1998] IRLR 23 CA**
Wheeler
The general principle in assessing compensation is that, as far as possible, complainants should be placed in the same position as they would have been in but for the unlawful act.

Abbey National plc v   **[1999] IRLR 222 EAT**
Formoso
The correct approach in awarding compensation for a discriminatory dismissal is to ask what were the chances, in percentage terms, that the employer would have dismissed the claimant had she not been pregnant and had a fair procedure been followed, rather than what a "reasonable employer" would have done. The "reasonable employer" approach is appropriate when considering the fairness of a dismissal, but not when assessing the loss flowing from a discriminatory dismissal.

RACE DISCRIMINATION

GROUNDS OF RACE

2(a). Direct discrimination shall be taken to occur where one person is treated less favourably than another is, has been or would be treated in a comparable situation on grounds of racial or ethnic origin.

RACE DISCRIMINATION DIRECTIVE 2000/43 – Article 2

Centrum voor Gelijkheid van Kansen   **[2008] IRLR 732 ECJ**
en voor Racismebestrijding v
Firma Feryn NV
The fact that an employer states publicly that it will not recruit employees of a certain ethnic or racial origin constitutes direct discrimination in respect of recruitment within the meaning of Article 2(2)(a) of the EC Race Discrimination Directive, such statements being likely strongly to dissuade certain candidates from submitting their candidature and, accordingly, to hinder their access to the labour market. The existence of such direct discrimination is not dependent on the identification of a complainant who claims to have been the victim.

MEANING OF RACE

(1) Race includes –
(a) colour;
(b) nationality;
(c) ethnic or national origins.

(2) In relation to the protected characteristic of race –
(a) a reference to a person who has a particular protected characteristic is a reference to a person of a particular racial group;
(b) a reference to persons who share a protected characteristic is a reference to persons of the same racial group.

(3) A racial group is a group of persons defined by reference to race; and a reference to a person's racial group is a reference to a racial group into which the person falls.

(4) The fact that a racial group comprises two or more distinct racial groups does not prevent it from constituting a particular racial group.

EQUALITY ACT 2010 – s.9

R (on the application of E) v   **[2010] IRLR 136 SC**
Governing Body of JFS
The definition of "racial grounds" includes "ethnic or national origins". Origins require one to focus on descent.

Mandla v   **[1983] IRLR 209 HL**
Lee
A group can be defined by reference to its "ethnic origins" if it constitutes a separate and distinct community by virtue of characteristics which are commonly associated with common racial origin. "Ethnic" is used in a sense appreciably wider than strictly racial or biological.
Per Lord Fraser of Tullybelton: For a group to constitute an ethnic group for the purposes of race relations legislation, it must regard itself, and be regarded by others, as a distinct community by virtue of certain characteristics. It is essential that there is (1) a long shared history, of which the group is conscious as distinguishing it from other groups, and the memory of which keeps it alive; (2) a cultural tradition of its own, including family and social customs and manners, often but not necessarily associated with religious observance. In addition, there are other relevant characteristics, one or more of which will commonly be found and will help to distinguish the group from the secondary community; (3) either a common geographical origin, or descent from a small number of common ancestors; (4) a common language, not necessarily peculiar to the group; (5) a common literature peculiar to the group; (6) a common religion different from that of the neighbouring groups or from the general community surrounding it; (7) a sense of being a minority or being an oppressed or a dominant group within a larger community.

CRE v   **[1989] IRLR 8 CA**
Dutton
Whether there is an identifiable group of persons who are defined by reference to ethnic origins is essentially a question of fact, to be determined on the evidence, applying the approach set out by Lord Fraser in *Mandla v Lee*.

CRE v   **[1989] IRLR 8 CA**
Dutton
If there remains a discernible minority of a religious, racial or ethnic group which adheres to the group it may still be a "racial group" within Lord Fraser's criteria, even though a substantial proportion of the group have become assimilated in the general public.

Mandla v   **[1983] IRLR 209 HL**
Lee
Sikhs are a group defined by "ethnic origins".

CRE v   **[1989] IRLR 8 CA**
Dutton
Gipsies, using the narrower meaning of the word "gipsies" as "a wandering race (by themselves called 'Romany'), of Hindu origin" rather than the larger, amorphous group of "travellers" or "nomads", are an identifiable group defined by reference to "ethnic origins" within the meaning of the definition of "racial group".

CRE v   **[1989] IRLR 8 CA**
Dutton
"Travellers" are not synonymous with "gipsies". Therefore, a notice in a pub stating "no travellers" did not indicate an intention by the licensee to discriminate on racial grounds,

since the prohibited class included all those of a nomadic way of life and all nomads were treated equally whatever their race.

Dawkins v   **[1993] IRLR 284 CA**
Department of the Environment
Rastafarians are not a separate "racial group". Although they are a separate group with identifiable characteristics, they have not established some separate identity by reference to their ethnic origins. "Ethnic" has a racial flavour. Comparing Rastafarians with the rest of the Jamaican community in England or with the rest of the Afro-Caribbean community, there was nothing to set them aside as a separate ethnic group.

BBC Scotland v   **[2001] IRLR 150 CS**
Souster
Neither the English nor the Scots are an "ethnic group" because the distinctive racial element required for recognition as an ethnic group is lacking.

Seide v   **[1980] IRLR 427 EAT**
Gillette Industries Ltd
Being "Jewish" can mean a member of a race or a particular ethnic origin as well as being a member of a particular religious faith.

BBC Scotland v   **[2001] IRLR 150 CS**
Souster
The phrase "national origins" is not limited to "nationality" in the legal sense and thus to citizenship which an individual acquires at birth. An individual can become a member of a racial group defined by reference to "origins" through adherence, as for instance by marriage.

BBC Scotland v   **[2001] IRLR 150 CS**
Souster
There can be direct or indirect racial discrimination within Great Britain arising from the fact that a person is of Scots or English national origins.

Tejani v   **[1986] IRLR 502 CA**
The Superintendent Registrar for
  the District of Peterborough
"National origins" refers only to a particular place or country of origin in accordance with the decision of the House of Lords in *Ealing London Borough Council v Race Relations Board* that "national origins" means "national" in the sense of "race" and not "citizenship". Therefore, there was no discrimination on grounds of "national origins" where the complainant was treated less favourably on grounds that he had been born abroad, without any particular reference to any particular place or country of origin, notwithstanding that a person born in the UK would not have been treated in the same way.

R (on the application of Elias) v   **[2006] IRLR 934 CA**
Secretary of State for Defence
"Place of birth" is not identical to "national origins" and therefore not inextricably linked to a forbidden ground of discrimination.

BBC Scotland v   **[2001] IRLR 150 CS**
Souster

"Nationality" is not defined exclusively by reference to citizenship. Nationality can encompass a change in nationality, and can be referable to present nationality.

BBC Scotland v   **[2001] IRLR 150 CS**
Souster

A claimant can be discriminated against on grounds of his English nationality where that nationality has been acquired by adherence or adoption since his birth or because he has been perceived to have become a member of the racial group, the English. It will be for the claimant to prove that he is English, whether that be because his national origins are English or because he has acquired English nationality or that he is perceived to be English.

Dziedziak v   **[2012] EqLR 543 EAT**
Future Electronics Ltd

A Polish national was subjected to direct discrimination on grounds of her nationality when she was instructed by her line manager not to speak "in her own language" at work. The use of those words in context demonstrated an intrinsic link with the claimant's nationality. There are some labels or descriptions, such as the use of those particular words in this context, that include within themselves the fact of a difference in treatment on the ground of the relevant protected characteristic.

Dhatt v   **[1991] IRLR 130 CA**
McDonalds Hamburgers Ltd

An application form which distinguished between British citizens and EC nationals on the one hand and claimants who were not British citizens or EC nationals on the other hand did not discriminate on grounds of nationality.

Simon v   **[1987] IRLR 307 CA**
Brimham Associates

In determining whether an act was done on "racial grounds", which means by reason of the racial group to which the complainant belongs, although it cannot be conclusive that the alleged discriminator did not know of the racial origin of the complainant, the knowledge or lack of knowledge of the alleged discriminator must be material.

Vicarious discrimination

Redfearn v   **[2006] IRLR 623 CA**
Serco Ltd

The expression "on racial grounds" does not cover every case in which the discriminator's less favourable act was significantly influenced by racial considerations, even if the race was that of a third party. That would mean that it could be an act of direct discrimination for an employer, who was trying to improve race relations in the workplace, to dismiss an employee, whom he discovered had committed an act of race discrimination, such as racist abuse, against a fellow employee or customer.

Redfearn v   **[2006] IRLR 623 CA**
Serco Ltd

A bus driver was not discriminated against "on racial grounds" when the employers discovered his candidature as a British National Party councillor, and decided that he should be dismissed on health and safety grounds having regard to the significant number of passengers and employees who were of Asian origin. It was a non-sequitur to argue that the claimant was dismissed "on racial grounds" because the circumstances leading up to his dismissal included a relevant racial consideration, such as the race of fellow employees and customers and the policies of the BNP on racial matters. The claimant was no more dismissed "on racial grounds" than an employee who is dismissed for racially abusing his employer, a fellow employee or a valued customer.

Moxam v   **[2012] EqLR 202 EAT**
Visible Changes Ltd

Derogatory statements made to the claimant about immigrants by a senior person in the company amounted to racial discrimination or harassment of the claimant, even though she was not an immigrant herself. It did not matter what racial group the claimant came from. She was entitled to be offended and to bring claims where she suffered as a result of any discriminatory language and conduct. She did not have to be an immigrant to complain of language of a racist nature used about a customer.

Segregation

(5) If the protected characteristic is race, less favourable treatment includes segregating B from others.
EQUALITY ACT 2010 – s.13

PEL Ltd v   **[1980] IRLR 142 EAT**
Modgill

Segregation means the employer keeping apart one person from others on grounds of his race. "Congregating" does not amount to "segregating". Where the fact that all the workers are of a particular racial group arises by the acts of those working in the particular shop themselves, the failure by the employer to intervene and to insist on workers of other racial groups going into the shop, to introduce their friends, contrary to the wishes of the employees in the shop, does not constitute the act of segregating persons on racial grounds.

DIRECT DISCRIMINATION

Discriminatory treatment

Commissioners of   **[2002] IRLR 776 EAT**
  Inland Revenue v
Morgan

There is no statutory or other offence consisting of a body being institutionally racist. While it would be possible to imagine a body whose habitual rules or practices were such that one could fairly say of the body that as an institution it was racist, the charge would be relevant only as a step in the reasoning toward a conclusion that the body was or was not guilty of some unlawful discrimination that fell within the Act.

Motive

R (on the application of European   [2005] IRLR 115 HL
    Roma Rights Centre) v
Immigration Officer at Prague Airport
If a person acts on racial grounds, the reason why he does so is irrelevant.

Stereotypical assumptions

Bradford Hospitals NHS Trust v   [2003] IRLR 4 EAT
Al-Shahib
Whilst it may sometimes be legitimate for a tribunal to take into account differences in behaviour which reflect racial and cultural differences, it is wrong for a tribunal to make findings based on the existence of such differences unless there is some evidential basis for them, such as expert evidence. For a tribunal simply to assume that a particular ethnic group has a specific characteristic is fundamentally wrong, even if the assumption is made for benign purposes.

Royal Bank of Scotland plc v   [2012] EqLR 406 EAT
Morris
When a senior manager, to whom the claimant complained about the behaviour of his white line manager, said that he was concerned that the claimant, who is black, was alleging racial discrimination, but the claimant had done nothing to provoke that comment, it followed that the senior manager did so as a result of a stereotype that a black employee complaining about his treatment by a white colleague must, or at least may, be alleging race discrimination. Since it was very unlikely that if the white line manager had been complaining about the claimant's conduct then the senior manager would have accused him of playing the race card, his comment, therefore, was made on racial grounds.

Statutory comparison

Dhatt v   [1991] IRLR 130 CA
McDonalds Hamburgers Ltd
The nationality of someone seeking work is a relevant circumstance because Parliament itself recognises and seeks to enforce by reference to nationality a general division between those who by reason of their nationality are free to work and those who require permission. Although nationality is itself discriminatory in racial terms, it is discrimination which has been sanctioned by statute.

Central Manchester University   [2012] EqLR 318 EAT
    Hospitals NHS Foundation Trust v
Browne
In concluding that a white hypothetical comparator would have been treated more favourably than the claimant, a divisional director who was of black African Caribbean racial origin, the employment tribunal was entitled to rely, in part, upon the respondent's treatment of two white divisional directors in non-identical but not wholly dissimilar circumstances. Comparing the treatment of those in non-identical but not wholly dissimilar cases is a permissible means of judging how a hypothetical comparator would have been treated.

INDIRECT DISCRIMINATION

Osborne Clarke Services v   [2009] IRLR 341 EAT
Purohit
A policy of not considering any application for solicitor training contracts from individuals requiring permission from the Border and Immigration Agency to work in the UK, which had a disproportionate impact on non-EEA nationals, had not been shown to be objectively justified where the employers had made no attempts to apply for a work permit. In the absence of any clear evidence as to the likelihood of failure, the employers' own conjecture that they could not apply or would not be successful was insufficient. The Code of Practice on racial equality and employment makes it clear that as far as possible selection should be based purely on merit, and that work permit issues should only come into consideration at the later stage of selection. It also makes it clear that as far as possible employers should make an application leaving it up to the immigration authorities to determine the outcome.

DISCRIMINATION BY EMPLOYERS

Promotion, transfer or training

West Midlands Passenger Transport   [1988] IRLR 186 CA
    Executive v
Singh
Since the suitability of candidates can rarely be measured objectively and often requires subjective judgments, evidence of a high percentage rate of failure to achieve promotion at particular levels by members of a particular racial group may indicate that the real reason for refusal is a conscious or unconscious racial attitude which involves stereotyped assumptions about members of that group.

Mecca Leisure Group plc v   [1993] IRLR 531 EAT
Chatprachong
The employers did not discriminate against an Asian-born employee on grounds of race by failing to provide him with English language training in order to prepare him for promotion where there was no evidence to suggest that the employers would have given special speech training to any member of staff not of Asian origin who had difficulties.

Eke v   **[1981] IRLR 334 EAT**
Commissioners of Customs and Excise

A refusal to investigate complaints of unfair treatment, whether based on grounds of race or otherwise, may amount to a refusal of access to "any other benefits, facilities or services". To be a breach of the Act, however, the refusal to investigate must be one which itself is "on racial grounds".

Wakeman v   **[1999] IRLR 424 CA**
Quick Corporation

Locally recruited British managers were not discriminated against on racial grounds by being paid substantially less than managers seconded from Japan. The fact that locally hired Japanese were paid on the same scale as other locally hired nationals at their level indicated that locally recruited staff were treated equally regardless of race, and that the secondees' pay depended on the place of their permanent employment rather than their racial origin.

Detrimental treatment

BL Cars Ltd v   **[1985] IRLR 193 EAT**
Brown

The issuing of a written instruction to check the identity of black employees and the setting up of a regime under which black employees would have to undergo special investigation before they could have access to their place of work was capable of amounting to a "detriment" to those employees. It could not be accepted that the "detriment" could only arise when the instruction issued was implemented.

Garry v   **[2001] IRLR 681 CA**
London Borough of Ealing

An employee was subjected to a "detriment" when, for reasons connected with her ethnic origin, an investigation by her employers into her activities was continued longer than an ordinary investigation would have been, even though she was unaware that the investigation was continuing.

RELIGION OR BELIEF DISCRIMINATION

EU RELIGION OR BELIEF DISCRIMINATION LAW

Jivraj v   **[2011] IRLR 827 UKSC**
Hashwani   **[2011] EqLR 1088 UKSC**

The reference to the "conditions for access to employment, to self-employment or to occupation" in Article 3(1)(a) of the Directive is concerned with preventing discrimination from qualifying or setting up as a solicitor, plumber, greengrocer or arbitrator. It is not concerned with discrimination by a customer who prefers to contract with one of their competitors once they have set up in business.

UK RELIGION OR BELIEF DISCRIMINATION LAW

MEANING OF RELIGION OR BELIEF

(1) Religion means any religion and a reference to religion includes a reference to a lack of religion.

(2) Belief means any religious or philosophical belief and a reference to belief includes a reference to a lack of belief.

(3) In relation to the protected characteristic of religion or belief –
> *(a) a reference to a person who has a particular protected characteristic is a reference to a person of a particular religion or belief;*
> *(b) a reference to persons who share a protected characteristic is a reference to persons who are of the same religion or belief.*

EQUALITY ACT 2010 – s.10

Eweida v   **[2009] IRLR 78 EAT**
British Airways plc

The protection afforded to those holding a religious or philosophical belief is a broad one. The belief can be intensely personal and subjective. Accordingly, it is not necessary for a belief to be shared by others in order for it to be a religious belief, nor need a specific belief be a mandatory requirement of an established religion for it to qualify as a religious belief.

Grainger plc v   **[2010] IRLR 4 EAT**
Nicholson

There must be some limits placed upon the definition of "philosophical belief". These are that the belief must be genuinely held; it must be a belief and not an opinion or viewpoint based on the present state of information available; it must be a belief as to a weighty and substantial aspect of human life and behaviour; it must attain a certain level of cogency, seriousness, cohesion and importance;

and it must be worthy of respect in a democratic society, be not incompatible with human dignity and not conflict with the fundamental rights of others. Moreover, in order for a belief to be protected, it is necessary for it to have a similar status or cogency to a religious belief. It is not a bar, however, to a philosophical belief being protected that it is a one-off belief, not shared by others.

McClintock v   **[2008] IRLR 29 EAT**
Department for Constitutional Affairs
To constitute a belief there must be a religious or philosophical viewpoint in which one actually believes. It is not enough to have an opinion based on some real or perceived logic or based on information or lack of information available.

Grainger plc v   **[2010] IRLR 4 EAT**
Nicholson
There is nothing in the make-up of a philosophical belief which would disqualify a belief based on a political philosophy. Therefore, belief in the political philosophies of socialism, Marxism, communism or free-market capitalism might qualify.

Grainger plc v   **[2010] IRLR 4 EAT**
Nicholson
A belief in man-made climate change and the environment is capable, if genuinely held, of being a "philosophical belief" .

EXCLUSIONS AND EXCEPTIONS

Occupational requirements

(3) A person (A) with an ethos based on religion or belief does not contravene a provision mentioned in paragraph 1(2) by applying in relation to work a requirement to be of a particular religion or belief if A shows that, having regard to that ethos and to the nature or context of the work –

(a) it is an occupational requirement,
(b) the application of the requirement is a proportionate means of achieving a legitimate aim, and
(c) the person to whom A applies the requirement does not meet it (or A has reasonable grounds for not being satisfied that the person meets it).

               EQUALITY ACT 2010 – Sch. 9

Jivraj v   **[2011] IRLR 827 UKSC**
Hashwani   **[2011] EqLR 1088 UKSC**
In determining whether being of a particular religion or belief is a genuine occupational requirement, it must be shown that in all the circumstances of the case the requirement was not only genuine but was also legitimate and justified. This is an objective question for the court.

Glasgow City Council v   **[2007] IRLR 476 EAT**
McNab
The local education authority was not entitled to have recourse to the genuine occupational requirement exception in respect of a teaching post in a maintained Roman

Catholic school because they could not show that they were an employer who had "an ethos based on religion or belief". An education authority does not have a religious ethos. The fact that it operates a statutory system under which it enables denominations to advance their ethos through schools maintained by it, does not mean that they espouse the same ethos at all.

Glasgow City Council v   **[2007] IRLR 476 EAT**
McNab
Had it been intended that an employer could qualify for the statutory protection if only part of their organisation had a religious ethos, it would have been expected that such a right would have been expressly stated by the legislature.

DIRECT DISCRIMINATION

McFarlane v   **[2010] IRLR 872 CA**
Relate Avon Ltd
There is an important distinction between the law's protection of the right to hold and express a belief and the law's protection of that belief's substance or content. The common law and Article 9 of the European Convention on Human Rights offer vigorous protection of every person's right to hold and express his or her beliefs. They do not offer any protection whatever of the substance or content of those beliefs on the ground only that they are based on religious precepts.

Power v   **[2011] EqLR 16 EAT**
Greater Manchester Police Authority
A distinction falls to be drawn between treatment on the grounds of a person's beliefs and treatment on the grounds of the manifestation of those beliefs.

McFarlane v   **[2010] IRLR 196 EAT**
Relate Avon Ltd
The right to hold religious beliefs and the right to manifest them in conduct are not inseparable. There will be cases in which the fact that the employee's motivation for the conduct in question may be found in his wish to manifest his religious belief does not mean that that belief is the ground of the employer's action.

Statutory comparison

(1) On a comparison of cases for the purposes of section 13, 14, or 19 there must be no material difference between the circumstances relating to each case.

               EQUALITY ACT 2010 – s.23

London Borough of Islington v   **[2009] IRLR 154 EAT**
Ladele
The proper hypothetical or statutory comparator for a registrar claiming that she was discriminated against on grounds of religion or belief by being disciplined for refusing to conduct civil partnerships was another registrar who

refused to conduct civil partnership work because of antipathy to the concept of same-sex relationships but which antipathy was not based upon religious belief. If such a person would equally have been required to carry out civil partnership duties and would have been subject to the similar disciplinary process if they had refused, there would be no direct discrimination on grounds of religion or belief.

INDIRECT DISCRIMINATION

Disproportionate impact

Chatwal v   [2011] EqLR 942 EAT
Wandsworth Borough Council
An employment tribunal erred in holding that the claimant had adduced no evidence from which it could be established that members of the particular branch of the Sikh religion of which he was a member, which requires its members to be vegetarian, would be put at a particular disadvantage by a requirement on employees that they participate in a rota for cleaning a departmental kitchen fridge in which meat and meat products were stored.

Justifiable

Eweida v   [2010] IRLR 322 CA
British Airways plc
BA's staff dress code, which forbade the wearing of visible neck adornment and so prevented a Christian from wearing with her uniform a small, visible cross, was not disproportionate in circumstances in which the employee's objection to the dress code was entirely personal, neither arising from any doctrine of her faith nor interfering with her observance of it, and never raised by any other employee.

Ladele v   [2010] IRLR 211 CA
London Borough of Islington
The fact that a Christian registrar's refusal to perform civil partnerships was based on her religious views of marriage could not justify the conclusion that the local authority should not be allowed to implement its aim to the full, namely that all registrars should perform civil partnerships as part of its Dignity for All policy. The claimant was employed in a public job and was working for a public authority; she was being required to perform a purely secular task, which was being treated as part of her job; her refusal to perform that task involved discriminating against gay people in the course of that job; she was being asked to perform the task because of the council's Dignity for All policy, whose laudable aim was to avoid, or at least minimise, discrimination both among the council's employees and as between it (and its employees) and those in the community they served. The claimant's refusal was causing offence to at least two of her gay colleagues; her objection was based on her view of marriage, which was not a core part of her religion; and the council's requirement in no way prevented her from worshipping as she wished.

McFarlane v   [2010] IRLR 872 CA
Relate Avon Ltd
A requirement that counsellors should be prepared to make their services available without differentiation to same-sex and heterosexual couples was justified, notwithstanding that it put those holding traditional Christian views at a disadvantage. There was no real difference between the position of a body such as Relate and the situation considered in *Ladele*, in which the EAT held that an employer may properly insist on all employees participating in the services in question, even if to do so is in conflict with their religious beliefs, because to do otherwise would be inconsistent with the principle which it regards as fundamental to its own ethos.

Cherfi v   [2011] EqLR 825 EAT
G4S Security Services Ltd
Although a requirement that the claimant remain on the site where he worked as a security guard during his lunch time, with the consequence that he was unable to attend Friday prayers in congregation at a local mosque, constituted a provision, criterion or practice which placed him at a disadvantage as a practising Muslim, the respondent's actions were justified as a proportionate means of achieving the legitimate aim of meeting its operational needs by complying with its contractual obligations towards a third party to provide a specific number of security officers at that site.

HARASSMENT

Saini v   [2009] IRLR 74 EAT
All Saints Haque Centre
The prohibition on harassment on grounds of religion or belief will be breached not only where an employee is harassed on the grounds that he holds certain religious or other relevant beliefs but also where he is harassed because someone else holds certain religious or other beliefs.

SEX DISCRIMINATION

SEX AS A DETERMINING FACTOR

2. Member States may provide, as regards access to employment including the training leading thereto, that a difference of treatment which is based on a characteristic related to sex shall not constitute discrimination where, by reason of the nature of the particular occupational activities concerned or of the context in which they are carried out, such a characteristic constitutes a genuine and determining occupational requirement, provided that the objective is legitimate and the requirement is proportionate.

EQUAL TREATMENT DIRECTIVE 2006/54 – Article 14

Johnston v   **[1986] IRLR 263 ECJ**
The Chief Constable of the Royal
  Ulster Constabulary
[Article 14(2)] of the Equal Treatment Directive, being a derogation from an individual right laid down in the Directive, must be interpreted strictly, and in determining the scope of any derogation, the principle of proportionality must be observed. That principle requires that derogations remain within the limits of what is appropriate and necessary for achieving the aim in view and requires the principle of equal treatment to be reconciled as far as possible with the requirement which constituted the decisive factor as regards the context of the activity in question. It is for the national court to ensure that the principle of proportionality is observed.

Sirdar v   **[2000] IRLR 47 ECJ**
The Army Board
There is no general exception in the EC Treaty covering all measures taken by Member States for reasons of public security. Therefore, application of the principle of equal treatment is not subject to any general reservation as regards measures for the organisation of the armed forces. However, the UK Government might be entitled under the Equal Treatment Directive to exclude women from service in special combat units such as the Royal Marines.

Commission of the European   **[1984] IRLR 29 ECJ**
  Communities v
United Kingdom of Great Britain
  and Northern Ireland
Reconciliation of the principle of equality of treatment with the principle of respect for private life is one of the factors which must be taken into consideration in determining the scope of the exception provided for in [Article 14(2)] of the Equal Treatment Directive.

POSITIVE ACTION

(4) With a view to ensuring full equality in practice between men and women in working life, the principle of equal treatment shall not prevent any Member State from maintaining or adopting measures providing for specific advantages in order to make it easier for the underrepresented sex to pursue a vocational activity or to prevent or compensate for disadvantages in professional careers.

EC TREATY – Article 141

Member States may maintain or adopt measures within the meaning of art. 141(4) of the Treaty with a view to ensuring full equality in practice between men and women in working life.

EQUAL TREATMENT DIRECTIVE 2006/54 – Article 3

Abrahamsson v   **[2000] IRLR 732 ECJ**
Fogelqvist
The Equal Treatment Directive does not preclude a rule of national case law under which a candidate belonging to the underrepresented sex may be granted preference over a competitor of the opposite sex, provided that the candidates possess equivalent or substantially equivalent merits and the candidatures are subjected to an objective assessment which takes account of the specific personal situations of all the candidates.

Abrahamsson v   **[2000] IRLR 732 ECJ**
Fogelqvist
The Equal Treatment Directive precludes national legislation which provides for positive discrimination in recruitment in favour of candidates of the under-represented sex by automatically granting preference to candidates belonging to the under-represented sex, so long as they are sufficiently qualified, subject only to the proviso that the difference between the merits of the candidates of each sex is not so great as to result in a breach of the requirement of objectivity in making appointments. Such legislation was ultimately based on the mere fact of belonging to the under-represented sex.

Abrahamsson v   **[2000] IRLR 732 ECJ**
Fogelqvist
Although Article 141(4) allows the Member States to maintain or adopt measures providing for special advantages intended to prevent or compensate for disadvantages in professional careers in order to ensure full equality between men and women in professional life, it cannot be inferred that it allows a selection method which is disproportionate to the aim pursued.

Kalanke v   **[1995] IRLR 660 ECJ**
Freie Hansestadt Bremen
National rules which guarantee women absolute and unconditional priority for appointment or promotion go beyond promoting equal opportunities and overstep the limits of the exception to the principle of equal treatment in the Equal Treatment Directive.

EFTA Surveillance Authority v   **[2003] IRLR 318 EFTA Ct**
Kingdom of Norway
The Equal Treatment Directive is based on the recognition of the right to equal treatment as a fundamental right

of the individual. National rules and practices derogating from that right can only be permissible when they show sufficient flexibility to allow a balance between the need for the promotion of the under-represented gender and the opportunity for candidates of the opposite gender to have their situation objectively assessed. There must, as a matter of principle, be a possibility that the best-qualified candidate obtains the post. Therefore, national legislation which allows a number of academic posts to be reserved exclusively for women because they are under-represented in the particular post went beyond the scope of the Directive insofar as it gave absolute and unconditional priority to female candidates.

Marschall v   [1998] IRLR 39 ECJ
Land Nordrhein-Westfalen

It is not contrary to the Equal Treatment Directive for equally-qualified women to be given preference for promotion where there are fewer women than men in the relevant post, so long as male candidates are guaranteed that women are not to be given priority if reasons specific to an individual equally-qualified man tilt the balance in his favour.

Application by Badek   [2000] IRLR 432 ECJ

A measure which is intended to give priority in promotion to women in sectors of the public service where they are underrepresented is compatible with Community law if it does not automatically and unconditionally give priority to women when women and men are equally qualified, and the candidatures are the subject of an objective assessment which takes account of the specific personal situations of all candidates.

Application by Badek   [2000] IRLR 432 ECJ

The Equal Treatment Directive does not preclude a rule for the public service which allocates at least half the training places to women in occupations in which women are under-represented and for which the State does not have a monopoly of training. Nor does it preclude a rule for the public service which guarantees, in sectors in which women are underrepresented, that where male and female candidates have equal qualifications, either all women who are qualified will be given an interview, or that no more male candidates than female candidates will be interviewed.

Lommers v   [2002] IRLR 430 ECJ
Minister van Landbouw,
Natuurbeheer en Visserij

Provision of a limited number of subsidised nursery places to female staff only is permissible in principle under the Equal Treatment Directive, where the scheme has been set up by the employer to tackle extensive under-representation of women, in a context characterised by a proven insufficiency of proper, affordable child-care facilities, so long as male employees who take care of their children by themselves are allowed to have access to the scheme on the same conditions as female employees. The fact that the policy did not guarantee access to nursery places to employees of both sexes on an equal footing was not contrary to the principle of proportionality.

ACCESS TO JOBS

1. There shall be no direct or indirect discrimination on grounds of sex in the public or private sectors, including public bodies, in relation to:

> *(a) conditions for access to employment, to self-employment or to occupation, including selection criteria and recruitment conditions, whatever the branch of activity and at all levels of the professional hierarchy, including promotion;*

EQUAL TREATMENT DIRECTIVE 2006/54 – Article 14

Johnston v   [1986] IRLR 263 ECJ
The Chief Constable of the Royal
Ulster Constabulary

The application of the principle of equal treatment to the conditions governing access to jobs, as set out in [Article 14(1)] of the Equal Treatment Directive, is unconditional and sufficiently precise so that it may be relied upon by individuals as against a Member State where that Member State fails to implement it correctly.

Gerster v   [1997] IRLR 699 ECJ
Freistaat Bayern

Legislation which treats part-time employees less favourably than full-time employees by providing for them to accrue length of service more slowly, and perforce gain promotion later, results in discrimination against women as compared with men and must in principle be regarded as contrary to the Equal Treatment Directive, unless the distinction is justified by objective reasons unrelated to any discrimination on grounds of sex. There would be no infringement of the Equal Treatment Directive if the national court found that part-time employees are generally slower than full-time employees in acquiring job-related abilities and skills, and that the competent authorities were in a position to establish that the measures chosen reflected a legitimate social policy aim, were an appropriate means of achieving that aim and were necessary in order to do so. However, a requirement that part-time employees must complete a longer period of service than a full-time employee in order to have approximately the same chance of promotion must be regarded as contrary to the Equal Treatment Directive if the national court concludes that there is no special link between length of service and acquisition of a certain level of knowledge or experience.

Kording v   [1997] IRLR 710 ECJ
Senator Für Finanzen

Legislation which treats a part-time employee less favourably than a full-time employee, by providing that the total length of professional experience required for exemption from a qualifying examination is to be extended on a pro rata basis for part-time workers, gives rise to indirect discrimination against women if substantially fewer men than women work part-time and must in principle be regarded as contrary to the Equal Treatment Directive. However, such inequality of treatment would be compatible with the Directive if it were justified by objective factors unrelated to any discrimination on grounds of sex.

Meyers v   **[1995] IRLR 498 ECJ**
Adjudication Officer

A benefit such as family credit in the UK falls within the scope of [Article 14(1)] of the Equal Treatment Directive, since its subject-matter is access to employment in that the benefit is intended to keep poorly-paid workers in employment. The fact that a scheme of benefits is part of a national social security system cannot exclude it from the scope of the Directive.

ACCESS TO TRAINING

1. There shall be no direct or indirect discrimination on grounds of sex in the public or private sectors, including public bodies, in relation to:

> *(b) access to all types and to all levels of vocational guidance, vocational training, advanced vocational training and retraining, including practical work experience;*

EQUAL TREATMENT DIRECTIVE 2006/54 – Article 2

Johnston v   **[1986] IRLR 263 ECJ**
The Chief Constable of the Royal
  Ulster Constabulary

The application of the principle of equal treatment to the conditions governing access to training, as set out in [Article 14(1)] of the Equal Treatment Directive, is unconditional and sufficiently precise so that it may be relied upon by individuals as against a Member State where that Member State fails to implement it correctly.

WORKING CONDITIONS AND DISMISSAL

1. There shall be no direct or indirect discrimination on grounds of sex in the public or private sectors, including public bodies, in relation to:

> *(c) employment and working conditions, including dismissals, as well as pay as provided for in Article 141 of the Treaty;*

EQUAL TREATMENT DIRECTIVE 2006/54 – Article 2

Marshall v   **[1986] IRLR 140 ECJ**
Southampton and South-West
  Hampshire Area Health Authority

[Article 2(1)] of the Equal Treatment Directive may be relied upon as against a State authority acting in its capacity as employer, in order to avoid the application of any national provision which does not conform to [Article 2(1)]. [Article 2(1)] is sufficiently precise and unconditional to be relied on by individuals and to be applied by national courts. The provision, taken by itself, prohibits any discrimination on grounds of sex with regard to working conditions in a general manner and in unequivocal terms. It does not confer on Member States the right to limit the application of the principle of equality of treatment in its field of operation or to subject it to conditions.

Meyers v   **[1995] IRLR 498 ECJ**
Adjudication Officer

To confine the concept of a working condition within the meaning of [Article 2(1)] solely to those working conditions which are set out in the contract of employment or applied by the employer in respect of a worker's employment would remove situations directly covered by an employment relationship from the scope of the Directive. Therefore, a benefit such as family credit, which is necessarily linked to an employment relationship, constitutes a working condition within the meaning of [Article 2(1)] of the Directive.

Discriminatory retirement ages

Burton v   **[1982] IRLR 116 ECJ**
British Railways Board

"Dismissal" for the purposes of [Article 2(1)] of the Equal Treatment Directive must be widely construed.

Marshall v   **[1986] IRLR 140 ECJ**
Southampton and South-West
  Hampshire Area Health Authority

A general policy concerning dismissal involving the dismissal of a woman solely because she has attained the qualifying age for a State pension, which age is different under national legislation for men and women, constitutes discrimination on grounds of sex contrary to [Article 2(1)] of the Equal Treatment Directive. In accordance with the decision of the European Court in *Burton v British Railways Board*, the term "dismissal" in [Article 2(1)] must be given a wide meaning. An age limit for the compulsory dismissal of workers pursuant to an employer's general policy concerning retirement relates to the conditions governing dismissal, to be determined in accordance with the Equal Treatment Directive, even if the dismissal involved the grant of a retirement pension.

Pensionsversicherungsanstalt v   **[2011] EqLR 70 CJEU**
Kleist

A rule found in a collective agreement which permitted an employer to compulsorily retire its employees when they reached pensionable age, where pensionable age was 60 years for women and 65 years for men, was direct discrimination on grounds of sex contrary to the Equal Treatment Directive.

INDIRECT DISCRIMINATION UNDER EC LAW

R v   **[1999] IRLR 253 ECJ**
Secretary of State for Employment
  ex parte Seymour-Smith

In order to establish whether a measure adopted by a Member State has disparate effect as between men and women to such a degree as to amount to indirect discrimination for the purposes of Article 141, the national court must verify whether the statistics indicate that a considerably smaller percentage of women than men is able to satisfy the condition required. That would be evidence of apparent sex discrimination. That could also be the case if the statistical evidence revealed a lesser but persistent and relatively constant disparity over a long period between men and women who satisfy the requirement.

R v   **[1999] IRLR 253 ECJ**
Secretary of State for Employment
   ex parte Seymour-Smith

The best approach for determining whether a rule has a more unfavourable impact on women than on men is to consider the respective proportions of men in the workforce able to satisfy the requirement and those unable to do so, and to compare those proportions as regards women in the workforce.

Jørgensen v   **[2000] IRLR 726 ECJ**
Foreningen af Speciallæger

In order to determine whether a collective agreement indirectly discriminates on grounds of sex, the Equal Treatment Directive requires a separate assessment to be made of each of the key conditions laid down in the contested provisions, in so far as those key elements constitute in themselves specific measures based on their own criteria of application and affecting a significant number of persons belonging to a determined category. An overall assessment of all the elements which might be involved in a scheme or a set of provisions would not allow effective review of the application of the principle of equal treatment and might not comply with the rules governing the burden of proof in matters relating to indirect discrimination on grounds of sex.

R v   **[1999] IRLR 253 ECJ**
Secretary of State for Employment
   ex parte Seymour-Smith

If a considerably smaller percentage of women than men is capable of fulfilling a statutory requirement, such as the service qualification for unfair dismissal, it is for the Member State, as the author of the allegedly discriminatory rule, to show that the said rule reflects a legitimate aim of its social policy, that that aim is unrelated to any discrimination based on sex, and that it could reasonably consider that the means chosen were suitable for attaining that aim.

Nolte v   **[1996] IRLR 225 ECJ**
Landesversicherrungsanstalt Hannover

A legislative measure is based on objective factors unrelated to discrimination on grounds of sex where the measure chosen reflects a legitimate social policy of the Member State, is appropriate to achieve that aim and necessary in order to do so. However, social policy is a matter for the Member States. Consequently, the Member States have a broad margin of discretion in exercising their competence to choose the measures capable of achieving the aim of their social and employment policy.

Kruger v   **[1999] IRLR 808 ECJ**
Kreiskrankenhaus Ebersberg

The exclusion of persons in "minor" employment from the scope of a collective agreement providing for the grant of

a special annual bonus was indirect discrimination within the meaning of Article 141 where it affected a considerably higher percentage of women than men. The exclusion was not justified since an exclusion from the benefit of a collective agreement is a different situation from that in *Nolte* and *Megner*, in which the Court held that the exclusion of persons in minor employment from social insurance fell within the broad margin of discretion of Member States to choose the measures for achieving the aims of their social and employment policy.

R v   **[1999] IRLR 253 ECJ**
Secretary of State for Employment
   ex parte Seymour-Smith

In order to show that a measure is justified by objective factors unrelated to any discrimination based on sex, it is not sufficient for a Member State to show that it was reasonably entitled to consider that the measure would advance a social policy aim. Although, in the *Nolte* case, the Court observed that, in choosing the measures capable of achieving the aims of their social and employment policy, the Member States have a broad margin of discretion, that cannot have the effect of frustrating the implementation of a fundamental principle of Community law such as that of equal pay for men and women. Mere generalisations concerning the capacity of a specific measure to encourage recruitment are not enough to show that the aim of the disputed rule is unrelated to any discrimination based on sex nor to provide evidence on the basis of which it could reasonably be considered that the means chosen were suitable for achieving that aim.

Jørgensen v   **[2000] IRLR 726 ECJ**
Foreningen af Speciallæger

Budgetary considerations cannot in themselves justify discrimination on grounds of sex. Although budgetary considerations may underlie a Member State's choice of social policy and influence the nature or scope of the social protection measures which it wishes to adopt, they do not in themselves constitute an aim pursued by that policy and cannot therefore justify discrimination against one of the sexes.

Kutz-Bauer v   **[2003] IRLR 368 ECJ**
Freie und Hansestadt Hamburg

An employer cannot justify discrimination solely because avoidance of such discrimination would involve increased costs.

Kachelmann v   **[2001] IRLR 49 ECJ**
Bankhaus Hermann Lampe KG

The Equal Treatment Directive does not preclude a selection process for dismissal when a part-time job is abolished on economic grounds that does not compare full-time workers with part-time workers, even though this may create an indirect disadvantage for part-time workers. If comparability between full-time and part-time workers were to be introduced in the selection process, that would have the effect of placing part-time workers at an advantage, while putting full-time workers at a disadvantage since, in the event of their jobs being abolished, part-time workers would have to be offered a full-time job, even if their employment contract did not entitle them to one.

DIRECT DISCRIMINATION UNDER UK LAW

James v　　　　　　　　　　**[1990] IRLR 288 HL**
Eastleigh Borough Council
Since the statutory pensionable age is itself a criterion which directly discriminates between men and women in that it treats women more favourably than men "on the ground of their sex", any other differential treatment of men and women which adopts the same gender-based criterion must equally involve discrimination "on the ground of sex".

Smith v　　　　　　　　　　**[1996] IRLR 456 CA**
Safeway plc
There is an important distinction between discrimination between the sexes and discrimination against one or other of the sexes. Discrimination is not failing to treat men and women the same. If discrimination is to be established, it is necessary to show, not merely that the sexes are treated differently, but that the treatment accorded to one is less favourable than the treatment accorded to the other.

James v　　　　　　　　　　**[1989] IRLR 318 CA**
Eastleigh Borough Council
There is direct discrimination if the overt basis for affording less favourable treatment was sex or, if the overt reason does not in terms relate to sex, it is shown that the overt reason was not the true reason and the true reason is the desire to treat women less favourably than men.

Hosso v　　　　　　　　　　**[2012] IRLR 235 CA**
European Credit Management Ltd　**[2012] EqLR 155 CA**
A claim regarding the difference in the allocation of share options paid to the claimant and those paid to her male comparator pursuant to a discretionary share option scheme had to be brought as a sex discrimination claim and not as an equal pay claim.

Kulikaoskas v　　　　　　　　**[2010] EqLR 276 EAT**
Macduff Shellfish
Neither EU law nor the Sex Discrimination Act prohibits an employer from affording less favourable treatment to a man on the ground of a woman's pregnancy. A claim of associative discrimination, where one person suffers less favourable treatment because of the pregnancy of another person, is not permitted.

INDIRECT DISCRIMINATION

Disproportionate impact

Hacking & Paterson v　　　　　**[2011] EqLR 19 EAT**
Wilson
It is not inevitable that women would be disproportionately adversely affected by a refusal to allow flexible working.

Many women return to full-time employment after childbirth. The childcare arrangements available to some women are such that they cannot work full time. However, some women who are able to access childcare arrangements that would enable them to work full time do not want to do so. For them, part-time working is a choice rather than necessity. More men are taking on childcare responsibilities. People (both male and female) seek flexible working for different reasons including, for instance, enabling them to combine jobs, pursue other interests or follow educational courses. A negative response to the request for flexible working may, accordingly, give rise to differing effects. Where the effect is on an employee who is able to work full time but does not wish to do so, it is difficult to see that it would be correct to talk in terms of that employee being disadvantaged. Where the effect does amount to a disadvantage, the question of whether it amounts to a particular disadvantage that is liable to be experienced by women as opposed to men arises. The claimant would have to address the issue of whether or not a refusal of the request for flexible working puts women at a "particular disadvantage".

Shackletons Garden Centre Ltd v　**[2010] EqLR 138 EAT**
Lowe
Although a requirement to work weekends on a rotational basis put women at a particular disadvantage compared with men because of their childcare commitments, there was insufficient evidence to support a finding that the claimant was put at an individual disadvantage by this because childcare arrangements would not be available.

Justifiable

London Underground Ltd v　　　**[1997] IRLR 157 EAT**
Edwards (No.2)
The employment tribunal was entitled to find that the employers had not justified indirectly discriminatory rostering arrangements requiring employees to make an early start. There was good evidence that the employers could have made arrangements which would not have been damaging to their business plans but which would have accommodated the reasonable demands of their employees.

Shackletons Garden Centre Ltd v　**[2010] EqLR 138 EAT**
Lowe
An employment tribunal erred in failing to address whether a requirement to work weekends on a rotational basis, if it put the claimant at a disadvantage on gender discriminatory grounds, was nonetheless a proportionate means of achieving a legitimate aim. There was ample material to suggest that the employers were addressing a legitimate aim, namely the need to provide cover at weekends, and to play fair with all of their employees, each of whom was expected to work at weekends in accordance with the rota.

R v　　　　　　　　　　　　**[2000] IRLR 363 HL**
Secretary of State for Employment
　　ex parte Seymour-Smith (No.2)
The Secretary of State had discharged the burden of showing that he was reasonably entitled in 1985 to consider that

　　　　　　　　　　　　　GUIDE TO DISCRIMINATION LAW

the extension of the unfair dismissal qualifying period from one to two years was justified by objective factors unrelated to sex, and that the 1985 Order was still objectively justified in 1991.

Allen v   **[2008] IRLR 690 CA**
GMB

An employment tribunal did not err in finding that the union had failed to justify its agreement with Middlesbrough Council over implementation of the local government single status scheme which disadvantaged women by prioritising pay protection and future pay rather than maximising claims for past unequal pay.

SEXUAL ORIENTATION DISCRIMINATION

EU SEXUAL ORIENTATION DISCRIMINATION LAW

Maruko v   **[2008] IRLR 450 ECJ**
Versorgungsanstalt der Deutschen Bühnen

Recital 22 of the preamble to the Framework Employment Equality Directive, which provides that the Directive is "without prejudice to national laws on marital status and the benefits dependent thereon", cannot affect application of the Directive.

Maruko v   **[2008] IRLR 450 ECJ**
Versorgungsanstalt der Deutschen Bühnen

The Framework Employment Equality Directive precludes legislation under which, after the death of his life partner, the surviving partner does not receive a survivor's benefit equivalent to that granted to a surviving spouse.

Römer v   **[2011] EqLR 921 CJEU**
Freie und Hansestadt Hamburg

National legislation which allowed for more favourable taxation treatment of married pensioners as regards occupational pensions than pensioners who had entered into a registered life partnership would be regarded as discrimination on grounds of sexual orientation contrary to Framework Employment Equality Directive 2000/78 if life partners were held to be in a legal and factual situation comparable to that of a married person as regards that pension.

UK SEXUAL ORIENTATION DISCRIMINATION LAW

ORGANISED RELIGION

2(1) A person (A) does not contravene a provision mentioned in sub-paragraph (2) by applying in relation to employment a requirement to which sub-paragraph (4) applies if A shows that –
    (a) the employment is for the purposes of an organised religion,
    (b) the application of the requirement engages the compliance or non-conflict principle, and
    (c) the person to whom A applies the requirement does not meet it (or A has reasonable grounds for not being satisfied that the person meets it).

(2) The provisions are –
    (a) section 39(1)(a) or (c) or (2)(b) or (c);
    (b) section 49(3)(a) or (c) or (6)(b) or (c);
    (c) section 50(3)(a) or (c) or (6)(b) or (c);
    (d) section 51(1).

(3) A person does not contravene section 53(1) or (2)(a) or (b) by applying in relation to a relevant qualification (within the meaning of that section) a requirement to which sub-paragraph (4) applies if the person shows that –

> *(a) the qualification is for the purposes of employment mentioned in sub-paragraph (1)(a), and*
> *(b) the application of the requirement engages the compliance or non-conflict principle.*

(4) This sub-paragraph applies to –

> *(a) a requirement to be of a particular sex;*
> *(b) a requirement not to be a transsexual person;*
> *(c) a requirement not to be married or a civil partner;*
> *(d) a requirement not to be married to, or the civil partner of, a person who has a living former spouse or civil partner;*
> *(e) a requirement relating to circumstances in which a marriage or civil partnership came to an end;*
> *(f) a requirement related to sexual orientation.*

(5) The application of a requirement engages the compliance principle if the requirement is applied so as to comply with the doctrines of the religion.

(6) The application of a requirement engages the non-conflict principle if, because of the nature or context of the employment, the requirement is applied so as to avoid conflicting with the strongly held religious convictions of a significant number of the religion's followers.

EQUALITY ACT 2010 – Sch. 9

R (on the application of Amicus –   **[2004] IRLR 430 HC**
    MSF section) v
Secretary of State for Trade and Industry
The exception is very narrow. It has to be construed strictly since it is a derogation from the principle of equal treatment; and it has to be construed purposively so as to ensure, so far as possible, compatibility with the Directive. When its terms are considered in light of those interpretative principles, they can be seen to afford an exception only in very limited circumstances. The fact that the exception applies "for the purposes of an organised religion" is an important initial limitation since that is a narrower expression than "for the purposes of a religious organisation" or "an ethos based on religion or belief" as used in the Regulations relating to discrimination on grounds of religion or belief. Thus, employment as a teacher in a faith school is likely to be for the "purposes of a religious organisation" but not for the "purposes of an organised religion".

R (on the application of Amicus –   **[2004] IRLR 430 HC**
    MSF section) v
Secretary of State for Trade
    and Industry
The condition that the employer must apply the requirement "so as to comply with the doctrines of the religion" is an objective test whereby it must be shown that employment of a person not meeting the requirement would be incompatible with the doctrines of the religion. That is very narrow in scope.

DIRECT DISCRIMINATION

R (on the application of Amicus –   **[2004] IRLR 430 HC**
    MSF section) v
Secretary of State for Trade and Industry
The protection against discrimination on grounds of sexual orientation relates as much to the manifestation of that orientation in the form of sexual behaviour as it does to sexuality as such.

Lisboa v   **[2011] EqLR 267 EAT**
Realpubs Ltd
The claimant was treated less favourably on grounds of sexual orientation by being required to carry out a policy of discrimination against customers on grounds of sexual orientation when his employer's strategy to relaunch a formerly gay pub as a "gastropub" was done in such a way as to discriminate against gay clientele by making them feel less welcome than the desired "straight" and family clientele.

Bivonas LLP v   **[2012] EqLR 216 EAT**
Bennett
A gay man was subjected to a detriment when he found an aide-memoire created by a partner in the appellant law firm, in which a reference was made to the claimant's "batty boy mate". The aide-memoire implicitly referred to the claimant's own sexual orientation as a gay man, was insulting to him personally and suggested that the claimant as a gay man was passing work to somebody else because they were gay and not for meritorious reasons. There was no doubt that it was reasonable for a worker to take the contents of the aide-memoire as being to his detriment, so that there was no need to construct a hypothetical reasonable worker and consider how he might have reacted to the insulting memorandum.

HARASSMENT

Grant v   **[2011] IRLR 748 CA**
HM Land Registry   **[2011] EqLR 872 CA**
The employment tribunal erred in concluding that the claimant had been discriminated against on grounds of sexual orientation when his new line manager informed one of his new prospective work colleagues that he was gay and when at a dinner attention was drawn to the fact that the claimant was gay by the same line manager in front of new work colleagues whom the claimant believed were unaware of his sexuality. There was no detriment to the claimant in respect of either incident because he had already voluntarily revealed his sexuality at his original place of work for the respondent. In those circumstances, having made his sexual orientation generally public, any grievance which the claimant had about his sexual orientation being revealed to others was unreasonable and unjustified.

Grant v   **[2011] IRLR 748 CA**
HM Land Registry   **[2011] EqLR 872 CA**
In the absence of a finding that a line manager who disclosed the claimant's sexual orientation to his new work

colleagues had done so with the purpose of humiliating him or embarrassing him or for some other ill purpose, even if in fact the disclosure had been unwanted and the claimant had been upset by it, the effect could not amount to a violation of dignity, nor could it properly be described as creating an intimidating, hostile, degrading, humiliating or offensive environment. Employment tribunals must not cheapen the significance of these words. They are an important control to prevent trivial acts causing minor upsets being caught by the concept of harassment. The claimant was no doubt upset that he could not release the information about his sexuality in his own way, but that was far from attracting the epithets required to constitute harassment.

Grant v   **[2011] IRLR 748 CA**
HM Land Registry   **[2011] EqLR 872 CA**
The fact that an individual has revealed their sexual orientation at work does not mean that remarks or references to his sexuality could not constitute discrimination. They may do so, particularly where the remarks made are vituperative or offensive. Everything depends upon the particular circumstances and so it will generally be relevant to know to whom the remark was made, in what terms and for what purpose. An individual may choose to make generally known in the workplace certain aspects of his or her private life. If that information is discussed in the course of conversation, even in idle gossip, provided at least that there was no ill intent, that would not make the disclosure of that information an act of discrimination. That is so even if the victim is upset at the thought that he or she will be the subject of such idle conversation. By putting these facts into the public domain, the employee takes the risk that he or she may become the focus of conversation and gossip.

English v   **[2009] IRLR 206 CA**
Thomas Sanderson Blinds Ltd
A person who is taunted by "homophobic banter" is subject to harassment on the ground of sexual orientation, even though he is not gay; he is not perceived or assumed to be gay by his colleagues; and he accepts they do not believe him to be gay. Harassment is on grounds of sexual orientation where the claimant's sexual orientation, whether real or supposed, is the basis of the harassment directed at him or her.

Thomas Sanderson Blinds Ltd v   **[2011] EqLR 688 EAT**
English (No.2)
In rejecting the claimant's claims of harassment on grounds of sexual orientation, the employment tribunal was required to take into account the claimant's subjective perception of the homophobic comments and innuendo to which he was subject by his fellow workers (with whom he remained genuinely good friends), including the fact that the claimant himself had engaged in similar conduct. It was necessary to do so in order to determine whether the effect of the unwanted conduct (if in fact it was unwanted) was to violate the claimant's dignity or create an adverse environment for him.

Thomas Sanderson Blinds Ltd v   **[2011] EqLR 688 EAT**
English (No.2)
There is no general rule applicable to answer the question whether, when fellow workers use homophobic or sexist language to each other, or language relating to any other protected characteristic, both commit unlawful harassment, one commits unlawful harassment, or neither does. The answer lies in an application of the statutory test to each individual case. In many cases, both employees will have committed unlawful harassment; each will commit conduct having the effect of violating the dignity or creating an adverse environment for the other, and in many cases that will have been the purpose of the conduct.

10.   EQUAL PAY

Each Member State shall during the first stage ensure and sub-sequently maintain the application of the principle that men and women should receive equal pay for equal work.

For the purpose of this Article, "pay" means the ordinary basic or minimum wage or salary and any other consideration, whether in cash or in kind, which the worker receives, directly or indirectly, in respect of his employment from his employer.

Equal pay without discrimination based on sex means:

(a) that pay for the same work at piece rates shall be calculated on the basis of the same unit of measurement;

(b) that pay for work at time rates shall be the same for the same job.

EC TREATY – Article 141

For the same work or for work to which equal value is attributed, direct and indirect discrimination on grounds of sex with regard to all aspects and conditions of remuneration shall be eliminated. In particular, where a job classification system is used for determining pay, it shall be based on the same criteria for both men and women and so drawn up as to exclude any discrimination on grounds of sex.

EQUAL TREATMENT DIRECTIVE 2006/54 – Article 4

Member States shall introduce into their national legal systems such measures as are necessary to ensure real and effective compensation or reparation as the Member States so determine for the loss and damage sustained by a person injured as a result of discrimination on grounds of sex, in a way which is dissuasive and proportionate to the damage suffered. Such compensation or reparation may not be restricted by the fixing of a prior upper limit, except in cases where the employer can prove that the only damage suffered by an applicant as a result of discrimination within the meaning of this Directive is the refusal to take his/her job application into consideration.

EQUAL TREATMENT DIRECTIVE 2006/54 – Article 18

Worringham v [1981] IRLR 178 ECJ
Lloyds Bank Ltd
Article 141 applies directly in Member States, so as to confer enforceable Community rights upon individuals, to all forms of discrimination which may be identified solely with the aid of the criteria of equal work and equal pay referred to by that Article, without national or Community measures being required to define them with greater precision in order to permit of their application. In such a situation the court is in a position to establish all the facts enabling it to decide whether a woman receives less pay than a man engaged in the same work, or work of equal value.

Allonby v [2004] IRLR 224 ECJ
Accrington & Rossendale College
The term "worker" used in Article 141 has a Community meaning and cannot be defined by reference to the legislation of Member States. A "worker" for the purposes of Article 141 is a person who, for a certain period of time, performs services for and under the direction of another person for which they receive remuneration. The term "worker" does not include independent providers of services who are not in a relationship of subordination with the person who receives the services. However, provided that a person is a "worker" within the meaning of Article 141, the nature of their legal relationship with the other party to the employment relationship is of no consequence in regard to the application of that Article.

Gerster v [1997] IRLR 699 ECJ
Freistaat Bayern
Article 141 applies to employment relationships arising in the public service.

Worringham v [1981] IRLR 178 ECJ
Lloyds Bank Ltd
National courts have a duty to ensure the protection of the rights which Article 141 vests in individuals.

Barber v [1996] IRLR 209 CA
Staffordshire County Council
Article 141 can be relied upon by a claimant to disapply barriers to a claim which are incompatible with Community law.

Smith v [1994] IRLR 602 ECJ
Avdel Systems Ltd
Application of the principle of equal treatment between men and women in relation to pay by employers must be immediate and full. Achievement of equality cannot be made progressive on a basis that still maintains discrimination, even if only temporarily.

CLAIM IN TIME

Biggs v [1996] IRLR 203 CA
Somerset County Council
UK domestic law time limits apply to a claim relying on Article 141 of the Treaty, unless it can be shown that they are less favourable than those relating to similar actions of a domestic nature or are such as to make it impossible in practice to exercise the rights under Article 141.

Magorrian v [1998] IRLR 86 ECJ
Eastern Health and Social Services Board
EC law precludes the application, to a claim based on Article 141, of a national rule, such as that in the Occupational Pensions Regulations, which limits the entitlement of a claimant to join an occupational pension scheme to a period which starts to run from two years prior to the date proceedings were commenced. The rule was such as to render any action by individuals relying on Community law impossible in practice, in that its application in the present case would deprive the claimants of the additional benefits under the scheme to which they were entitled, since those benefits could be calculated only by reference to periods of service completed by them as from two years prior to commencement of proceedings.

Barber v   **[1996] IRLR 209 CA**
Staffordshire County Council
Article 141 does not confer any right to a redundancy payment or to unfair dismissal compensation. Community law does not create rights of action which have an existence apart from domestic law.

Setiya v   **[1995] IRLR 348 EAT**
East Yorkshire Health Authority
It would not be just to grant an employee, whose unfair dismissal complaint was dismissed by an employment tribunal in 1992 on grounds that he worked less than eight hours per week, an extension of time for appealing to the EAT against the tribunal's decision, in light of the decision of the House of Lords in 1994 that the hours per week qualification contravened EC law. To be granted an extension of time, it is not sufficient for the appellant simply to point to a subsequent decision of a higher court to the effect that the decision sought to be appealed against was wrongly decided.

SAME WORK

Brunnhofer v   **[2001] IRLR 571 ECJ**
Bank der österreichischen Postsparkasse
In order to determine whether employees perform the same work or work to which equal value can be attributed, it is necessary to ascertain whether, taking account of a number of factors such as the nature of the activities actually entrusted to each of the employees, the training requirements for carrying them out and the working conditions, those persons are in fact performing the same or comparable work.

Angestelltenbetriebsrat der Wiener   **[1999] IRLR 804 ECJ**
   Gebietskrankenkasse v
Wiener Gebietskrankenkasse
Two groups of employees who have different professional qualifications cannot be regarded as employed on "the same work" for the purpose of Article 141, even where the same activities are performed over a considerable length of time, if the different groups cannot be considered to be in a comparable situation. Professional training is not merely one of the factors that may be an objective justification for giving different pay for doing the same work; it is also one of the possible criteria for determining whether or not the same work is being performed.

Brunnhofer v   **[2001] IRLR 571 ECJ**
Bank der österreichischen Postsparkasse
The fact that the employees concerned are classified in the same job category under a collective agreement is not in itself sufficient for concluding that they perform the same work or work of equal value. The general indications provided in a collective agreement are only one indication amongst others and must, as a matter of evidence, be corroborated by precise and concrete factors based on the activities actually performed by the employees concerned.

BURDEN OF PROOF

Brunnhofer v   **[2001] IRLR 571 ECJ**
Bank der österreichischen Postsparkasse
The burden is normally on the employee to establish that the conditions giving rise to a presumption that there is unequal pay are fulfilled by proving by evidence that the pay she receives is less than that of her chosen comparator, and that she does the same work or work of equal value, comparable to that performed by him.

Brunnhofer v   **[2001] IRLR 571 ECJ**
Bank der österreichischen Postsparkasse
In comparing the pay of men and women in order to determine whether the principle of equal pay is being complied with, genuine transparency, permitting an effective review, is assured only if each aspect of remuneration is compared, rather than any general overall assessment of all the consideration paid to the workers.

Jämställdhetsombudsmannen v   **[2000] IRLR 421 ECJ**
Örebro Läns Landsting
Where the work of two groups can be regarded as of equal value, the national court must verify whether there is a substantially higher proportion of women than men in the disadvantaged group. If so, Article 141 requires the employer to justify the difference by showing that there are objective reasons for the difference in pay which are unrelated to any discrimination on grounds of sex.

Handels- og Kontorfunktionærernes   **[1989] IRLR 532 ECJ**
   Forbund i Danmark v
Dansk Arbejdsgiverforening
   (acting for Danfoss)
Pursuant to [Article 18 of the Equal Treatment Directive], Member States, in accordance with their national circumstances and their legal systems, must take the measures necessary in order to guarantee the application of the principle of equal pay and to ensure the existence of effective means to see to it that this principle is observed. The concern for effectiveness which therefore underlies the Directive must lead to an interpretation requiring adjustments to national rules relating to the burden of proof in specific situations where such adjustments are essential for the effective implementation of the principle of equality.

Handels- og Kontorfunktionaerernes   **[1989] IRLR 532 ECJ**
   Forbund i Danmark v
Dansk Arbejdsgiverforening
   (acting for Danfoss)
The EC [Equal Treatment Directive] must be interpreted as meaning that when an undertaking applies a pay system which is characterised by a total lack of transparency, the burden of proof is on the employer to show that his pay practice is not discriminatory where a female worker establishes, by comparison with a relatively large number of employees, that the average pay of female workers is lower than that of male workers.

Specialarbejderforbundet   **[1995] IRLR 648 ECJ**
  i Danmark v
Dansk Industri, acting for Royal Copenhagen
The mere finding that in a piecework pay scheme the average pay of a group of workers consisting predominantly of women carrying out one type of work is appreciably lower than the average pay of a group of workers consisting predominantly of men carrying out another type of work to which equal value is attributed does not suffice to establish that there is discrimination with regard to pay, since that difference may be due to differences in individual output of the workers constituting the two groups. However, in a piecework pay system where individual pay includes a variable element depending on each worker's output and it is not possible to identify the factors which determined the rates or units of measurement used to calculate the variable element in the pay, the burden of proving that the differences found are not due to sex discrimination may shift to the employer in order to avoid depriving the workers concerned of any effective means of enforcing the principle of equal pay.

Specialarbejderforbundet   **[1995] IRLR 648 ECJ**
  i Danmark v
Dansk Industri, acting for Royal Copenhagen
Where a comparison between workers of different sexes for work to which equal value is attributed involves the average pay of two groups paid by the piece, the national court must satisfy itself that the two groups each encompass all the workers who, taking account of factors such as the nature of the work, the training requirements and the working conditions, can be considered to be in a comparable situation. A comparison is not relevant where it involves groups formed in an arbitrary manner so that one comprises predominantly women and the other predominantly men with a view to carrying out successive comparisons. The comparison must also cover a relatively large number of workers in order to ensure that the differences found are not due to purely fortuitous or short-term factors or to differences in the individual output of the workers concerned.

MEANING OF "PAY"

Garland v   **[1982] IRLR 111 ECJ**
British Rail Engineering Ltd
"Pay", for the purposes of Article 141, comprises any consideration, whether in cash or in kind, whether immediate or future, that the worker receives, albeit indirectly, in respect of his employment from his employer.

Barber v   **[1990] IRLR 240 ECJ**
Guardian Royal Exchange
  Assurance Group
Although many advantages granted by an employer also reflect considerations of social policy, the fact that a benefit is in the nature of pay cannot be called in question where the worker is entitled to receive it from his employer by reason of the existence of the employment relationship. Therefore, a redundancy payment made by an employer cannot cease to constitute a form of pay on the sole ground

that, rather than deriving from the contract of employment, it is a statutory or ex gratia payment.

Barber v   **[1990] IRLR 240 ECJ**
Guardian Royal Exchange
  Assurance Group
Since Article 141 applies to discrimination arising directly from legislative provisions, benefits provided for by law may come within the concept of "pay".

Hill v   **[1998] IRLR 466 ECJ**
Revenue Commissioners
A system for classifying workers converting from jobsharing to full-time employment comes within the concept of "pay" for the purposes of Article 141, since it determines the progression of pay due to those workers.

Lewen v   **[2000] IRLR 67 ECJ**
Denda
A Christmas bonus constitutes "pay" within the meaning of Article 141, even if it is paid voluntarily by the employer as an exceptional allowance.

Jämställdhetsombudsmannen v   **[2000] IRLR 421 ECJ**
Örebro Läns Landsting
Differences in normal working time relate to working conditions and therefore fall under the Equal Treatment Directive rather than Article 141. The fact that the fixing of certain working conditions may have pecuniary consequences is not sufficient to bring such conditions within the scope of Article 141. However, any differences that might exist in the hours worked by two groups whose pay is being compared may constitute objective reasons unrelated to any discrimination on grounds of sex such as to justify a difference in pay.

Lommers v   **[2002] IRLR 430 ECJ**
Minister van Landbouw, Natuurbeheer
  en Visserij
A scheme under which an employer makes nursery places available to employees is to be regarded as a "working condition" within the meaning of the Equal Treatment Directive rather than as "pay" within the meaning of Article 141, notwithstanding that the cost of the nursery places was partly borne by the employer.

Gerster v   **[1997] IRLR 699 ECJ**
Freistaat Bayern
Rules concerning access to career advancement do not fall within the scope of Article 141, even though they are indirectly linked to pay. Such a rule is primarily designed to lay down conditions for inclusion on a list of persons eligible for promotion and only indirectly affects the level of pay to which the person concerned is entitled upon completion of the promotions procedure.

Legislation

Rinner-Kühn v   **[1989] IRLR 493 ECJ**
FWW Spezial-Gebäudereinigung GmbH
A legislative provision which results in practice in dis-

crimination between male and female workers is, in principle, to be regarded as contrary to the objective pursued by Article 141. It would only be otherwise if the different treatment between the two categories of workers was justified by objective factors unrelated to any discrimination on grounds of sex.

Rinner-Kühn v   **[1989] IRLR 493 ECJ**
FWW Spezial-Gebäudereinigung GmbH
The mere fact that a legislative provision affects a considerably greater number of female than of male workers cannot be regarded as an infringement of Article 141 if a Member State can establish before the national court that the means selected correspond to an objective necessary for its social policy and are appropriate and necessary to the attainment of that objective.

Allonby v   **[2004] IRLR 224 ECJ**
Accrington & Rossendale College
Where State legislation is at issue, the applicability of Article 141 to an undertaking is not subject to a condition that the worker concerned can be compared with a worker of the other sex who is or has been employed by the same employer and has received higher pay for equal work or work of equal value. A woman may rely on statistics to show that a clause in State legislation is contrary to Article 141 because it discriminates against female workers, and may invoke Article 141 against the employer concerned.

KB v   **[2004] IRLR 240 ECJ**
National Health Service Pensions Agency
Legislation which, in breach of the European Convention on Human Rights, prevents transsexuals from fulfilling a marriage requirement which must be met for one of them to be able to have the benefit of a survivor's pension, must be regarded as being in principle incompatible with the requirements of Article 141 of the EC Treaty.

Collective agreements

Kowalska v   **[1990] IRLR 447 ECJ**
Freie und Hansestadt Hamburg
Article 141 is sufficiently precise to be relied upon by an individual before a national court in order to have any national provision, including a collective agreement, contrary to Article 141 set aside.

Kowalska v   **[1990] IRLR 447 ECJ**
Freie und Hansestadt Hamburg
Article 141 precludes the application of a provision of a collective agreement under which part-time workers are excluded from a benefit where a considerably smaller percentage of men than of women work part time, unless the employer shows that the provision is justified by objective factors unrelated to any discrimination on grounds of sex. It is for the national court to determine whether and to what extent a provision of a collective agreement which in practice affects more women than men is justified on objective grounds unrelated to any discrimination based on sex.

Kowalska v   **[1990] IRLR 447 ECJ**
Freie und Hansestadt Hamburg
Where there is indirect discrimination in a provision of a collective agreement, the members of the group which is disadvantaged because of that discrimination must be treated in the same way and have the same system applied to them as the other workers, in proportion to their hours of work.

Nimz v   **[1991] IRLR 222 ECJ**
Freie und Hansestadt Hamburg
Where there is indirect discrimination in a provision of a collective agreement, the national court is required to disapply that provision, without requesting or awaiting its prior removal by collective negotiation or any other procedure. It would be incompatible with the nature of Community law for a judge to refuse to do all that is necessary, at the time when Community law is applied, to set aside any provisions of a collective agreement which might prevent Community standards from attaining their full effect.

Overtime

Stadt Lengerich v   **[1995] IRLR 216 ECJ**
Helmig
It is compatible with Article 141 and with the [Equal Treatment Directive] for a collective agreement to provide for the payment of overtime supplements only for hours worked in excess of the normal working hours for full-time employees fixed by the agreement and to exclude any overtime supplement for part-time employees for hours worked in excess of their individual working hours if those hours do not exceed the number determined by the agreement. There was no unequal treatment as between part-time and full-time employees, since the overall pay was the same for the same number of hours worked, and therefore no discrimination incompatible with Article 141 and the Directive.

Elsner-Lakeburg v   **[2005] IRLR 209 ECJ**
Land Nordrhein-Westfalen
Legislation which provides that both part-time and full-time teachers do not receive any remuneration for additional hours worked when the additional work does not exceed three hours per calendar month is contrary to Article 141 and the [Equal Treatment Directive] if it affects considerably more women than men, and if there is no objective unrelated to sex which justifies that different treatment or if it is not necessary to achieve the objective pursued. Part-time workers are entitled to have the same scheme applied to them as that applied to other workers, on a basis proportional to their working time. In this case, three additional hours was in fact a greater burden for part-time teachers than it was for full-time teachers since a full-time teacher must work an additional 3% extra in order to be paid for additional hours, whereas a part-time teacher must work 5% extra. Since the number of additional teaching hours giving entitlement to pay was not reduced for part-time teachers in a manner proportionate to their working hours, they received different treatment compared with full-time teachers as regards pay for additional teaching hours.

Sick pay

Rinner-Kühn v [1989] IRLR 493 ECJ
FWW Spezial-Gebäudereinigung GmbH
The continued payment of wages to a worker in the event of illness falls within the definition of "pay" within the meaning of Article 141.

Rinner-Kühn v [1989] IRLR 493 ECJ
FWW Spezial-Gebäudereinigung GmbH
Article 141 of the EC Treaty precludes national legislation which permits employers to exclude employees whose normal working hours do not exceed 10 hours a week or 45 hours a month from the continued payment of wages in the event of illness, where that measure affects a considerably greater number of women than men, unless the Member State shows that that legislation is justified by objective factors unrelated to any discrimination on grounds of sex.

Rinner-Kühn v [1989] IRLR 493 ECJ
FWW Spezial-Gebäudereinigung GmbH
A submission that workers who work less than 10 hours a week or 45 hours a month are not integrated in and connected with the undertaking in a way comparable to that of other workers only represented generalised statements concerning categories of workers and could not be regarded as objective criteria unrelated to any discrimination on grounds of sex.

Pregnancy

North Western Health Board v [2005] IRLR 895 ECJ
McKenna
A sick leave scheme which treats female workers suffering from a pregnancy-related illness in the same way as other workers suffering from an illness that is unrelated to pregnancy is "pay" within the scope of Article 141 EC.

HK (acting on behalf of [1999] IRLR 55 ECJ
  Hoj Pedersen) v
Fællesforeningen for Danmarks Brugsforeninger
  (acting on behalf of Kvickly Skive)
It is contrary to Article 141 and the [Equal Treatment Directive] to deprive a woman of her full pay when she is unfit for work before the beginning of her maternity leave as a result of a pregnancy-related condition, when a worker is in principle entitled to receive full pay in the event of incapacity for work on grounds of illness.

North Western Health Board v [2005] IRLR 895 ECJ
McKenna
A rule of a sick leave scheme which provides for a reduction in pay where the absence exceeds a certain duration as regards both female workers absent prior to maternity leave by reason of an illness related to their pregnancy and male workers absent by reason of any other illness does not constitute discrimination on grounds of sex contrary to Article 141 and the [Equal Treatment Directive], so long as the amount of payment made is not so low as to undermine the objective of protecting pregnant workers.

North Western Health Board v [2005] IRLR 895 ECJ
McKenna
It is not contrary to Article 141 and the [Equal Treatment Directive] for a sick leave scheme to treat all illnesses in an identical manner for the purpose of determining the maximum total number of days of paid sick leave to which a worker is entitled during a given period, and not to take any account of the special nature of pregnancy-related illnesses. However, the offsetting of absences during pregnancy on grounds of a pregnancy-related illness against a maximum total number of days of paid sick leave to which a worker is entitled over a specified period cannot have the effect that, during the absence affected by that offsetting after the maternity leave, the female worker receives pay that is below the minimum amount to which she was entitled over the course of the illness which arose during her pregnancy. Special provisions must be implemented in order to prevent such an effect.

Maternity pay

Gillespie v [1996] IRLR 214 ECJ
Northern Health and Social
  Services Board
The principle of equal pay does not require that women should continue to receive full pay during maternity leave. Women taking maternity leave are in a special position, which requires them to be afforded special protection, but which is not comparable with that of a man or a woman actually at work. Although the benefit paid by an employer to a woman on maternity leave constitutes "pay" within the meaning of Article 141 and the [Equal Treatment Directive], discrimination involves the application of different rules to comparable situations or the application of the same rule to different situations. Therefore, neither Article 141 or the Directive requires that women should continue to receive full pay during maternity leave.

Todd v [1997] IRLR 410 NICA
Eastern Health and Social Services Board
Gillespie v
Northern Health and Social Services Board (No.2)
A healthy pregnancy did not come within the contractual provisions relating to sickness and disability. Pregnancy cannot be compared with sickness.

Clark v [1996] IRLR 578 CA
Secretary of State for Employment
Special provisions which are made for women who are absent from work because of pregnancy or confinement are a separate code. The code provides pregnant women with special protection, but when in receipt of payments under the code their position cannot be "compared" with that of a man or with that of a woman in work.

Gillespie v [1996] IRLR 214 ECJ
Northern Health and Social Services Board
A woman on maternity leave must receive a pay rise awarded before or during maternity leave.

Alabaster v   **[2004] IRLR 486 ECJ**
Woolwich plc

The principle of non-discrimination requires that a woman who still has a contract of employment or employment relationship during maternity leave must, like any other worker, benefit from any pay rise which is awarded between the beginning of the reference period and the end of maternity leave. To deny such an increase to a woman on maternity leave would discriminate against her since, had she not been pregnant, she would have received the pay rise. Therefore, a woman who receives a pay increase before the start of her maternity leave is entitled, in accordance with Article 141 of the EC Treaty and the judgment in *Gillespie v Northern Health and Social Services Board*, to have the increase taken into consideration in the calculation of the earnings-related element of her statutory maternity pay, even though the pay rise was not back-dated to the relevant reference period for calculating her entitlement under the Statutory Maternity Pay (General) Regulations.

Alabaster v   **[2005] IRLR 576 CA**
Barclays Bank plc (No.2)

In accordance with Article 141 and the judgment of the European Court of Justice, the claimant was entitled to have a pay increase which she received before the start of her maternity leave taken into consideration in the calculation of the earnings-related element of her statutory maternity pay, even though the pay rise was not backdated to the relevant reference period for calculating her entitlement under the Statutory Maternity Pay (General) Regulations. In order to give effect in national law to the rights of a woman on maternity leave in a way which complies with the requirements of EC law, it was appropriate to disapply those parts of s.1 of the Equal Pay Act which impose a requirement for a male comparator. In that way, the claimant could succeed in her claim for sex discrimination without the need for such a comparator.

Gillespie v   **[1996] IRLR 214 ECJ**
Northern Health and Social Services Board

It is for national legislature to set the amount of maternity pay, provided the amount is not so low as to undermine the purpose of maternity leave, namely the protection of women before and after giving birth. In order to assess the adequacy of the amount payable, the national court must take account of other forms of social protection afforded by national law in the case of justified absence from work, as well as the length of maternity leave.

Abdoulaye v   **[1999] IRLR 811 ECJ**
Régie Nationale des Usines Renault

The principle of equal pay presupposes that male and female workers whom it covers are in comparable situations. Women on maternity leave are in a different situation than men since there are occupational disadvantages, inherent in maternity leave, which arise as a result of being away from work. Therefore, it is not contrary to Article 141 to make a lump-sum payment to female workers who take maternity leave, and not to men who become fathers, notwithstanding women on maternity leave receive full pay, where the lump-sum payment is designed to offset the

occupational disadvantages which arise for those workers as a result of their being away from work.

Todd v   **[1997] IRLR 410 NICA**
Eastern Health and Social Services Board
Gillespie v
Northern Health and Social Services Board (No.2)

Contractual maternity pay which was at a higher level than statutory sickness benefit could not be held to be inadequate, or such as to undermine the purpose of maternity leave, so as to fall within the proviso to the ruling of the European Court in the *Gillespie* case.

Parental leave

Lewen v   **[2000] IRLR 67 ECJ**
Denda

Article 141 of the EC Treaty precludes an employer from entirely excluding women on parental leave from the benefit of a Christmas bonus without taking account of the work done in the year in which the bonus is paid or of periods of maternity leave during which they were prohibited from working, where that bonus is awarded retroactively as pay for work performed in the course of that year. If the Christmas bonus is retroactive pay for work performed, refusal to award a bonus, even one reduced proportionately, to workers on parental leave who worked during the year in which the bonus was granted, on the sole ground that their contract of employment is suspended when the bonus is granted, places them at a disadvantage as compared with those whose contract is not suspended at the time of the award. Such a refusal constitutes discrimination within the meaning of Article 141, since female workers are far more likely to be on parental leave when the bonus is awarded than male workers.

Time off

Arbeiterwohlfahrt der Stadt   **[1992] IRLR 423 ECJ**
   Berlin eV v
Bötel

Compensation in the form of paid leave or overtime pay for participation in training courses given by an employer to staff committee members in accordance with statutory provisions falls within the concept of "pay" within the meaning of Article 141 of the EC Treaty and the [Equal Treatment Directive]. Although such compensation does not arise from the contract of employment, it is nevertheless paid by the employer by virtue of legislative provisions and by reason of the existence of an employment relationship with an employee.

Kuratorium für Dialyse und   **[1996] IRLR 637 ECJ**
   Nierentransplantation eV v
Lewark

National legislation which causes indirect discrimination against women by limiting to their individual working hours the compensation which staff council members employed on a part-time basis receive from their employer for attending training courses held during full-time working hours but which exceed their individual part-time working hours, when staff council members employed full-time receive compensation for attendance at the same courses on the basis of their full-time working hours, can be justified by objective factors unrelated to any discrimination based on sex. The mere fact that a legislative provision affects far more women workers than men cannot be regarded as a breach of Article 141 if the Member State is able to show that the measures chosen reflect a legitimate aim of its social policy, are appropriate to achieve that aim and are necessary in order to do so.

Arbeiterwohlfahrt der Stadt   **[1992] IRLR 423 ECJ**
   Berlin eV v
Bötel
Article 141 and the [Equal Treatment Directive] preclude national legislation which applies to a considerably greater number of women than men limiting to their individual working hours the compensation which members of staff committees employed part-time should receive from their employer in the form of paid leave or overtime pay, in respect of their participation in training courses providing the knowledge and skills required for the running of staff committees and which are organised during the full-time working hours applicable in the undertaking but exceeding their own working hours as part-time employees, whereas the members of staff committees participating in the same courses who are full-time employees are paid compensation up to the limit of the full-time working hours. It remains open to the Member State to establish that the said legislation is justified by objective factors unrelated to any discrimination on grounds of sex.

Davies v   **[1999] IRLR 769 EAT**
Neath Port Talbot County Borough Council
Part-time workers have a right under Article 141 to be paid on the same basis as their full-time counterparts when attending union-run training courses away from work.

Pension schemes

Scope of Article 141

Barber v   **[1990] IRLR 240 ECJ**
Guardian Royal Exchange
   Assurance Group
A pension paid under a contracted-out private occupational scheme constitutes consideration paid by the employer to the worker in respect of his employment and consequently falls within the scope of the definition of "pay" in Article 141.

Bestuur van het Algemeen   **[1995] IRLR 103 ECJ**
   Burgerlijk Pensioenfonds v
Beune
In order to determine whether the benefits provided by a pension scheme are within the scope of Article 141, the only possible decisive criterion is whether the pension is paid to the worker by reason of the employment relationship between him and his former employer.

Barber v   **[1990] IRLR 240 ECJ**
Guardian Royal Exchange
   Assurance Group
It is contrary to Article 141 to impose an age condition which differs according to sex in respect of pensions paid under a contracted-out scheme, even if the difference between the pensionable age for men and that for women is based on the one provided for by the national statutory scheme.

Coloroll Pension Trustees Ltd v   **[1994] IRLR 586 ECJ**
Russell
The principles laid down in the *Barber* judgment, and the limitation of its effects in time, concern not only contracted-out occupational schemes but also non-contracted-out occupational schemes.

Bestuur van het Algemeen   **[1995] IRLR 103 ECJ**
   Burgerlijk Pensioenfonds v
Beune
A civil service pension scheme, which essentially relates to the employment of the person concerned, forms part of the pay received by that person and comes within the scope of Article 141. If the pension paid by the public employer concerns only a particular category of workers, if it is directly related to the period of service, and if its amount is calculated by reference to the civil servant's last salary, it is entirely comparable to the pension paid by a private employer to its former employees.

Bestuur van het Algemeen   **[1995] IRLR 103 ECJ**
   Burgerlijk Pensioenfonds v
Beune
Article 141 precludes national legislation which applies different rules for calculating the occupational pension of married men and married women. Married men placed at a disadvantage by the discrimination are entitled to be treated in the same way and have the same scheme applied to them as is applied to married women.

Ten Oever v   **[1993] IRLR 601 ECJ**
Stichting Bedrijfspensioenfonds voor
   het Glazenwassers- en Schoonmaakbedrijf
A survivor's pension provided by an occupational pension scheme, whose rules were agreed between both sides of the industry concerned and which was funded by the industry's employees and employers to the exclusion of any financial contribution from the public purse, falls within the concept of "pay" within the meaning of Article 141 of the EC Treaty, notwithstanding that, by definition, a survivor's pension is not paid to the employee.

Coloroll Pension Trustees Ltd v   **[1994] IRLR 586 ECJ**
Russell
Article 141 may be relied upon by an employee's dependants.

Coloroll Pension Trustees Ltd v   **[1994] IRLR 586 ECJ**
Russell
Article 141 may be relied upon against the trustees of an occupational pension scheme. Since the trustees are required to pay benefits which are "pay" within the mean-

ing of Article 141, they are bound, in so doing, to do everything within the scope of their powers to ensure compliance with the principle of equal treatment.

Coloroll Pension Trustees Ltd v   **[1994] IRLR 586 ECJ**
Russell
Employers and trustees cannot rely on the rules of their pension scheme, or those contained in the trust deed, in order to evade their obligation under Article 141 to ensure equal treatment in the matter of pay. In so far as the rules of national law prohibit them from acting beyond the scope of their powers or in disregard of the provisions of the trust deed, employers and trustees are bound to use all the means available under domestic law to ensure compliance with the principle of equal treatment, such as recourse to the national courts to amend the provisions of the pension scheme or of the trust deed.

Worringham v   **[1981] IRLR 178 ECJ**
Lloyds Bank Ltd
A contribution to a retirement benefits scheme which is paid by an employer in the name of male employees only, by means of an addition to gross salary, is discrimination in the form of unequal pay for men and women contrary to Article 141, even though the salary of men after deduction of the contributions is comparable with that of women who do not pay contributions, since the amount of the gross salary determined the amount of certain benefits and social advantages to which workers of both sexes are entitled.

Barber v   **[1990] IRLR 240 ECJ**
Guardian Royal Exchange
  Assurance Group
It is contrary to Article 141 for a man made compulsorily redundant to be entitled to claim only a deferred pension payable at the normal pension age, when a woman in the same position is entitled to an immediate retirement pension as a result of the application of an age condition that varies according to sex in the same way as is provided for by the national statutory pension scheme.

Neath v   **[1994] IRLR 91 ECJ**
Hugh Steeper Ltd
The use of actuarial factors differing according to sex in funded defined-benefit occupational pension schemes to take account of the fact that women live on average longer than men does not fall within the scope of Article 141. Therefore, inequality of employers' contributions to funded defined-benefit pension schemes, which is due to the use of actuarial factors differing according to sex, is not prohibited by Article 141. Unlike periodic payment of pensions, the funding arrangement chosen to secure the adequacy of the funds necessary to cover the cost of the pensions promised is outside the concept of "pay" in Article 141 as it not a consequence of the employer's commitment to pay employees defined benefits or to grant them specific advantages and therefore does not come within the corresponding expectations of the employees as to the benefits which will be paid by the employer or the advantages with which they will be provided.

Coloroll Pension Trustees Ltd v   **[1994] IRLR 586 ECJ**
Russell
Transfer benefits and capital-sum benefits, whose value depends on the funding arrangements chosen, do not constitute "pay". Consequently, Article 141 does not cover an inequality where a reduced pension is paid when the employer opts for early retirement or in the amount of a reversionary pension payable to a dependant in return for the surrender of part of the annual pension.

Coloroll Pension Trustees Ltd v   **[1994] IRLR 586 ECJ**
Russell
Article 141 does not cover additional benefits stemming from additional voluntary contributions by employees, where the pension scheme does no more than provide the membership with the necessary arrangements for management.

Smith v   **[1994] IRLR 602 ECJ**
Avdel Systems Ltd
Article 141 does not preclude an employer from raising the retirement age for women to that for men in order to comply with the *Barber* judgment. Article 141 does not preclude measures which achieve equal treatment by reducing the advantages of the persons previously favoured. It merely requires that men and women should receive the same pay for the same work without imposing any specific level of pay. However, once discrimination in pay has been found to exist, so long as measures for bringing about equal treatment have not been adopted by the scheme, the only proper way of complying with Article 141 is to grant the persons in the disadvantaged class the same advantages as those enjoyed by the persons in the favoured class. In the present case, that meant that, as regards the period between the date of the Barber judgment and the date on which the scheme adopted measures to achieve equality, the pension rights of men must be calculated on the basis of the same retirement age as that for women.

Smith v   **[1994] IRLR 602 ECJ**
Avdel Systems Ltd
Where the retirement age for women is raised to that of men in order to remove discrimination in relation to occupational pensions, Article 141 does not allow transitional measures designed to limit the adverse consequences for women as regards benefits payable in respect of future periods of service.

Van Den Akker v   **[1994] IRLR 616 ECJ**
Stichting Shell Pensioenfonds
Article 141 does not allow an occupational pension scheme to maintain in force after the date of the *Barber* judgment a condition as to retirement age differing according to sex, even where that difference is due to giving female employees an option before the *Barber* judgment to maintain a retirement age lower than that for men.

Smith v   **[1994] IRLR 602 ECJ**
Avdel Systems Ltd
Article 141 precludes an occupational pension scheme, even where there are objectively justifiable considerations relating to the needs of the undertaking or of the scheme

concerned, from retrospectively raising the retirement age for women in relation to periods of service between the date of the *Barber* judgment and the date of entry into force of the measures designed to achieve equal treatment.

Coloroll Pension Trustees Ltd v   **[1994] IRLR 586 ECJ**
Russell

The national court is bound to ensure correct implementation of Article 141 and, in order to do so, may make use of all means available to it under domestic law, such as by ordering the employer to pay additional sums into the scheme, ordering that any sum payable by virtue of Article 141 must be paid out of surplus funds or out of the scheme's assets. Any problems arising because the funds held by the trustee are insufficient or the employer cannot provide sufficient funds to equalise benefits must be resolved on the basis of national law in accordance with the principle of equal pay.

Coloroll Pension Trustees Ltd v   **[1994] IRLR 586 ECJ**
Russell

The rights accruing to a worker from Article 141 cannot be affected by the fact that he changes his job and has to join a new pension scheme, with his acquired pension rights being transferred to the new scheme. A worker entering retirement is entitled to expect the scheme of which he is then a member to pay him a pension calculated in accordance with the principle of equal treatment, and to increase benefits accordingly, even where the capital transferred is inadequate due to the discriminatory treatment under the first scheme. However, in accordance with the *Barber* judgment, neither the scheme which transferred rights nor the scheme which accepted them is required to take the financial steps necessary to bring about equality in relation to periods of service prior to 17 May 1990.

Bilka-Kaufhaus GmbH v   **[1986] IRLR 317 ECJ**
Weber von Hartz

Article 141 is restricted to pay discrimination and therefore does not have the effect of requiring an employer to organise an occupational pension scheme in such a manner as to take into account the particular difficulties faced by persons with family responsibilities in meeting the conditions for entitlement to such a pension.

Coloroll Pension Trustees Ltd v   **[1994] IRLR 586 ECJ**
Russell

Article 141 is not applicable to pension schemes which at all times have had members of only one sex.

Moroni v   **[1994] IRLR 130 ECJ**
Firma Collo GmbH

The provisions of EC Occupational Social Security Directive 86/378 cannot limit the scope of Article 141.

Temporal limitation

Barber v   **[1990] IRLR 240 ECJ**
Guardian Royal Exchange
  Assurance Group

The direct effect of Article 141 may not be relied upon in order to claim entitlement to a pension with effect from a date prior to that of the judgment in this case (17 May 1990), except in the case of those who have before that date initiated legal proceedings or raised an equivalent claim under the applicable national law.

Ten Oever v   **[1993] IRLR 601 ECJ**
Stichting Bedrijfspensioenfonds voor
  het Glazenwassers- en Schoonmaakbedrijf

The direct effect of Article 141 may be relied upon, for the purpose of claiming equal treatment in the matter of occupational pensions, only in relation to benefits payable in respect of periods of employment subsequent to 17 May 1990, the date of the *Barber* decision, subject to the exception in favour of those who before that date initiated legal proceedings or raised an equivalent claim under the applicable national law.

Coloroll Pension Trustees Ltd v   **[1994] IRLR 586 ECJ**
Russell

Where a benefit is not linked to the actual length of service, such as a lump-sum payment in the event of the employee's death during employment, the limitation of the effects in time of the *Barber* judgment applies only where the operative event occurred before 17 May 1990. After that date, such benefits must be granted in accordance with the principle of equal treatment without distinguishing between periods of service prior to and subsequent to the *Barber* judgment.

Vroege v   **[1994] IRLR 651 ECJ**
NCIV Instituut voor
  Volkshuisvesting BV

The temporal limitation of the *Barber* judgment concerns only those kinds of discrimination which employers and occupational pension schemes could reasonably have considered to be permissible owing to the transitional derogations provided by Community law in respect of equal treatment with regard to the determination of pensionable age.

Quirk v   **[2002] IRLR 353 CA**
Burton Hospitals NHS Trust

The decisions of the European Court of Justice reveal a difference in the treatment of "access cases" relating to the right to join or to be fully admitted to a pension scheme and its benefits, and claims relating to the calculation of the level of benefits under a pension scheme. The Court of Justice has applied the temporal limitation to level of benefit cases but not to access cases.

Quirk v   **[2002] IRLR 353 CA**
Burton Hospitals NHS Trust

The provision in the NHS Pension Scheme Regulations allowing a woman retiring before age 60 to receive benefits calculated by reference to all of her pensionable service, whereas the pension payable to men before age 60 is calculated only by reference to service from 17 May 1990, the date of the *Barber* decision, did not discriminate against a man contrary to Article 141 since the claim was caught by the temporal limitation contained in the European Court's decision in the *Barber* case and in the *Bar-*

ber Protocol to the EC Treaty, in that it was a complaint about the level of benefit payable, rather than a complaint relating to access to benefits under a pension scheme. The essence of the complaint was not that the claimant was denied the right to be a member of the pension scheme, but that, unlike the case of a female nurse, the calculation of pension benefits on his retirement at age 55 would not take account of his years of pensionable service prior to 17 May 1990.

Howard v   **[1995] IRLR 570 EAT**
Ministry of Defence
The exclusion from the temporal limitation imposed by the European Court on the *Barber* decision for those who had made a claim "equivalent" to legal proceedings in national law, is restricted to where a dispute has been raised before an independent third party with power to determine the dispute conclusively, such as an administrative or arbitration tribunal, and does not extend to a person who only asserts a claim.

Admission

Bilka-Kaufhaus GmbH v   **[1986] IRLR 317 ECJ**
Weber von Hartz
The conditions for admission to an occupational pension scheme, where the benefits paid to employees constitute consideration received by the worker from the employer in respect of employment, fall within the scope of the definition of "pay" in Article 141 of the EC Treaty; such a scheme does not constitute a social security scheme governed directly by statute, which would be outside the scope of Article 141.

Vroege v   **[1994] IRLR 651 ECJ**
NCIV Instituut voor
   Volkshuisvesting BV
Article 141 of the EC Treaty covers the right to join an occupational pension scheme, as well as entitlement to benefits paid by an occupational pension scheme. Therefore, an occupational pension scheme which excludes part-time workers will contravene Article 141 if the exclusion affects a much greater number of women than men, unless the employer shows that it may be explained by objectively justified factors unrelated to any discrimination on grounds of sex.

Trustees of Uppingham School   **[2002] IRLR 792 CA**
   Retirement Benefit Scheme for
   Non-Teaching Staff v
Shillcock
Exclusion of the claimant part-time employee from membership of the appellant's occupational pension scheme on grounds that she earned less than the lower earnings limit for Class I national insurance contributions was not indirectly discriminatory on grounds of sex against women contrary to Article 141. Subtracting the lower earnings limit from the earnings of every employee for the purpose of assessing pensionable salary involved a consistent, and not a discriminatory, approach to all categories of employee.

Allonby v   **[2004] IRLR 224 ECJ**
Accrington & Rossendale College
A requirement of being employed under a contract of employment as a precondition for membership of a pension scheme for teachers, set up by State legislation, must be disapplied unless it is objectively justified, where it is shown that among the teachers who are "workers" within the meaning of Article 141 there is a much higher percentage of women than of men who fulfil all the conditions for membership of the scheme except that of being employed under a contract of employment as defined by national law.

Preston v   **[2004] IRLR 96 EAT**
Wolverhampton Healthcare
   NHS Trust (No.3)
There is a breach of the Equal Pay Act where pension scheme membership is compulsory for full-time staff but part-time staff are excluded, regardless of whether an employee joined the scheme when it became open to them. However, there is no breach of the Equal Pay Act where pension scheme membership is compulsory for full-time staff and optional for part-time staff.

Schröder v   **[2000] IRLR 353 ECJ**
Deutsche Telekom AG
Where the exclusion of part-time workers from an occupational pension scheme has been found to constitute indirect discrimination prohibited by Article 141, the only limitation in time on the possibility of relying on the direct effect of Article 141 in relation to membership of the scheme and the subsequent payment of a pension is that resulting from *Defrenne (No.2)*, that periods of service of such workers are to be taken into account only from 8 April 1976 onwards. The limitation in time of the *Barber* decision and the *Barber* Protocol concerns only those kinds of discrimination which employers and pension schemes could reasonably have considered to be permissible under Community law. Since it has been clear since the judgment in *Bilka* that any discrimination, based on sex, in the right to join an occupational pension scheme infringes Article 41, there was no reason to suppose that those concerned could have been mistaken as to the applicability of Article 41 to the right to join an occupational scheme.

Vroege v   **[1994] IRLR 651 ECJ**
NCIV Instituut voor
   Volkshuisvesting BV
The *Barber* Protocol to Article 141, which provides that benefits under occupational social security schemes shall not be considered as remuneration if and in so far as they are attributable to periods of employment prior to 17 May 1990, does not affect the right to join an occupational pension scheme. The Protocol is applicable to benefits paid under an occupational pension scheme, since that is all that is mentioned in the Protocol. Neither the Protocol, nor the *Barber* judgment, dealt with, or made any provision for, the conditions of membership of occupational schemes, which continues to be governed by the *Bilka* judgment.

Dietz v   **[1996] IRLR 692 ECJ**
Stichting Thuiszorg Rotterdam
The *Barber* Protocol to the Treaty on European Union does not affect the right to payment of a retirement pension where the worker was excluded from membership of an occupational pension scheme in breach of Article 141.

Fisscher v   **[1994] IRLR 662 ECJ**
Voorhuis Hengelo BV
National rules relating to time limits for bringing actions under national law may be relied on against workers who assert their right under Community law to join an occupational pension scheme, provided that they are not less favourable for that type of action than for similar actions of a domestic nature and that they do not render the exercise of rights conferred by Community law impossible in practice.

Fisscher v   **[1994] IRLR 662 ECJ**
Voorhuis Hengelo BV
The fact that a worker can claim retroactively to join an occupational pension scheme does not allow the worker to avoid paying the contributions relating to the period of membership concerned. The worker cannot claim more favourable treatment, particularly in financial terms, than if the worker had been duly accepted as a member.

Bridging pensions

Birds Eye Walls Ltd v   **[1994] IRLR 29 ECJ**
Roberts
It is not contrary to Article 141 for an employer to reduce the amount of a bridging pension to take account of the amount of the State pension which the employee will receive, even though, in the case of men and women aged between 60 and 65, the result is that a female ex-employee receives a smaller bridging pension than that paid to her male counterpart.

Birds Eye Walls Ltd v   **[1994] IRLR 29 ECJ**
Roberts
It is not contrary to Article 141 for an employer, when calculating a bridging pension, to take account of the full State pension which a married woman would have received if she had not opted in favour of paying contributions at a reduced rate. Nor is it contrary to Article 141 for an employer to take account of the widow's pension which may be drawn by the woman concerned.

Notice payment

Clark v   **[1995] IRLR 421 EAT**
Secretary of State for Employment
Sums payable by an employer to an employee for failing to give notice to which the employee is entitled are "pay" within the meaning of Article 141, because such payment is in respect of the employee's employment.

Clark v   **[1996] IRLR 578 CA**
Secretary of State for Employment
The exclusion of women absent from work because of pregnancy from the categories specified in para.2 of Schedule 3 to the Employment Protection (Consolidation) Act, which determines the liability of an employer for the statutory minimum notice period, did not amount to discrimination on the ground of sex contrary to Article 141. Discrimination on grounds of sex means either that different rules are applied to men and women in comparable situations or that the same rule is applied to men and women in different situations. Women taking maternity leave, however, are in a special position, since men are never in a "comparable situation".

Redundancy payment

Barber v   **[1990] IRLR 240 ECJ**
Guardian Royal Exchange
  Assurance Group
Benefits paid by an employer to a worker in connection with the latter's compulsory redundancy fall within the scope of Article 141 of the EC Treaty, whether they are paid under a contract of employment, by virtue of legislative provisions or on a voluntary basis.

McKechnie v   **[1991] IRLR 283 EAT**
UBM Building Supplies (Southern) Ltd
The decision of the European Court in *Barber v Guardian Royal Exchange Assurance Group Ltd* removed any possible doubt that both a statutory redundancy payment and an ex-gratia payment based on the statutory payment provided by a collective agreement are properly to be regarded as coming within the definition of "pay" in Article 141.

Commission of the European   **[1993] IRLR 404 ECJ**
  Communities v
Kingdom of Belgium
Payments in addition to unemployment benefit provided under Belgian law to men who are made redundant between ages 60 and 65 constitute "pay" within the scope of Article 141 of the EC Treaty, rather than a social security benefit falling outside Article 141, since the payment is the responsibility of the last employer of the employee dismissed, is due by reason of the employment relationship which existed, and has its origins in an agreement between the social partners.

Rankin v   **[1993] IRLR 69 EAT**
British Coal Corporation
The general policy in legislation, concerned not only with redundancy but with similar statutory claims such as equal pay and racial and sexual discrimination provisions, suggests that a period for bringing claims directly under Article 141 in the region of three to six months could not properly be stigmatised as unreasonable, given that the starting date for the running of the period is also reasonable.

Rankin v   **[1993] IRLR 69 EAT**
British Coal Corporation
Balancing the requirements of certainty and the protection

of rights under the Treaty, a claim in respect of a discriminatory statutory redundancy payment brought within a reasonable period of time after the coming into force of the amending legislation which removed the discrimination should be regarded as timeous.

Severance pay

Barry v   **[1999] IRLR 581 HL**
Midland Bank plc
A security of employment agreement, whereby severance pay was calculated on the basis of the employee's current pay at the date of termination, was not indirectly discriminatory against women contrary to Article 141, even though the scheme made no allowance for employees whose hours of work fluctuated, thereby disadvantaging part-time workers by not taking into account any full-time service they may have had. The scheme did not have a discriminatory effect and thus did not infringe the principle of equal pay for equal work, since the same rules applied to women and men, to both full-time and part-time workers.

Unfair dismissal compensation

R v   **[1999] IRLR 253 ECJ**
Secretary of State for Employment
    ex parte Seymour-Smith
An award of unfair dismissal compensation constitutes "pay" within the meaning of Article 141, since it is paid to the employee by reason of his employment, which would have continued but for the unfair dismissal.

R v   **[1999] IRLR 253 ECJ**
Secretary of State for Employment
    ex parte Seymour-Smith
The conditions determining whether an unfairly dismissed employee is entitled to compensation fall within the scope of Article 141 rather than the Equal Treatment Directive, since the condition concerns access to a form of pay. However, where a dismissed employee seeks reinstatement or re-engagement, the conditions laid down by national law concern working conditions or the right to take up employment and would therefore fall under the Equal Treatment Directive.

Travel facilities

Garland v   **[1982] IRLR 111 ECJ**
British Rail Engineering Ltd
Travel facilities accorded to employees after retirement are "pay" within the meaning of Article 141, so that an employer who provided special travel facilities for former male employees to enjoy after their retirement discriminated within the meaning of Article 141 against former female employees who did not receive the same facilities.

CLAIM IN TIME

(1) This section applies to –
    (a) a complaint relating to a breach of an equality clause or rule;
    (b) an application for a declaration referred to in section 127(3) or (4).

(2) Proceedings on the complaint or application may not be brought in an employment tribunal after the end of the qualifying period.

(3) If the complaint or application relates to terms of work other than terms of service in the armed forces, the qualifying period is, in a case mentioned in the first column of the table, the period mentioned in the second column.

Case	Qualifying period
A standard case	*The period of 6 months beginning with the last day of the employment or appointment.*
A stable work case (but not if it is also a concealment or incapacity case (or both))	*The period of 6 months beginning with the day on which the stable working relationship ended.*
A concealment case (but not if it is also an incapacity case)	*The period of 6 months beginning with the day on which the worker discovered (or could with reasonable diligence have discovered) the qualifying fact.*
An incapacity case (but not if it is also a concealment case)	*The period of 6 months beginning with the day on which the worker ceased to have the incapacity.*
A case which is a concealment case and an incapacity case.	*The period of 6 months beginning with the later of the days on which the period would begin if the case were merely a concealment or incapacity case.*

EQUALITY ACT 2010 – s.129

(1) This section applies for the purposes of section 129.

(2) A standard case is a case which is not –
    (a) a stable work case,
    (b) a concealment case,
    (c) an incapacity case, or
    (d) a concealment case and an incapacity case.

(3) A stable work case is a case where the proceedings relate to a period during which there was a stable working relationship between the worker and the responsible person (including any time after the terms of work had expired).

(4) A concealment case in proceedings relating to an equality clause is a case where –
    (a) the responsible person deliberately concealed a qualifying fact from the worker, and
    (b) the worker did not discover (or could not with reasonable diligence have discovered) the qualifying fact until after the relevant day.

EQUALITY ACT 2010 – s.130

Preston v   [2000] IRLR 506 ECJ
Wolverhampton Healthcare NHS Trust

Community law does not preclude a national procedural rule, which requires that a claim for membership of an occupational pension scheme must be brought within six months of the end of the employment to which the claim relates, provided that that limitation period is not less favourable for actions based on Community law than for those based on domestic law. The setting of reasonable limitation periods for bringing proceedings satisfies the Community law principle of effectiveness, inasmuch as it constitutes an application of the fundamental principle of legal certainty, even if expiry of the limitation period results in the dismissal of the claimant's action.

Preston v   [2001] IRLR 237 HL
Wolverhampton Healthcare
   NHS Trust (No.2)

The limitation requiring a claim to be brought within six months of the end of the employment to which the claim relates, is not less favourable than the time limit of six years for bringing a claim for breach of contract. Therefore, the principle of equivalence is not breached.

Secretary of State for Health v   [2007] IRLR 665 EAT
Rance

The time limit for bringing an equal pay claim is one of jurisdiction. A tribunal is precluded from hearing a claim that is not presented within the relevant time. Consequently, the jurisdictional provisions cannot be waived by the parties.

National Power plc v   [2001] IRLR 32 CA
Young

The word "employment" does not relate to the particular job on which the woman bases her claim to an equality clause. "Employed in the employment" means employed under a contract of service.

Slack v   [2009] IRLR 463 CA
Cumbria County Council

There was a new contract of employment where the claimant signed a document which included terms that differed from previous contracts and expressly stated that it superseded any previous contract of employment. However, the time limit is not triggered where the new contract was part of a succession of contracts in respect of the same employment within a stable employment relationship. A stable employment relationship is not confined to cases of a succession of contracts with breaks between the contracts. There can be a stable employment relationship where there is an unbroken succession of contracts.

Potter v   [2009] IRLR 900 EAT
North Cumbria Acute Hospitals
   NHS Trust (No.2)

Fundamental as well as minor contractual changes can be effected by consensual variation. Parties can agree both the content and the mechanism for effecting contractual change. Where parties do not expressly agree the mechanism for a change in terms and conditions of employment,

their intention is to be objectively ascertained from all the relevant circumstances. In the present case, the changes in health service terms and condition brought about by Agenda for Change did not amount to a termination of the claimants' contracts of employment and replacement with new contracts, thereby triggering the time limit. The changes, which were restricted to pay, were not fundamental and were a variation to existing contracts of employment.

Powerhouse Retail Ltd v   [2006] IRLR 381 HL
Burroughs

Where there has been a relevant transfer under the Transfer of Undertakings Regulations, time begins to run, for the purposes of an equal pay claim against a transferor, from the date of the relevant TUPE transfer rather than from the end of an employee's employment with the transferee.

Gutridge v   [2009] IRLR 721 CA
Sodexo Ltd

The *Powerhouse* judgment is not limited in its application to occupational pension schemes. Accordingly, where there is a transfer of an undertaking, a claim for breach of the equality clause by the transferor must be brought against the transferee within six months of the termination of her employment with the transferor. That time limit, however, does not apply to any discrimination by the transferee which occurs during the course of the transferred employment.

Foley v   [2012] EqLR 1019 EAT
NHS Greater Glasgow & Clyde

The six-month limitation period for bringing an equal pay claim runs from the date of transfer in non-TUPE cases as well as to cases of TUPE transfers.

Preston v   [2000] IRLR 506 ECJ
Wolverhampton Healthcare NHS Trust

Where there has been a stable employment relationship resulting from a succession of short-term contracts concluded at regular intervals in respect of the same employment to which the same pension scheme applies, Community law precludes a procedural rule, which has the effect of requiring a claim for membership of an occupational pension scheme to be brought within six months of the end of each contract of employment to which the claim relates.

Preston v   [2004] IRLR 96 EAT
Wolverhampton Healthcare
   NHS Trust (No.3)

The features that characterise a "stable employment relationship" are that there is (1) a succession of short-term contracts, meaning three or more contacts for an academic year or shorter; (2) concluded at regular intervals, in that they are clearly predictable and can be calculated precisely, or where the employee is called upon frequently whenever a need arises; (3) relating to the same employment; and (4) to which the same pension scheme applies. A stable employment relationship ceases for this purpose when a succession of short-term contracts is superseded by a permanent contract.

Secretary of State for Health v   **[2007] IRLR 665 EAT**
Rance
In order for there to be a "stable employment relationship", the work done under the contract must be the same throughout. If there is a fundamental difference, time will begin to run.

North Cumbria University   **[2010] IRLR 804 EAT**
   Hospitals NHS Trust v
Fox
There was a stable employment relationship where, following implementation of Agenda for Change, the claimants continued to do the same work for the employer without any break in either the work itself or the succession of contracts. The only difference was that there were new terms and conditions, but there was no suggestion that the nature of their jobs changed materially.

REFERENCE BY COURT TO TRIBUNAL

(1) If it appears to a court in which proceedings are pending that a claim or counter-claim relating to an equality clause or rule could more conveniently be determined by an employment tribunal, the court may strike out the claim or counter-claim.

(2) If in proceedings before a court a question arises about an equality clause or rule, the court may (whether or not on an application by a party to the proceedings) –
> *(a) refer the question, or direct that it be referred by a party to the proceedings, to an employment tribunal for determination, and*
> *(b) stay or sist the proceedings in the meantime.*

EQUALITY ACT 2010 – s.128

Birmingham City Council v   **[2012] EqLR 1147 UKSC**
Abdulla
Although s.2(3) of the Equal Pay Act provided that an equal pay claim brought in the ordinary courts could be struck out by the court if it could "more conveniently" be disposed of by an employment tribunal, a claim could never be more conveniently disposed of by an employment tribunal if it was known that the employment tribunal would decline jurisdiction on the grounds that the claim was time-barred.

Birmingham City Council v   **[2012] EqLR 1147 UKSC**
Abdulla
The reasons why a claimant did not lodge a claim in respect of the operation of the statutory equality clause in the employment tribunal within the applicable six-month time limit are not relevant in any way to the notion of "convenience" set out in the statutory provisions.

CHOICE OF COMPARATOR

(1) This section applies for the purposes of this Chapter.

(2) If A is employed, B is a comparator if subsection (3) or (4) applies.

(3) This subsection applies if –
> *(a) B is employed by A's employer or by an associate of A's employer, and*
> *(b) A and B work at the same establishment.*

(4) This subsection applies if –
> *(a) B is employed by A's employer or an associate of A's employer,*
> *(b) B works at an establishment other than the one at which A works, and*
> *(c) common terms apply at the establishments (either generally or as between A and B).*

(9) For the purposes of this section, employers are associated if –
> *(a) one is a company of which the other (directly or indirectly) has control, or*
> *(b) both are companies of which a third person (directly or indirectly) has control.*

EQUALITY ACT 2010 – s.79

Ainsworth v   **[1977] IRLR 74 EAT**
Glass Tubes & Components Ltd
An employment tribunal cannot substitute its own choice of comparator for the comparator selected by the claimant.

Thomas v   **[1978] IRLR 451 EAT**
National Coal Board
There is no requirement that the comparator selected by the claimant should be representative of a group.

Macarthys Ltd v   **[1980] IRLR 210 ECJ**
Smith
The principle of equal pay in Article 141 is not confined to situations in which men and women are contemporaneously doing equal work and therefore applies where it is established that, having regard to the nature of her services, a woman has received less pay than a man who was employed prior to her employment and who did equal work for the employer.

Walton Centre for Neurology and   **[2008] IRLR 588 EAT**
   Neurosurgery NHS Trust v
Bewley
A claimant cannot bring an equal pay claim using their successor as a comparator. The exercise of comparing with a successor is too hypothetical.

Pointon v   **[1979] IRLR 119 CA**
The University of Sussex
A complaint under the equal pay legislation must relate to a term in the claimant's contract of employment that is less favourable than the equivalent term in the contract of the man with whom she is comparing herself. The equal pay legislation cannot be used to establish a claim that a claimant should have been paid more than her comparator.

Macarthys Ltd v   **[1980] IRLR 210 ECJ**
Smith

Comparisons under Article 141 are confined to parallels which may be drawn on the basis of concrete appraisals of the work actually performed by employees of different sex within the same establishment or service.

Allonby v   **[2004] IRLR 224 ECJ**
Accrington & Rossendale College

Although Article 141 is not limited to situations in which men and women work for the same employer and may be invoked in cases of discrimination arising directly from legislative provisions or collective agreements, as well as in cases in which work is carried out in the same establishment or service, where the differences identified in the pay conditions of workers performing equal work or work of equal value cannot be attributed to a single source, there is no body which is responsible for the inequality and which could restore equal treatment. Such a situation does not come within the scope of Article 141. Therefore, a woman whose contract of employment was not renewed and who was immediately made available to her previous employer through another undertaking to provide the same services was not entitled to rely on Article 141 in a claim against the new employer, using as a basis for comparison the remuneration received for equal work or work of the same value by a man employed by the woman's previous employer.

Robertson v   **[2005] IRLR 363 CA**
Department for Environment, Food
  and Rural Affairs

Having a common employer is not necessarily the same as being "in the same employment" or having pay and conditions attributed to a "single source". The critical question is whether there is a single body responsible for the discriminatory pay differences of which complaint is made. This is not determined by only addressing the formal legal question of the identity of the employer.

Robertson v   **[2005] IRLR 363 CA**
Department for Environment, Food
  and Rural Affairs

The Crown is not the "single source" responsible for unequal pay as between employees who worked in different civil service departments, since pay and conditions of civil servants are no longer negotiated or agreed centrally on a civil service-wide basis but are the responsibility of each individual department.

Armstrong v   **[2006] IRLR 124 CA**
Newcastle Upon Tyne NHS Hospital Trust

Claimants employed by a hospital trust could not use employees at another hospital of the same trust as comparators notwithstanding that the hospital trust had taken some part in the negotiation of terms and conditions at departmental level and there was some evidence of the harmonisation of terms and conditions, in circumstances in which it was found that the trust had not assumed responsibility for the terms and conditions of all the employees for the purposes of the *Robertson* test.

North Cumbria Acute Hospitals   **[2009] IRLR 176 EAT**
  NHS Trust v
Potter

The equal pay legislation does not require a single source for terms and conditions as between the claimant and her comparator.

South Ayrshire Council v   **[2002] IRLR 256 CS**
Morton

In determining whether men and women receive unequal pay for equal work, the scope of the inquiry is not always confined to the claimant's own workplace or to the claimant's own employer. If a case falls within para.21 of the decision in *Defrenne (No.2)*, as being direct discrimination having its origin in legislative provisions or in a collective agreement, a comparison is admissible and there is no need to apply the further test in para.22 of *Defrenne (No.2)* as to whether the work of the claimant and the work of the comparator is carried out in the same establishment or service.

South Ayrshire Council v   **[2002] IRLR 256 CS**
Morton

A claimant and her comparator who are in the same branch of public service and who are subject to a uniform system of national pay and conditions set by a statutory body whose decision is binding on their employers are engaged in the same "service" in the sense in which that expression is used in *Defrenne (No.2)*. Therefore, a female headteacher employed by a local education authority in Scotland was entitled to bring an equal pay claim relying on Article 141 to compare herself with a male headteacher employed by a different education authority in Scotland.

South Ayrshire Council v   **[2003] IRLR 153 CS**
Milligan

A comparator who is earning the same or less than the claimant is a valid comparator in a contingent equal pay claim, founded on the case of a comparator whose success in her own claim could result in discrimination against the claimant. Therefore, a male primary school headteacher was entitled to present his equal pay claim on a contingent basis, by naming as a comparator a female primary school headteacher whose pay currently was the same as his or less, and to have his case adjourned pending resolution of the comparator's equal pay claim comparing her work to that of male secondary school headteachers.

McLoughlin v   **[1978] IRLR 127 EAT**
Gordons (Stockport) Ltd

The equal pay legislation, is *res judicata* and cannot be heard again unless there can be shown to be some appreciable difference in the facts.

Same establishment

City of Edinburgh Council v   **[2012] IRLR 202 CS**
Wilkinson   **[2012] EqLR 54 CS**

The claimants, who worked for the respondent council primarily in schools, hostels, libraries or in social work, were not employed at the "same establishment" as their chosen male comparators also employed by the respondent but in manual roles such as road workers, refuse collectors, gardeners and grave diggers and at different physical locations. The council's undertaking did not constitute a single "establishment". The legislation treats the notion of an establishment as something distinct from the whole undertaking of the employer or associated employer and there is no presumption that an employer's whole undertaking should constitute a single establishment. The use of the preposition "at" rather than "in" in the phrase "at an establishment" conveys an association with a locality. Accordingly, the term "establishment" is largely directed to an individual's place of work, in the sense of a complex or the grouping of buildings as a whole such as a particular factory complex, campus or school.

Common terms and conditions

Lawson v   **[1988] IRLR 53 EAT**
Britfish Ltd
Once it is found that the claimants and the comparator are employed at the same establishment, whether there are common terms and conditions does not arise.

Beddoes v   **[2011] EqLR 838 EAT**
Birmingham City Council
The natural construction of the term "same employment" is that all employees of the same employer are available as comparators for equal pay purposes provided they satisfy the establishment criterion. The EAT could not accept the argument that EU law requires that in applying the concept of the "same employment", a comparison should only be between persons whose terms and conditions derived from a "single source".

British Coal Corporation v   **[1996] IRLR 404 HL**
Smith
"Common terms and conditions of employment" means terms and conditions which are substantially comparable on a broad basis, rather than the same terms and conditions subject only to de minimis differences. It is sufficient for the claimant to show that her comparator at another establishment and at her establishment were or would be employed on broadly similar terms.

North v   **[2011] IRLR 239 CS**
Dumfries and Galloway Council   **[2011] EqLR 187 CS**
In order for it to be found that as between two different establishments, "common terms and conditions of employment are observed either generally or for employees of the relevant classes", it had to be shown that were the comparators to be transferred to the claimants' place of employment their terms and conditions would be unchanged by that hypothetical transposition.

City of Edinburgh Council v   **[2012] IRLR 202 CS**
Wilkinson   **[2012] EqLR 54 CS**
The claimants, who worked for the respondent primarily in schools, hostels, libraries or in social work, and their male comparators employed in manual roles, were employed at different establishments where common terms and conditions of employment were observed, notwithstanding that the claimants and their comparators were not engaged on the

same terms and conditions since they had different pay, holiday and bonus provisions. A collective agreement may cover a variety of categories of employees, with different provision being made for each category. When considering whether the same terms and conditions are observed at different establishments, the relevant question to ask is whether, if the claimant's comparator, employed to do manual work, were to be transferred to the same establishment as the claimant for the performance of that job, would he continue to be employed on terms and conditions applicable to manual workers that were broadly similar?

South Tyneside Metropolitan   **[2007] IRLR 715 CA**
   Borough Council v
Anderson
"Common", as applied to terms and conditions, means sufficiently similar for a broad comparison to be made. Once it is found that the two employees' terms and conditions are "broadly similar", it is open to the employer to show a genuine material difference.

Leverton v   **[1989] IRLR 28 HL**
Clwyd County Council
Terms and conditions of employment governed by the same collective agreement represent the paradigm, though not necessarily the only example, of common terms and conditions of employment. Therefore, a nursery nurse was entitled to bring an equal value complaint comparing her work with that of male clerical workers employed by the respondents in different establishments where she and her comparators were employed on terms and conditions derived from the same collective agreement, notwithstanding that there were differences between her hours of work and holiday entitlement and those of her comparators.

Thomas v   **[1987] IRLR 451 EAT**
National Coal Board
There were "common terms and conditions of employment" between establishments for the relevant employees, notwithstanding that locally negotiated and varying bonus payments and concessionary entitlements formed a substantial part of remuneration, where the entitlement to bonuses and concessions was negotiated nationally, and it was only the amount which varied locally, so that the basic similarity of terms and conditions was not affected.

South Tyneside Metropolitan   **[2007] IRLR 715 CA**
   Borough Council v
Anderson
There were common terms and conditions as between local authority female school support staff and men employed by the local authority on the same grades, notwithstanding that none of the men worked in schools.

Associated employers

Hasley v   **[1989] IRLR 106 NICA**
Fair Employment Agency
The first limb of the statutory definition of associated employers, correctly interpreted, means that two employ-

ers are to be treated as associated if one employer is a company of which the other employer (not necessarily a company) has control. The second limb covers where both employers are companies of which a third person (not necessarily a company) has control.

Hasley v   **[1989] IRLR 106 NICA**
Fair Employment Agency
A statutory body corporate is not a "company" within the meaning of the statutory definition of associated employers.

LIKE WORK

(2) A's work is like B's work if –
    (a) A's work and B's work are the same or broadly similar, and
    (b) such differences as there are between their work are not of practical importance in relation to the terms of their work.

(3) So on a comparison of one person's work with another's for the purposes of subsection (2), it is necessary to have regard to –
    (a) the frequency with which differences between their work occur in practice, and
    (b) the nature and extent of the differences.

EQUALITY ACT 2010 – s.65

Capper Pass Ltd v   **[1976] IRLR 366 EAT**
Lawton
Whether a man and a woman are employed on like work is to be approached in two stages. First, is the work which she does and the work which he does of the same or of a broadly similar nature? This can be answered by a general consideration of the type of work involved and the skill and knowledge required to do it. Second, if it is work of a broadly similar nature, are the differences between the things she does and the things he does of practical importance in relation to terms and conditions of employment? Once it is determined that work is of a broadly similar nature, it should be regarded as being "like work" unless the differences are plainly of a kind which the employment tribunal in its experience would expect to find reflected in the terms and conditions of employment. Trivial differences, or differences not likely in the real world to be reflected in terms and conditions of employment, ought to be disregarded.

Capper Pass Ltd v   **[1976] IRLR 366 EAT**
Lawton
In deciding whether the work done by a woman and the work done by a man is "like work", the employment tribunal has to make a broad judgment. The intention is that the employment tribunal should not be required to undertake too minute an examination, nor be constrained to find that work is not like work, merely because of insubstantial differences.

Maidment and Hardacre v   **[1978] IRLR 462 EAT**
Cooper & Co (Birmingham) Ltd
The equal pay legislation does not allow for a gap in remuneration to be narrowed so that it truly reflects the difference in the value of the work done by a claimant and her comparator. If the complainant and her comparator are not employed on like work, it is irrelevant that the gap in remuneration between them is in no way commensurate to the difference in the work which they do.

DIFFERENCES OF PRACTICAL IMPORTANCE

E Coomes (Holdings) Ltd v   **[1978] IRLR 263 CA**
Shields
The equal pay legislation requires a comparison to be made

between the things that the woman and the man actually do and the frequency with which they are done, rather than between their respective contractual obligations.

Electrolux Ltd v   **[1976] IRLR 410 EAT**
Hutchinson

For differences in contractual obligations to amount to a difference of practical importance in relation to terms and conditions, it must be shown that, as well as being contractually obliged to do additional different duties, the duties are performed to some significant extent.

British Leyland Ltd v   **[1978] IRLR 57 EAT**
Powell

In determining whether differences in the things done by a man and those done by a woman are of "practical importance in relation to terms and conditions of employment", a practical guide is whether the differences (which ex hypothesi are not sufficient to make the work not of the same or a broadly similar nature) are such as to put the two employments into different categories or grades in an evaluation study.

Responsibility

Eaton Ltd v   **[1977] IRLR 71 EAT**
Nuttall

In considering whether there is like work, the circumstances in which the man and the woman do their work should not be disregarded. One of the circumstances properly to be taken into account is the degree of responsibility involved in carrying out the job. A factor such as responsibility may be decisive where it can be seen to put one employee into a different grade from another with whom comparisons are being made.

Waddington v   **[1977] IRLR 32 EAT**
Leicester Council for Voluntary
   Services

An obligation to supervise, to take responsibility or to control, if it is discharged, falls within the words "the things she does and the things they do".

Thomas v   **[1987] IRLR 451 EAT**
National Coal Board

The additional responsibility entailed in working permanently at night, alone and without supervision can amount to a "difference of practical importance in relation to terms and conditions of employment".

Time of work

Dugdale v   **[1976] IRLR 368 EAT**
Kraft Foods Ltd

In determining whether men and women are employed on like work, the mere time at which the work is performed should be disregarded when considering the differences between the things that the women do and the things which the men do.

National Coal Board v   **[1978] IRLR 122 EAT**
Sherwin

If the man and the woman do the same work, the mere fact that they do it at different times is of no importance. The disadvantage of working at night, or at other inconvenient times, can be compensated by an additional night shift premium or other appropriate arrangement, but there is no reason why the man should receive by way of remuneration a sum which is greater than necessary to recognise the fact that he works at night, or at other inconvenient times, and if he does there is no reason why the woman should not be remunerated to the extent of the excess. An employment tribunal is entitled to adjust the woman's remuneration upon a claim by her so that it is at the same rate as the man's, discounting for the fact that he works at inconvenient hours, and she does not.

Maidment and Hardacre v   **[1978] IRLR 462 EAT**
Cooper & Co (Birmingham) Ltd

In applying the test of like work, it is not permissible to ignore some part of the work which the man actually does on the ground that his pay includes an additional element in respect of that work, which can be discounted. There is no warrant for the exclusion or hiving-off of some part of the activities of the comparator. There can be no question of discounting, or of applying the equality clause, until it has been established that the man and the woman are employed on like work, so that it cannot be right in order to determine that question to pray in aid a result which could only be arrived at after deciding that they were engaged on like work.

WORK RATED AS EQUIVALENT

(4) A's work is rated as equivalent to B's work if a job evaluation study –

(a) gives an equal value to A's job and B's job in terms of the demands made on a worker, or

(b) would give an equal value to A's job and B's job in those terms were the evaluation not made on a sex-specific system.

(5) A system is sex-specific if, for the purposes of one or more of the demands made on a worker, it sets values for men different from those it sets for women.

EQUALITY ACT 2010 – s.65

Bromley v   **[1988] IRLR 249 CA**
H & J Quick Ltd

A job evaluation scheme must be "analytical" in order to comply with the equal pay legislation. The word "analytical" indicates conveniently the general nature of what is required by the section, viz that the jobs of each worker covered by the study must have been valued in terms of the demand made on the worker under various headings. It is not enough that benchmark jobs have been evaluated on a factor demand basis as required by the equal pay legislation if the jobs of the claimants and their comparators were not.

Eaton Ltd v   **[1977] IRLR 71 EAT**
Nuttall

The equal pay legislation can only apply to a valid evaluation study – that is, a study satisfying the test of being thorough in analysis and capable of impartial application. It should be possible by applying the study to arrive at the position of a particular employee at a particular point in a particular salary grade without taking other matters into account, except those unconnected with the nature of the work. An evaluation study which does not satisfy that test, and which requires the management to make a subjective judgment concerning the nature of the work before the employee can be fitted in at the appropriate place in the appropriate salary grade would not be a valid study for the purposes of equal pay legislation.

Arnold v   **[1982] IRLR 307 EAT**
Beecham Group Ltd

Before the equal pay legislation can be applied, there must be a completed job evaluation study, and there is no complete job evaluation study unless and until the parties who have agreed to carry out the study have accepted its validity. However, it is not the stage of implementing the study by using it as the basis of the payment of remuneration that makes it complete; it is the stage at which it is accepted as a study.

O'Brien v   **[1980] IRLR 373 HL**
Sim-Chem Ltd

Once a job evaluation study has been undertaken and has resulted in a conclusion that the job of a woman is of equal value with that of a man, then a comparison of their respective terms and conditions is made feasible and, subject to the material factor defence, the equality clause can take effect. It is not necessary for the pay structure to have been adjusted as a result of the conclusions of the job evaluation study.

Springboard Sunderland Trust v   **[1992] IRLR 261 EAT**
Robson

In determining whether two jobs have been given an equal value, so as to be work rated as equivalent, it is necessary to have regard to the full results of the job evaluation scheme, including the allocation to grade or scale at the end of the evaluation process.

EQUAL VALUE

(6) A's work is of equal value to B's work if it is –
(a) neither like B's work nor rated as equivalent to B's work, but
(b) nevertheless equal to B's work in terms of the demands made on A by reference to factors such as effort, skill and decision-making.

EQUALITY ACT 2010 – s.65

(6) The tribunal must determine that A's work is not of equal value to B's work unless it has reasonable grounds for suspecting that the evaluation contained in the study –
(a) was based on a system that discriminates because of sex, or
(b) is otherwise unreliable.

(7) For the purposes of subsection (6)(a), a system discriminates because of sex if a difference (or coincidence) between values that the system sets on different demands is not justifiable regardless of the sex of the person on whom the demands are made.

EQUALITY ACT 2010 – s.131

SCOPE FOR COMPARISON

Pickstone v   **[1988] IRLR 357 HL**
Freemans plc
The equal pay legislation does not preclude a woman employed on like work or work rated as equivalent with one man from claiming that she is employed on work of equal value to that of another man.

Murphy v   **[1988] IRLR 267 ECJ**
Bord Telecom Eireann
Article 141 of the EC Treaty must be interpreted as covering the case where a worker who relies on that provision to obtain equal pay within the meaning thereof is engaged in work of higher value than that of the person with whom a comparison is to be made.

Redcar & Cleveland Borough   **[2008] IRLR 776 CA**
    Council v
Bainbridge (No.2)
Claimants are entitled to put forward all their equal pay claims cumulatively, although the amount of the arrears of pay recovered as a result of successfully putting the equal pay claim in one way will reduce the amount recoverable as a result of successfully putting the claim in a different way.

Redcar & Cleveland Borough   **[2008] IRLR 776 CA**
    Council v
Bainbridge (No.2)
It is not permissible to allege a new cause of action in respect of a particular pay period in another action under the same head for the same pay period simply by selecting a different comparator. For a new cause of action for the same period it would be necessary to bring the equal pay claim under a different head, which would normally involve different comparators as well.

JOB EVALUATION

(5) Subsection (6) applies where –
(a) a question arises in the proceedings as to whether the work of one person (A) is of equal value to the work of another (B), and
(b) A's work and B's work have been given different values by a job evaluation study.

Burden of proof

Dibro Ltd v   **[1990] IRLR 129 EAT**
Hore
Provided that a job evaluation scheme is analytical and a valid one and relates to facts and circumstances existing at the time when the equal value proceedings were instituted, it does not matter that it came into existence after the initiation of proceedings. It is open to an employer to utilise such a scheme as evidence at any stage up to the final hearing, after the independent expert's report has been admitted, at which the tribunal gives its decision on the whole of the evidence.

Bainbridge v   **[2007] IRLR 494 EAT**
Redcar & Cleveland Borough
    Council (No.2)
An equal rating under a job evaluation scheme is not the same as establishing that the two jobs so rated are necessarily of equal value. There are two elements to a job evaluation study. There is the evaluation of the jobs; then there is the fixing of grade boundaries. It is not uncommon for jobs to be fitted into grades where there may be real distinctions in the value of the jobs.

Hovell v   **[2009] IRLR 734 CA**
Ashford and St Peter's Hospital
    NHS Trust
The fact that there is a small difference in the points given by a job evaluation study does not of itself establish that two jobs are of equal value. Equal value does not mean nearly equal value. However, jobs may be equal in value even though not precisely equal in points scored. It follows that a tribunal does not necessarily have to have the benefit of an independent expert before it can find equality where the claimant's job has been marked lower than the comparator's job in the job evaluation study.

Work rated unequal

Bromley v   **[1988] IRLR 249 CA**
H & J Quick Ltd
The equal pay legislation requires a study undertaken with a view to evaluating jobs in terms of the demand made on a worker under various headings (for instance effort, skill, decision). It is necessary that both the work of the woman

complainant and the work of her male comparator should have been valued in such terms of demand made on the worker under various headings.

Dibro Ltd v   **[1990] IRLR 129 EAT**
Hore
A job evaluation scheme advanced by the employer must compare the jobs as they were being carried out at the date the proceedings were issued and not compare a job or jobs which may have been changed since the initiation of proceedings.

Bromley v   **[1988] IRLR 249 CA**
H & J Quick Ltd
There was not a valid job-evaluation study where the jobs of the women and their comparators were slotted into the structure on a "whole job" basis and no comparison was made by reference to the selected factors between the demands made on the individual workers under the selected headings. That at an appeal stage two of the women's jobs were evaluated in terms of their demands under the selected factors made no difference to the outcome in their cases, since there was never any appeal by their comparator. Nor was it sufficient that every worker covered by the study had a right of appeal which if exercised would have led to an analysis of their jobs.

INDEPENDENT EXPERT'S REPORT

(1) Expert evidence shall be restricted to that which, in the opinion of the tribunal, is reasonably required to resolve the proceedings.

(3) No party may call an expert or put in evidence an expert's report without the permission of the tribunal. No expert report shall be put in evidence unless it has been disclosed to all other parties and any independent expert at least 28 days prior to the hearing.

(4) In proceedings in which an independent expert has been required to prepare a report on the question, the tribunal shall not admit evidence of another expert on the question unless such evidence is based on the facts relating to the question. Unless the tribunal considers it inappropriate to do so, any such expert report shall be disclosed to all parties and to the tribunal on the same date on which the independent expert is required to send his report to the parties and to the tribunal.

EMPLOYMENT TRIBUNALS (CONSTITUTION AND RULES OF PROCEDURE) REGULATIONS 2004: Schedule 6, rule 11

Leverton v   **[1989] IRLR 28 HL**
Clwyd County Council
An independent expert has to carry out what is, in effect, an ad hoc job evaluation study as between a complainant and her comparators and assess the demands of the job on a qualitative, rather than a quantitative, basis.

Leverton v   **[1989] IRLR 28 HL**
Clwyd County Council
Per Lord Bridge: Differences in hours of work and holidays between a complainant and her comparators are not a matter for assessment by the independent expert when considering the "demands" made upon them by their respective jobs.

Potter v   **[2009] IRLR 22 EAT**
North Cumbria Acute Hospitals NHS Trust
Whether a claimant's work and the work of comparator are of equal value must be considered in respect of every part of the claim period. Where there have, or may have, been material changes in a claimant's or comparator's job, or in its content, over the claim period, therefore, the facts will have to be found on a distinct basis in respect of the different parts of the period.

Tennants Textile Colours Ltd v   **[1989] IRLR 3 NICA**
Todd
The burden of proving an equal pay claim is on the claimant. The burden of proof is not transferred to the employer if the independent expert's report is in favour of the claimant.

Middlesbrough Borough Council v   **[2007] IRLR 981 EAT**
Surtees
Rule 11(4) does not deprive the tribunal of the power to hear an expert called by a party. What the party's expert

can give evidence about must exclude the facts that are not to be challenged and which represent a sacrosanct position following findings or agreement at an earlier stage in the proceedings. Given the restricted scope of challenge to facts, an expert is there to challenge methodology. The system of job evaluation is one which is susceptible to different methodologies.

DEFENCES

(1) The sex equality clause in A's terms has no effect in relation to a difference between A's terms and B's terms if the responsible person shows that the difference is because of a material factor reliance on which –

(a) does not involve treating A less favourably because of A's sex than the responsible person treats B, and

(b) if the factor is within subsection (2), is a proportionate means of achieving a legitimate aim.

(2) A factor is within this subsection if A shows that, as a result of the factor, A and persons of the same sex doing work equal to A's are put at a particular disadvantage when compared with persons of the opposite sex doing work equal to A's.

(3) For the purposes of subsection (1), the long-term objective of reducing inequality between men's and women's terms of work is always to be regarded as a legitimate aim.

(6) For the purposes of this section, a factor is not material unless it is a material difference between A's case and B's

EQUALITY ACT 2010 – s.69

BURDEN OF PROOF

Enderby v   **[1993] IRLR 591 ECJ**
Frenchay Health Authority and
Secretary of State for Health
There is a prima facie case of sex discrimination where valid statistics disclose an appreciable difference in pay between two jobs of equal value, one of which is carried out almost exclusively by women and other predominantly by men. It is for the national court to assess whether the statistics appear to be significant in that they cover enough individuals and do not illustrate purely fortuitous or short-term phenomena.

Enderby v   **[1993] IRLR 591 ECJ**
Frenchay Health Authority and
Secretary of State for Health
Where there is a prima facie case of discrimination, Article 141 of the EC Treaty requires the employer to show that the difference in pay is based on objectively justified factors unrelated to any discrimination on grounds of sex. Workers would be unable to enforce the principle of equal pay before national courts if evidence of a prima facie case did not shift to the employer the onus of showing that the pay differential is not in fact discriminatory.

Brunnhofer v   **[2001] IRLR 571 ECJ**
Bank der österreichischen
Postsparkasse
If the employee adduces evidence to show that the criteria for establishing the existence of a difference in pay between a woman and a man and for identifying comparable work are satisfied, a prima facie case of discrimination would exist, and it is then for the employer to prove that there was no breach of the principle of equal pay. To do this, the employer

could deny that the conditions for the application of the principle were met, by establishing that the activities actually performed by the two employees were not in fact comparable. The employer could also justify the difference in pay by objective factors, by proving that there was a difference unrelated to sex to explain the comparator's higher pay.

Glasgow City Council v Marshall [2000] IRLR 272 HL

If there is any evidence of sex discrimination, such as evidence that the difference in pay has a disparately adverse impact on women, the employer will be called upon to satisfy the tribunal that the difference in pay is objectively justifiable.

Bury Metropolitan Council v Hamilton [2011] IRLR 358 EAT [2011] EqLR 214 EAT
Council of the City of Sunderland v Brennan

An employer discharges the burden of proving an explanation simply by showing at a factual level how the state of affairs complained of came about. The real battleground comes at the next stage, where the tribunal has to consider whether there has in fact been sex discrimination, which will in turn, whenever the necessary gender disproportion is shown, turn on the issue of objective justification.

Gibson v Sheffield City Council [2010] IRLR 311 CA

A productivity bonus which applied only to men's work had a sexual taint and a disparately adverse effect on women's work as compared with men's work. Therefore, it had to be justified objectively by the employers.

Middlesbrough Borough Council v Surtees [2007] IRLR 869 EAT

Where the criterion which the employer chooses to differentiate pay scales impacts adversely on women because of the position of women in society, the pay arrangements are inevitably tainted by sex and the obligation to justify arises. Secondly, where the disadvantage to women as a group, typically gleaned from statistics, is sufficiently striking, it may be justified to draw the inference that the difference in pay reflects traditional attitudes about what is appropriate male and female work and pay, even though no obvious discriminatory factor is identified. A third situation is where the difference in pay is caused by a particular factor that is applied only to the predominantly male group. In those circumstances, it will be sex-tainted unless the employer can show that there are non-discriminatory reasons why the factor has been applied so as to only benefit the male group.

Coventry City Council v Nicholls [2009] IRLR 345 EAT

If it is possible to make a payment only to an almost exclusively male group, because of particular features of their job not shared by the female claimants, then it necessarily involves a form of prima facie indirect discrimination against those women in that the payment is being made by reference to characteristics of a job which in practice are held by job-holders who are predominantly of one sex only. Such payments will be unlawful unless they can be justified.

Cumbria County Council v Dow (No.1) [2008] IRLR 91 EAT

That there is job segregation along traditional sex lines does not inevitably mean that the particular differential must be sex tainted, but in such cases the difficulty of establishing otherwise will be a heavy one.

Barry v Midland Bank plc [1999] IRLR 581 HL

A claim of indirect discrimination contrary to Article 141 requires the claimant to show that she belongs to a group of employees which is differently and less well-treated than others, and that that difference affects considerably more women than men. If she can, the employer must show that the difference in treatment is objectively justified.

Grundy v British Airways plc [2008] IRLR 74 CA

In determining whether a pay disparity has a disproportionate adverse impact on women, there is no principle of law which requires the tribunal always to base its test on the advantaged cohort. The pool must be one which suitably tests the particular discrimination complained of, but this does not mean that there is a single suitable pool for every case. Provided it tests the allegation in a suitable pool, the tribunal cannot be said to have erred in law even if a different pool, with a different outcome, could equally legitimately have been chosen.

Cheshire & Wirral Partnership NHS Trust v Abbott [2006] IRLR 546 CA

Although in a case of indirect sex discrimination in pay it is for the employee to identify a comparator group and to produce statistical evidence to show an appreciable difference in pay for jobs of equal value, the employee is not entitled to identify an artificial or arbitrary group. In principle, the comparison should be between the disadvantaged group and the advantaged group. As a matter of statistics, a more reliable result is likely to be forthcoming if one takes as large a group as possible, so long as that group shares the relevant characteristics and can be seen as doing work of equal value.

Schonheit v Stadt Frankfurt am Main [2004] IRLR 983 ECJ

A difference in treatment between men and women may be justified, depending on the circumstances, by reasons other than those put forward when the measure introducing the differential treatment was adopted. It is for the Member State which has introduced such a measure, or the party who invokes it, to establish before the national court that there are objective reasons unrelated to any discrimination on grounds of sex such as to justify the measure concerned, and they are not bound in that respect by the intention expressed when the measure was adopted.

Cadman v Health and Safety Executive [2004] IRLR 971 CA

There is no rule of law that the justification must have consciously and contemporaneously featured in the decision-making processes of the employer, and cannot be "after the event" arguments.

British Airways plc v   **[2008] IRLR 815 CA**
Grundy (No.2)

There is a telling difference between cases in which the disparate impact of a new contractual provision has been recognised and its justifiability considered before adopting it, and cases in which the impact is initially not recognised, then denied, then found to exist and then sought to be justified. While justification in retrospect is perfectly admissible, it is probably going to start from a lower evidential base.

Tyldesley v   **[1996] IRLR 395 EAT**
TML Plastics Ltd

A differential which is explained by careless mistake, which could not possibly be objectively justified, amounts to a defence, provided the tribunal is satisfied that the mistake was of sufficient influence to be significant or relevant. If a genuine mistake suffices, so must a genuine perception, whether reasonable or not, about the need to engage an individual with particular experience, commitment and skills.

GROUNDS FOR THE PAY DIFFERENCE

Bilka-Kaufhaus GmbH v   **[1986] IRLR 317 ECJ**
Weber von Hartz

A policy which applies independently of a worker's sex but in fact affects more women than men will not constitute an infringement of Article 141 if the employer shows that the policy is objectively justified on economic grounds. This requires a finding by the national court that the measures chosen by the employer correspond to a real need on the part of the undertaking, are appropriate with a view to achieving the objectives pursued and are necessary to that end.

Rainey v   **[1987] IRLR 26 HL**
Greater Glasgow Health Board

Although the European Court in the *Bilka-Kaufhaus* case referred to "economic" grounds objectively justified, read as a whole the ruling of the European Court would not exclude objectively justified grounds which are other than economic, such as administrative efficiency in a concern not engaged in commerce or business.

Redcar & Cleveland Borough   **[2007] IRLR 91 EAT**
   Council v
 Bainbridge

It is inherent in the principle of proportionality that where different means of achieving a particular objective could be achieved, the one which has the least discriminatory impact should be chosen. A tribunal considering objective justification, therefore, is obliged to have regard to whether different and less discriminatory means could have been used to achieve the same objective.

Rainey v   **[1987] IRLR 26 HL**
Greater Glasgow Health Board

A difference between the woman's case and the man's must be "material", which means "significant and relevant".

Waddington v   **[1977] IRLR 32 EAT**
Leicester Council for Voluntary Services

Usually the material difference will not be differences between the things the woman does and the things the man does in the course of the work.

Davies v   **[1989] IRLR 439 EAT**
McCartneys

The factors which form the basis for a defence can also be factors relevant in determining the demands of the jobs for the purpose of assessing equal value. However, an employer should not be allowed simply to say, "I value one demand factor so highly that I pay more," unless his true reason for so doing is one which is found by the tribunal to be genuine and not attributable to sex.

Redcar & Cleveland Borough   **[2008] IRLR 776 CA**
   Council v
Bainbridge (No.2)

A tribunal has to find what the reason was for the pay differential and, if necessary, should look at the underlying reason and not merely the immediate reason or criterion for inclusion/exclusion. It is right to examine the underlying or historical position where that will throw light on the reason why one person is receiving an advantage and another is excluded from it.

Armstrong v   **[2006] IRLR 124 CA**
Newcastle Upon Tyne NHS Hospital Trust

It cannot be said that a failure to deprive male comparators of part of their income in the form of a bonus was discriminatory, if the assumption is that their original receipt of that part of their income was not discriminatory. Accordingly, an employment tribunal erred in finding that even if a disparity had been justified when it was introduced, the continuation over time of a system whereby more men than women received bonuses was indirectly discriminatory.

Secretary of State for Justice v   **[2012] IRLR 382 EAT**
Bowling   **[2012 EqLR 109 EAT**

An employer made out a valid defence when it established that the difference in pay paid to the claimant and her male comparator was due to the fact that he had been placed on a higher spinal point on an incremental scale on appointment, due to his greater skill and experience at that time, and then progressed up the salary scale ahead of her, notwithstanding that over time she "caught up" in terms of experience and skill. The original explanation was still the operative cause of the difference in pay and had nothing to do with gender.

SEX DISCRIMINATION

British Coal Corporation v   **[1994] IRLR 342 CA**
Smith
North Yorkshire County Council v
Ratcliffe

A "material factor" defence must fail if the employer

cannot prove that the material factor relied upon was not tainted by sex.

Glasgow City Council v Marshall
[2000] IRLR 272 HL

In order to discharge the burden of showing that the explanation for the variation is not tainted with sex the employer must satisfy the tribunal on several matters. First, that the proffered explanation, or reason, is genuine, and not a sham or pretence. Second, that the less favourable treatment is due to this reason. The factor relied upon must be the cause of the disparity. The factor must be "material" in a causative sense, rather than in a justificatory sense. Third, that the reason is not "the difference of sex", which is apt to embrace any form of sex discrimination, whether direct or indirect.

Bury Metropolitan Council v Hamilton
[2011] IRLR 358 EAT
[2011] EqLR 214 EAT

Council of the City of Sunderland v Brennan

The explanation, or cause, of a state of affairs is not definitively established simply by showing its historical origins. In the case of direct discrimination, it may be pertinent to consider not only why the differential in question first arose but why it was maintained, particularly if the relevant circumstances may have changed. In the case of indirect discrimination, gender proportions as between the advantaged and disadvantaged groups may have changed, or there may be reasons why a justification which was once good no longer remained so.

Snoxell v Vauxhall Motors Ltd
[1977] IRLR 123 EAT

An employer can never establish that a variation between the woman's contract and the man's contract is genuinely due to a material difference (other than the difference of sex) between her case and his when it can be seen that past sex discrimination has contributed to the variation.

Skills Development Scotland v Co Ltd
[2011] EqLR 955 EAT

Buchanan

The mere effluxion of time does not cause a gender-neutral explanation for a difference in pay to lose its "non–sex" character, although passage of time could be one amongst all the relevant factors relied upon by the claimant in any given case to challenge the genuine nature of the employer's explanation.

Coventry City Council v Nicholls
[2009] IRLR 345 EAT

Union hostility to change is incapable of constituting a new explanation for a difference in pay such that it can be said that a pay differential the roots of which lay firmly in sex discrimination has at some indeterminate point ceased to have anything to do with sex. The union's stance may explain why the discrimination was not removed earlier, but it does not replace the original discriminatory explanation for the difference in pay.

SPECIFIC DEFENCES

Collective agreements

Enderby v Frenchay Health Authority and Secretary of State for Health
[1993] IRLR 591 ECJ

The fact that the respective rates of pay of two jobs of equal value, one carried out almost exclusively by women and the other predominantly by men, were arrived at by collective bargaining processes which, although carried out by the same parties, were distinct, and conducted separately and without any discriminatory effect within each group, is not sufficient objective justification for the difference in pay between those two jobs.

British Road Services Ltd v Loughran
[1997] IRLR 92 NICA

Separate pay structures based on different collective agreements are not a sufficient defence if the claimants are members of a class of which a "significant" number are female. The European Court's use of the term "almost exclusively" women in Enderby was merely a reference to the facts of that case and did not intend to propound a principle that unless the disadvantaged group could be described as being composed "almost exclusively" of females, a presumption of discrimination could not arise.

Clark v Metropolitan Police Authority
[2011] EqLR 1026 Mayor's and City of London Ct

The mere fact that pay arrangements which treated part-time workers less favourably were the result of collective bargaining did not amount to a valid justification of the pay arrangement when, at the time of the pay negotiations, no consideration was given to the difference in treatment which resulted from the negotiated agreement or its impact on women or part-time employees in general.

Specialarbejderforbundet i Danmark v Dansk Industri, acting for Royal Copenhagen
[1995] IRLR 648 ECJ

The fact that rates of pay have been determined by collective bargaining or by negotiation at local level may be taken into account by the national court as a factor in its assessment of whether differences between the average pay of two groups of workers are due to objective factors unrelated to any discrimination on grounds of sex.

Redcar & Cleveland Borough Council v Bainbridge (No.2)
[2008] IRLR 776 CA

The fact that different jobs have been the subject of separate collective bargaining can be a defence to an equal pay claim in that the reason for the difference in pay for those jobs has been separate collective bargaining, not the difference of sex of the employees. Such a case could occur, for instance, where two different groups are of similar proportions by gender, but one of the groups earns less than the other. The position would be otherwise where there is a marked difference in the sex balance between the different groups, which would be evidence from which the tribunal could infer that the process was sex-tainted, unless the employer provided a different explanation.

Quality of work

Handels- og Kontorfunktionaerernes   **[1989] IRLR 532 ECJ**
  Forbund i Danmark v
Dansk Arbejdsgiverforening
  (acting for Danfoss)
EC Equal Pay legislation must be interpreted as meaning that the quality of the work carried out by the worker may not be used as a criterion for pay increments where its application shows itself to be systematically unfavourable to women. Where an assessment of the quality of work results in systematic unfairness to female workers, that could only be because the employer applied the criterion in an abusive manner. It is inconceivable that the work carried out by female workers would be generally of a lower quality.

Productivity

Council of the City of Sunderland v   **[2012] IRLR 507 CA**
Brennan   **[2012] EqLR 480 CA**
A finding of fact by the employment tribunal that bonuses paid to male comparators but not to the female claimants whose work was rated as equivalent were no longer related to productivity made the employer's argument that the bonuses were paid for a non-discriminatory reason unsustainable. Given the finding that the additional amount paid to the comparators no longer represented a reward for the level of work, the respondent could not discharge the burden of showing objective justification for the pay differential.

Cumbria County Council v   **[2008] IRLR 91 EAT**
Dow (No.1)
Improving productivity is a legitimate aim, but the means used must be proportionate to that aim. A tribunal is entitled to seek evidence that productivity had increased as a result of improvements in the performance of the workers themselves. Without a proper application of the scheme, the benefits were not being achieved. It cannot be proportionate to pay bonuses to achieve a legitimate objective if that objective is not in any meaningful way being realised. Where the payment cannot be justified, it is in essence part of the basic wage.

Additional obligations

Handels- og Kontorfunktionaerernes   **[1989] IRLR 532 ECJ**
  Forbund i Danmark v
Dansk Arbejdsgiverforening
  (acting for Danfoss)
EC Equal Pay legislation must be interpreted as meaning that where the adaptability of the employee to variable

work schedules and places of work is used as a criterion for pay increments and this works systematically to the disadvantage of female workers who, as a result of household and family duties, may have greater difficulty than male workers in organising their working time in a flexible manner, the employer may justify the use of the criterion by demonstrating that such adaptability is important for the performance of the specific duties entrusted to the worker.

National Coal Board v   **[1978] IRLR 122 EAT**
Sherwin
An employment tribunal that found that a difference between the woman's pay and the pay of a man employed on like work was greater than could be justified by the fact that the man worked permanently on the night shift alone was entitled to conclude that the employers had failed to show that the difference to which the variation in pay was genuinely due was other than a difference of sex. The tribunal were therefore entitled to order that the women should be paid at the same rate as the man after making a proper, but not excessive, discount for the fact that he worked permanently at night alone.

Training

Handels- og Kontorfunktionaerernes   **[1989] IRLR 532 ECJ**
  Forbund i Danmark v
Dansk Arbejdsgiverforening
  (acting for Danfoss)
EC Equal Pay legislation must be interpreted as meaning that where the worker's vocational training is used as a criterion for pay increments and this works systematically to the disadvantage of female workers, the employer may justify the use of the criterion of vocational training by demonstrating that such training is important for the performance of specific duties entrusted to the worker.

Service payments

Cadman v   **[2006] IRLR 969 ECJ**
Health & Safety Executive
An employer does not have to establish specifically that recourse to length of service as a determinant of pay is appropriate as regards a particular job to attain the legitimate objective of rewarding experience acquired which enables the worker to perform his duties better, unless the worker provides evidence capable of raising serious doubts in that regard.

Cadman v   **[2006] IRLR 969 ECJ**
Health & Safety Executive
Where the worker provides evidence capable of giving rise to serious doubts as to whether recourse to the criterion of length of service is, in the circumstances, appropriate to attain the objective of rewarding experience that enables the worker to perform his duties better, then it is for the employer to justify in detail recourse to the criterion of length of service by proving, as regards the job in question, that length

of service goes hand in hand with experience and that experience enables the worker to perform his duties better.

Cadman v   **[2006] IRLR 969 ECJ**
Health & Safety Executive
Where pay is based on a job evaluation system, if the objective pursued by using the criterion of length of service is to recognise experience, there is no need for the employer to show that an individual worker has acquired experience during the relevant period which has enabled him to perform his duties better.

Wilson v   **[2010] IRLR 59 CA**
Health & Safety Executive
An employer can be required to provide objective justification for use of a length of service criterion as well as its adoption in the first place. The employer must justify where the claimant has shown that there is evidence from which, if established at trial, it can properly be found that the general rule that a length of service criterion can be used should not apply because its adoption or use was disproportionate.

Hill v   **[1998] IRLR 466 ECJ**
Revenue Commissioners
Rules which treat full-time workers who previously job-shared at a disadvantage compared with other full-time workers by applying a criterion of service calculated by length of time actually worked in a post, and therefore placing them on the full-time pay scale at a level lower than that which they occupied on the pay scale applicable to jobsharing, must in principle be treated as contrary to Article 141, where 98% of those employed under jobsharing contracts are women.

Hill v   **[1998] IRLR 466 ECJ**
Revenue Commissioners
An employer cannot justify discrimination arising from a jobsharing scheme solely on the ground that avoidance of such discrimination would involve increased costs.

Protected pay

Snoxell v   **[1977] IRLR 123 EAT**
Vauxhall Motors Ltd
Where it can be shown that there is a group of employees who have had their wages protected for causes neither directly nor indirectly due to a difference of sex, and where male and female employees, doing the same work, who are not in this "red circle" are treated alike, an employer may succeed in establishing a defence.

Fearnon v   **[2009] IRLR 132 NICA**
Smurfit Corrugated Cases (Lurgan) Ltd
The judgment in *Snoxell* did not suggest that the length of time that a discrepancy in salary has endured because of red-circling is irrelevant to the question of whether it can continue to be a genuine material factor. To qualify as a contemporaneous genuine material factor accounting for the discrepancy in salary, the reasons for red-circling

at the time that the difference in earnings is challenged must be examined. Otherwise, it would be possible for an unscrupulous employer to allow a difference in earnings to persist while knowing that the initial reason for it no longer obtained. It is wrong to assume that because it was right to institute the system, it will remain right to maintain it indefinitely.

Bury Metropolitan Council v   **[2011] IRLR 358 EAT**
Hamilton   **[2011] EqLR 214 EAT**
Council of the City of Sunderland v
Brennan
There is no universal answer to the question of whether pay protection arrangements could be justified, nor even any single touchstone by which those arrangements that could be justified can be distinguished from those that could not. The question is one for the assessment of the tribunal, in each case applying the established test of proportionality. An important factor is the extent to which it must or should have been clear to the employer that its previous non-payment of bonus to claimants involved unlawful discrimination: whether, taking a broad view, the employer knew or should have known that its previous pay arrangements were discriminatory. Employers will not be able to justify withholding pay protection from claimants without advancing cogent and specific reasons for what is in effect a continuation (albeit limited) of past discrimination.

Redcar & Cleveland Borough   **[2008] IRLR 776 CA**
  Council v
Bainbridge (No.2)
Transitional arrangements that continue past indirect discrimination will not be unlawful if they can be justified. However, where the old indirect discrimination has been recognised, the employer will have great difficulty in justifying the continuation of any discriminatory element. That is because he must do his best to comply with the fundamental principle of equal pay. Nevertheless, it is still possible for an employer to justify where he is aware of the past discrimination by demonstrating that he had done all he could to minimise the effect of the continuing discrimination but was unable to eliminate it immediately. Where an employer is reorganising his pay structures and there is no reason to think that the old arrangements were directly or indirectly discriminatory, he will be entitled to bring in the new arrangements by transitional provisions. Thus, the employer's state of knowledge about the discriminatory effect of his provisions and the extent to which he tries to minimise that effect will be relevant considerations for whether the employer's discriminatory means are an appropriate and proportionate means of achieving his legitimate objective.

Redcar & Cleveland Borough   **[2008] IRLR 776 CA**
  Council v
Bainbridge (No.2)
Pay protection arrangements were rooted in past sex discrimination and had to be justified by the employer where the underlying reason the male comparators were receiving pay protection and the women claimants were not was because the women, unlike the men, did not suffer a drop in pay when a job evaluation scheme was implemented

because they had previously been discriminated against in terms of pay. If they had been paid their wage entitlement, they too would have suffered a drop in pay and would have been entitled to pay protection.

Redcar & Cleveland Borough Council v Bainbridge (No.2)
[2008] IRLR 776 CA

A large public employer might be able to demonstrate that the constraints on its finances were so pressing that it could not do other than it did and that it was justified in putting the need to cushion the men's pay reduction ahead of the need to bring the women up to parity with the men. However, that result is not a foregone conclusion and the employer must prove that what was done was objectively justified in the individual case.

United Biscuits Ltd v Young
[1978] IRLR 15 EAT

Where an employer seeks to discharge the onus of proof by a "red circle" defence, he must do so with respect to each employee who, it is claimed, is within the circle. The employer must prove that at the time when the employee was admitted to the circle his higher pay was related to a consideration other than sex.

Financial constraints

Benveniste v University of Southampton
[1989] IRLR 123 CA

That a woman was appointed at a lower point on a salary scale than men doing like work due to financial constraints did not constitute a material difference to justify her lower salary once the reason for the lower payment disappeared. The material difference between her case and the case of her comparators evaporated when the financial constraints were removed.

Redcar & Cleveland Borough Council v Bainbridge
[2007] IRLR 91 EAT

Although budgetary considerations cannot be the sole justification for failing to give effect to the principle of equal pay, they can be a factor to be weighed with other considerations when determining whether the difference in pay could be objectively justified, provided that if there are cost constraints, they are allocated in a way that limits any discriminatory impact as much as possible. For example, transitional arrangements to cushion the pay of those moving to lower pay will sometimes be appropriate. It would be theoretically possible to confer the benefit of the higher pay on everyone, but the cost may reinforce the justification limiting the benefit.

Bury Metropolitan Council v Hamilton
[2011] IRLR 358 EAT
[2011] EqLR 214 EAT
Council of the City of Sunderland v Brennan

A case of justification on the basis of cost can only be proved by adding sufficiently detailed evidence, both of the costs themselves and of the financial context, to enable the tribunal to reach an informed view. That need not involve an exhaustive review of the council's finances, but the tribunal must be put in a position where it could assess the broad picture.

Hours of work

Bilka-Kaufhaus GmbH v Weber von Hartz
[1986] IRLR 317 ECJ

An employer who excludes part-time workers from an occupational pension scheme is in breach of Article 141 if this exclusion affects significantly more women than men, unless the employer can show that the exclusion is based on objectively justified factors unrelated to any discrimination on grounds of sex.

Bilka-Kaufhaus GmbH v Weber von Hartz
[1986] IRLR 317 ECJ

An employer may justify the exclusion of part-time workers, irrespective of their sex, from an occupational pension scheme on the ground that it seeks to employ as few part-time workers as possible, where it is found that the means chosen for achieving that objective correspond to a real need on the part of the undertaking, are appropriate with a view to achieving the objective in question and are necessary to that end.

Kowalska v Freie und Hansestadt Hamburg
[1990] IRLR 447 ECJ

Article 141 precludes the application of a provision of a collective agreement under which part-time workers are excluded from the benefit of a severance payment in the case of termination of the employment relationship, when it is clear that in fact a considerably smaller percentage of men than of women work part time, unless the employer shows that the provision is justified by objective factors unrelated to any discrimination on grounds of sex.

Market forces

Enderby v Frenchay Health Authority and Secretary of State for Health
[1993] IRLR 591 ECJ

The state of the employment market, which may lead an employer to increase the pay of a particular job in order to attract candidates, may constitute an objectively justified economic ground for a difference in pay. If the national court is able to determine precisely what proportion of the increase in pay is attributable to market forces, it must necessarily accept that the pay differential is objectively justified to the extent of that proportion. If that is not the case, it is for the national court to assess whether the role of market forces in determining the rate of pay was sufficiently significant to provide objective justification for part or all of the difference. Therefore, it must determine, if necessary by applying the principle of proportionality, whether and to what extent the shortage of candidates for a job and the need to attract them by higher pay constitutes an objectively justified economic ground for the difference in pay between the jobs in question.

Rainey v   [1987] IRLR 26 HL
Greater Glasgow Health Board

A difference in pay between a female prosthetist and her male comparator, employed on like work but recruited from the private sector on his existing terms and conditions when the prosthetic service was established prior to her employment, fell within the statutory defence where the fact that the new service could never have been established within a reasonable time if the employees of private contractors had not been offered a scale of remuneration no less favourable than that which they were then enjoying was a good and objectively justified ground for offering that scale of remuneration. There was no suggestion that it was unreasonable to place the prosthetists on the particular point on the salary scale which was in fact selected, and it was not a question of the women being paid less than the norm but of the comparator being paid more because of the necessity to attract him.

Ratcliffe v   [1995] IRLR 439 HL
North Yorkshire County Council

A difference in pay, between the female school catering assistants and their male comparators employed in local government on work rated as equivalent, which resulted from a reduction in the women's wages from the local government rate because of the employer's need to tender for work at a commercially competitive rate, was not genuinely due to a material factor which was not the difference of sex. To reduce the women's wages below that of their male comparators was the very kind of discrimination in relation to pay which the Act sought to remove.

Cumbria County Council v   [2008] IRLR 91 EAT
Dow (No.1)

It is not enough for an employer to establish that some differential is justified by market forces without giving the tribunal a proper evidential basis for determining whether it is the whole amount or something short of that.

Cumbria County Council v   [2008] IRLR 91 EAT
Dow (No.1)

Lack of recruitment problems does not establish that the market rate was being paid. That is equally consistent with the employer paying over the odds. It is for the employer to show that the market dictated higher pay. It is not for the claimants to show that the pay is too high.

Albion Shipping Agency v   [1981] IRLR 525 EAT
Arnold

A change in an employer's trading position leading to reduced profitability was capable of constituting a defence to a woman's claim for equal pay with her male predecessor, provided the employers could show that they were not taking advantage of the complainant's sex to get the work done at a rate less than that for which a man would have worked.

EFFECT OF THE EQUALITY CLAUSE

(1) If the terms of A's work do not (by whatever means) include a sex equality clause, they are to be treated as including one.

(2) A sex equality clause is a provision that has the following effect –

> *(a) if a term of A's is less favourable to A than a corresponding term of B's is to B, A's term is modified so as not to be less favourable;*
>
> *(b) if A does not have a term which corresponds to a term of B's that benefits B, A's terms are modified so as to include such a term.*

EQUALITY ACT 2010 – s.66

Barber v   [1990] IRLR 240 ECJ
Guardian Royal Exchange
  Assurance Group

The application of the principle of equal pay must be ensured in respect of each element of remuneration and not only on the basis of a comprehensive assessment of the consideration paid to workers.

Jämställdhetsombudsmannen v   [2000] IRLR 421 ECJ
Örebro Läns Landsting

In comparing the pay of midwives and a clinical technician for the purpose of Article 141, the appropriate comparison was between the monthly basic salary of the two groups. No account was to be taken of a supplement paid to the midwives for working inconvenient hours. Genuine transparency, permitting effective judicial review, is assured only if the principle of equal pay applies to each of the elements of remuneration.

Hayward v   [1988] IRLR 257 HL
Cammell Laird Shipbuilders Ltd

The natural meaning of the word "term" is a distinct provision or part of the contract which has sufficient content to make it possible to compare it, from the point of view of the benefits it confers, with a similar provision or part in another contract. Therefore, if in the contract of a woman and the contract of a man employed on work of equal value there is "a term of a similar kind" – ie a term making a comparable provision for the same subject-matter – the two must be compared and if, on that comparison, the term of the woman's contract proves to be less favourable than the term of the man's contract, then the term in the woman's contract is to be treated as modified so as to make it not less favourable.

Hayward v   [1988] IRLR 257 HL
Cammell Laird Shipbuilders Ltd

If a contract contains provisions relating to basic pay, benefits in kind such as the use of a car, cash bonuses and sickness benefits, on the natural and ordinary meaning of the word "term", all these different terms cannot be lumped together as one "term" of the contract, simply because they can all together be considered as providing for the total "remuneration" for the services to be performed under the contract.

Degnan v   [2005] IRLR 615 CA
Redcar and Cleveland Borough Council
Attendance allowances paid to men employed on work rated as equivalent to that of the claimant women were a single term together with the hourly rate and fixed bonuses, rather than being a separate term of the men's contract for the purpose of the comparison with the terms of the women's contracts. The EAT correctly held that all monetary payments received by male comparators for normal working hours should be aggregated and divided by the number of hours in the working week, to give an hourly rate; if it is greater, the woman's hourly rate should be increased to eliminate the difference.

St Helens & Knowsley Hospitals NHS   [2011] IRLR 815 CA
Trust v   [2011] EqLR 968 CA
Brownbill
The terms in the female claimants' contracts regarding payment for working unsocial hours within their normal working week could be compared to terms of a similar kind in the contracts of their male comparators, notwithstanding that overall the women were paid more than their chosen comparators. The focus of the law is upon equality of terms and not of total pay actually received. The decision of the House of Lords in *Hayward v Cammell Laird Shipbuilders Ltd* applied. The present case was not like *Degnan v Redcar and Cleveland Borough Council*, which turned on its own particular facts, and where features of artificiality and historical anomaly tended to disguise the reality of the pay elements. The Court of Appeal's decision in *Degnan* did not, and was not intended to, give rise to an exception to the principle in *Hayward*.

Hayward v   [1988] IRLR 257 HL
Cammell Laird Shipbuilders Ltd
A woman who can point to a term of her contract which is less favourable than a term of a similar kind in the man's contract is entitled to have that term made not less favourable irrespective of whether she is as favourably treated as the man when the whole of her contract and the whole of his contract are considered. Therefore, a woman employee on work of equal value was entitled to the same basic hourly wage and overtime rates as her comparator, notwithstanding that she received additional holidays and better sickness benefits.

Dugdale v   [1976] IRLR 368 EAT
Kraft Foods Ltd
An equality clause has effect so as to modify any less favourable term of the women's contract so as to make it not less favourable. It need not produce equality if, though they are engaged on like work, the payment to the men includes something affecting them and not the woman, such as working at night.

Evesham v   [2000] IRLR 257 CA
North Hertfordshire Health Authority
A claimant's entitlement to have the relevant term of her contract of employment modified so as to be not less favourable than that of her male comparator means that she should mirror her comparator on the incremental pay scale, and therefore enter the scale at the lowest level, rather than that she should be placed on the pay scale for his post at a level appropriate to her actual years of service.

Sorbie v   [1976] IRLR 371 EAT
Trust House Forte Hotels Ltd
The effect of an equality clause is to strike out the less favourable rate and substitute the higher rate. Once a contract of employment has been modified in accordance with an equality clause, it is a contract providing remuneration at the higher rate. That contract remains so modified until something else happens, such as a further agreement between the parties, a further collective agreement, or a further statutory modification by reason of a further operation of the equality clause. Therefore, a modification to a woman's contract providing equal pay with a male comparator did not cease to operate when the man was no longer employed on like work.

Hartlepool Borough Council v   [2009] IRLR 796 EAT
Llewellyn
A male claimant is entitled to the benefit of a contractual term enjoyed by a female comparator even though the comparator herself has only acquired the benefit of that term as a result of the operation of the Act. The reference to a "term" in the man's (ie the comparator's) contract should be construed as a reference to either a term in the contract as actually agreed between the parties or a term acknowledged by the employer or declared by a tribunal to have been inserted or modified following a claim under the Act.

Clark v   [2011] EqLR 1026 Mayor's and City of London Ct
Metropolitan Police Authority
A part-time police inspector normally working 32 hours per week was entitled to be paid in respect of each hour that she actually worked and not just her normal hours of duty in circumstances where a full-time male inspector on like work normally working 40 hours per week would be paid for hours worked between 32 and 40. The practice of not paying for hours worked over and above normally required hours was less favourable to part-time workers, who were overwhelmingly women, and therefore tainted by indirect sex discrimination, which had not been objectively justified.

REMEDIES

(1) This section applies to proceedings before a court or employment tribunal on a complaint relating to a breach of an equality clause, other than a breach with respect to membership of or rights under an occupational pension scheme.

(2) If the court or tribunal finds that there has been a breach of the equality clause, it may –

    (a) make a declaration as to the rights of the parties in relation to the matters to which the proceedings relate;

    (b) order an award by way of arrears of pay or damages in relation to the complainant.

(3) The court or tribunal may not order a payment under subsection (2)(b) in respect of a time before the arrears day.

(4) In relation to proceedings in England and Wales, the arrears day is, in a case mentioned in the first column of the table, the day mentioned in the second column.

Case	Arrears day
A standard case	The day falling 6 years before the day on which the proceedings were instituted.
A concealment case or an incapacity case (or a case which is both).	The day on which the breach first occurred.

(5) In relation to proceedings in Scotland, the arrears day is the first day of –

    (a) the period of 5 years ending with the day on which the proceedings were commenced, or

    (b) if the case involves a relevant incapacity, or a relevant fraud or error, the period of 20 years ending with that day.

EQUALITY ACT – s.132

(1) This section applies to proceedings before a court or employment tribunal on a complaint relating to –

    (a) a breach of an equality rule, or

    (b) a breach of an equality clause with respect to membership of, or rights under, an occupational pension scheme.

(2) If the court or tribunal finds that there has been a breach as referred to in subsection (1) –

    (a) it may make a declaration as to the rights of the parties in relation to the matters to which the proceedings relate;

    (b) it must not order arrears of benefits or damages or any other amount to be paid to the complainant.

(3) Subsection (2)(b) does not apply if the proceedings are proceedings to which section 134 applies.

(4) If the breach relates to a term on which persons become members of the scheme, the court or tribunal may declare that the complainant is entitled to be admitted to the scheme with effect from a specified date.

(5) A date specified for the purposes of subsection (4) must not be before 8 April 1976.

(6) If the breach relates to a term on which members of the scheme are treated, the court or tribunal may declare that the complainant is, in respect of a specified period, entitled to secure the rights that would have accrued if the breach had not occurred.

(7) A period specified for the purposes of subsection (6) must not begin before 17 May 1990.

(8) If the court or tribunal makes a declaration under subsection (6), the employer must provide such resources to the scheme as are necessary to secure for the complainant (without contribution or further contribution by the complainant or other members) the rights referred to in that subsection.

EQUALITY ACT 2010 – s.133

Council of the City of   **[2005] IRLR 504 EAT**
  Newcastle upon Tyne v
Allan
Compensation for non-economic loss, such as for injury to feelings, aggravated or exemplary damages, is not recoverable in a claim brought under the Equal Pay Act.

Redcar & Cleveland Borough   **[2008] IRLR 776 CA**
  Council v
Bainbridge (No.2)
A job evaluation scheme does not have retroactive effect so as to entitle the claimant to rely on a person of the opposite sex, who is rated as equivalent under the job evaluation scheme, as a comparator for the purposes of a rated as equivalent claim for a period prior to the implementation of the job evaluation scheme.

Preston v   **[2000] IRLR 506 ECJ**
Wolverhampton Healthcare NHS Trust
The fact that a worker can claim retroactively to join an occupational pension scheme does not allow him to avoid paying the contributions relating to the period of membership concerned.

Copple v   **[2011] EqLR 1271 CA**
Littlewoods plc
A requirement that a claimant employed part time who alleged that an employer's rules regarding entitlement to membership of a pension scheme were in breach of the Equal Pay Act because they denied or restricted access to it to full-time workers must establish that she would have joined a pension scheme during the period that she was excluded from it in order to obtain a declaration as to her entitlement to membership was compatible with EU law. If the women would not have joined anyway, they would not have received the benefits of membership and accordingly no declaration of entitlement was appropriate.